At the Brink of Infinity

At
the Brink
of
Infinity

Poetic
Humility in
Boundless
American
Space

James E. von der Heydt

UNIVERSITY OF IOWA PRESS | IOWA CITY

for Margaret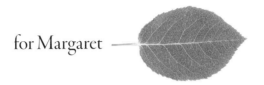

Contents

One value even of the smallest well is, that when you look into it you see that earth is not continent but insular. This is as important as that it keeps butter cool.

— H. D. Thoreau, *Walden*

Preface

If writing can be practical without being pragmatic, the most extreme instances of Emersonian poetic sight are the best places to find out how. What kind of writing can showcase the capacities of the senses, without representing any action? Henry David Thoreau tries his hand at answering this question, in an especially Emersonian mood: no pragmatic reader is ready for the challenge that results. In the epigraph on the facing page, Thoreau's vision neither complements nor comments upon his work as a delver. He looks into his well, he says, not just as an occasion to think about watery places, but to see, as a matter of routine sensory fact, that the well-water somehow surrounds the very land from which he dug it. There is no suggestion that anything will be accomplished in this way — and yet clearly this sentence is a recommendation. Thoreau is saying, in the most practical tone imaginable: You try it. Reader, you want to know what's important in the world: so, practice seeing the least obvious thing. You see that? Draw the wrong conclusion. Do not *imagine*, but simply make an effort and *notice* how, in your eyes, the object and its context swap roles — foreground becoming background and vice versa. Look, look how useless insight can be.

To the true practitioner of vision, Thoreau claims, a tiny body of water found with a shovel can transform the land — not into a homestead, but into an island. The liquidity we would cup in our hands in an instant surrounds us instead. This is a neglected element of the Emersonian agenda: the way it trains us to practice treating such useless insights as predominant; to know ourselves engulfed and uncontained; to believe that the feeding of the vision is as important as the pragmatic sustaining of the body. Even when stocking his domestic larder with butter, Thoreau derives that kind of import from the world abroad. Eyes can turn the world inside out. On this continent, the Emersonian believes, even delving or consuming should be an invocation of vastness.

To think in an American literary mode is to think big. Thoreau's brinkmanship in the remark about the well—bizarrely equating in importance the oceanic surround and a homesteader's handling of dairy—is an extreme version of the size contrast that makes American literature so edgy. If the lexicon of size were to disappear, the idea of a distinctive U.S. literary sensibility, with roots in the age of Emerson, would fade and shrivel. Largeness—of terrain, of spirit, of deed, and even of form—prominently marks the texts called typically American, from the enhanced visibility and expanded vision that John Winthrop claimed for his "city on a hill," to Walt Whitman's personal containment of "multitudes," to the frontier horizon an American archetype finds to be "commensurate with his capacity for wonder" in a key passage of *The Great Gatsby*. Without the peculiarly valenced metaphors of space that proliferate both within and around its canonical texts, American literature of the modern era would be nearly unrecognizable. It has other earmarks: experimentalism; a loose association with individualist egalitarianism; and the unique sensibility W. E. B. DuBois called double-consciousness. But if it could not speak of largeness, it would lack its most characteristic metaphors for versatility, for comprehension, and for artistic vision. The language of size invigorates the rhetoric of "American possibility" and provides terminology to almost every other aspect of the tradition. The celebration of bigness, almost irresistibly, becomes an element of the American writer's encounter with the world, and an image of what writing should do to its readers. Robert Frost, for example, maintained that "[m]y poems are all set to trip the reader head foremost into the boundless" (*Selected Letters* 344).

In dealing with American bigness, the writer must choose either to embrace vastness, or self-consciously to stave vastness off, or, somehow, both at once. Reconciliation of this choice, through patient negotiation, is the task of many U.S. novels: in literary practice, as opposed to transactional writing, none of the three options is as simple as it seems. The novelist hopes to create relations between the expansive self-sufficiency involved in the idea of "the American continent," on the one hand, and, on the other, the troubling insularity of the perceiving self. Hence U.S. protagonists strive to surmount, even as they are encompassed by, their social and material surroundings. A novel ranges over the space between small and large, the representative individual and the world of promise. Unlike an essay or a poem, it must somehow integrate the paradoxes of big and small into narrative's complex machinery. Thoreau looks into a well to create for himself a sense of openness—hardly a useful activity.

In different circumstances infinity can just be a useful figure of speech. To the marketer and the mythmaker, to the rhapsodist and the jingoist, the concept of open space has great instrumental value. As long as "infinity" is not taken too seriously, boundlessness can come to hand as a highly useful element of discursive culture. Indeed, in the United States the language of collective action and possibility seems to be constituted by contrasts in scale. Various pairings of the limitless and the prosaic consistently define the American ideas of mystique, destiny, sublimity, and mission.

Politically, invoking vast horizons makes sense; metaphors of "pioneering" seem basic to the American concept of leadership. But today boundlessness is deployed just as readily to reinforce the consumer culture of domesticity that Thoreau called into question. Infinity, as it is understood today, would have been used to sell him appliances and metaphors, to save him trips out of doors. The enormously popular Magnetic Poetry Kit, for example, some dozens of individual words to be arranged at whim on a refrigerator, advertises itself as a door onto openness. Shoppers read that it offers "literally billions of poetic possibilities"; it is "A Box of Words Searching for Meaning on a Sea of Metal." In the U.S. market, freedom of choice is maximized when the customer buys an itinerary into the boundless. The scope a refrigerator might give for self-expression is as important as the way that it keeps butter cool. As Thoreau's seemingly gratuitous mention of his butter supply suggested, transactions with infinity take on extra mystique when they involve small, mundane objects.

Such relations between imaginative awe and rapacious consumerism are brilliantly lampooned in the movie *Toy Story*: in the opening scenes an obsolescent cowboy doll, Woody, is supplanted by an astronaut action figure named Buzz Lightyear. In moments of determined intensity, Lightyear is given to pronouncements of his signature line: "To infinity — and beyond!" Warmheartedly, this parody of childlike (and corporate) one-upmanship reduces Emersonian mass culture to its essential, exultant vacuity. Wryness is an excellent attitude for such a culture to have toward itself (and in real life, Disney's version of the same toy sold well and unironically). At the same time, though, such bemusements may trace one line of their ancestry to the paradoxes of American philosophical writing. The marketer's skill, like that of literary forebears, is to link household items with extravagant possibilities.

These examples suggest that the entrancing magic of infinity is invoked most effectively when vastness is juxtaposed with something small. Indeed, extremity at both ends of the spectrum is the defining feature of American scale. This is true in politics as well as marketing: in his superbly crafted speech to Congress on September 20, 2001, President G. W. Bush made use of a similar pairing to seal his own political identity.

> In the months and years ahead, life will return almost to normal. . . .
> Some will remember an image of a fire, or a story of rescue. Some will carry memories of a face and a voice gone forever.
> — And I will carry this. It is the police shield of a man named George Howard, who died at the World Trade Center trying to save others. . . .
> This is my reminder of lives that ended, and a task that does not end.

Operation "Infinite Justice," the air campaign in Afghanistan, would begin a few weeks later. As the president clutched his small memento mori before Congress, and spoke of that which does not end, he activated both terms in a powerful American rhetoric of individuality and infinity. The well-known story of boundless possibility, the march of freedom always outward to new terrain, became a way of defining the freshly conceived "war on terror" as an unending task. Buzzword became policy. Imaginations were fired by this infinite challenge in part because of the way its emblem, Officer Howard's badge, could be held in the hand and tucked, somberly, day after day, into the pocket of one resolute and representative man.

American invocations of guns and butter, twinning horizons for collective action with the tokens of domestic identity, draw on a worthy literary heritage. Nothing so reliably captures U.S. attention as the claim that the sky is the limit, and that we are poised anew, alertly, on the brink of boundlessness. The electricity created by miniaturization and representation — a tingle anyone can feel in Bush's zeugma, "[America] will carry memories; *and I will carry this*" — drives much of the most effective American writing. It is more respectfully harnessed, with deference to representation's complexity, in American narrative art. Likewise, a thoughtful concern about what it means to be representative governs the ongoing progress of U.S. scholarship about American literature in historical context.

This book is not about that kind of action. It is concerned instead with unpragmatic representational practices — links made directly between opposite extremes, in lyric texts where no mediation can succeed and no action can begin to address the perennial longing to participate in something endless. Historicist criticism about U.S. literature seeks broader chronological or geographic perspectives rather than narrower, textual ones. It presupposes that no parochial evidentiary sample can suffice: a narrow context of analysis inevitably will yield less meaning than a larger one. Ironically, though, that scholarly axiom about the importance of increasing scope is itself deeply Emersonian — despite having been designed for the express purpose of challenging U.S. exceptionalism. In fact, few concepts bear more prominently the trademark of Ralph Waldo Emerson, that celebrated prime mover of American literature, than the vision of knowledge expanding to erase old boundaries. He believes that there is no end to the writer's campaign of description. That belief matches the central tenet of his idealism: the infinite human soul, inevitably (even if it looks into a well), finds itself in a world of infinite possibility. Hence the more the writer dreams of containing all, the more insular she knows her domain to be. A spirit of truly limitless imagination, insistent on fullness of scope, must constantly surmount, and inevitably scorn, the very things it accomplishes; "To infinity — and beyond," indeed.

At the end of this Emersonian line of thought is a discouraging proposition that tends to be neglected in research-oriented historical scholarship, with its assumption that when it comes to literary context, "more is more." No scholarly bigness of knowledge can encompass or objectively explain a discourse that is, itself, all about size. The purpose of this book, then, is not to take a larger perspective than other books about American poetry, but to be more self-conscious about the axioms of American reading. We should do more to examine the *idea* of size enabling the Emersonian to draw a horizon about herself — and not solely by measuring and dating that circle, to situate it within larger future histories. The analysis that follows interests itself primarily with the narrowest of contexts, at the sensorial epicenter of Emerson's expanding circles of American knowing — with the Big Bang of sensation, as it were, that opens space to cognition but also creates the limitless vacuum the mind can only dream of encompassing. That event is enacted in a discernible lineage of stark American poems. In these unpragmatic texts, it happens whenever the writer's eye opens onto openness. "The eye is the first circle," Emerson said; "the horizon which it forms is the second" ("Circles" II.179). That primal creation of the senses, a horizon of isolation that Thoreau could find even in a well, is embodied best in a succession of American poems uninterested in action. They are preoccupied with those fundamental elements of sight, eye-lens and skyline. Locating the poet before nature's barest tableau — the shoreline —

this book seeks both to describe and to emulate the Emersonian philosophical sensibility of a strain of poets that began with Emily Dickinson.

Within a lyric rather than a narrative frame, the idea of infinity ceases to be instrumental (instead, it is paralyzing). The shoreline-poem is about the writer's static encounter with the brink of infinity. On the beach, the reflective person feels very big and very small at the same time. Into that moment tragedy is immediately drawn. For Emerson, Dickinson, Robert Frost, Elizabeth Bishop, and James Merrill, the localized, practical experience of the brink offers more philosophical challenge than any "larger" chronological context. They shrink before their own grand visions of ocean horizon. They do not pretend to choose between humility and pride. Indeed, the lyric poet's most intense visions of infinity approach the zero point on the spectrum of cynicism —a spectrum that continues, in the United States, to stretch at the other end toward new and previously unimaginable frontiers.

The first chapter explains what makes Emersonian epistemology in boundless nature so complex. It culminates with a case study: a pair of mid-nineteenth-century poems about the relation between a seashell and a writer's experience of ocean. The next two chapters establish the two foci of the Emersonian poetics of infinity, focusing respectively on largeness and smallness: chapter 2 is about oceans in the work of each poet, and chapter 3, in like fashion, about houses. Such writing is marked both by outlandish abstraction and by pathetic materiality. The uncanniness of the lopsided poems in these two chapters indicates how essential each term is to the other: when largeness is not ballasted by the particular, or smallness is merely precious, the results may be more philosophically illustrative than beautiful. Poems by Emerson are included in these chapters, because in his lyrics he never developed a way to balance the twin demands his prose placed upon the writer of possibility. The book's remaining chapters examine the problems of sensation and size in the best work of four of America's best poets.

Futility should mark any rigorous attempt to mediate directly between infinite openness and human objects (including poems). Narrative artists, of course, can devise some plausible, indirect connection between terms as opposed as "ocean" and "house" — using a broad timeline, boats, patient teamwork, and the like. But when large and small are conceived as incommensurately extreme ideas, no temporal process can link them. There is no way to stage a truly coherent encounter between infinity and handiwork, to name felicitously what it feels like to be "golden averages, volitant stabilities . . . , houses founded upon the sea" (Emerson, "Montaigne" IV.91). Thus instead of time or process, a more awkward paradigm of space governs this distinct American poetics founded on incommensurability.

Chapters 4 through 7, then, consider in turn the static sensoria of four Emersonian successor-poets' gorgeous and paradoxical encounters with nature. In the Epilogue, and throughout, these poems are situated within a neglected lineage in the history of philosophy. It can seem stiff and unnatural to read philosophical poetry without recourse to narrative or even logical sequence — almost as unnatural as it is to write philosophy under the same constraint. Epistemology's beauty can be hard to see, and willfully bizarre poetic sight — like Thoreau's labeling North America an "island" — can seem adventitious or merely counterintuitive. The most rigorous of these poets, Dickinson and Bishop, were each initially dismissed for just such reasons as overly idiosyncratic, hermetic, or fussy. But readers' experience of the incommensurable gives such writings a stony permanence that no flow of culture can erode. Emerson advocated passionately for unmooring such immediate encounters, in all their difficulty, from history. In this he shared the iconoclasm — specifically, the deep-seated counter-Hegelianism — of the most modern philosopher of Christianity, Søren Kierkegaard. Coming fresh to what should be felt directly, and feeling all the pain of that encounter, these two writers ignore their historical contexts — not persuasively, but definitively — and in encountering the space of knowledge, they attempt something much harder than most writers ever contemplate.

Here that philosophical project matters because it is helpful in the interpretation of poems. In the narrowness and rigor of the Kierkegaardian mindset, energy can flow from infinite to particular — at immense cost to the person who reaches for both at once. She reveals and undergoes the paradoxes that are always, secretly, built in to the American's "manifestly destined" encounter with a boundless context. The national thought-experiment of limitlessness becomes in these texts, tragically and magnificently, an experience of the eyes and limbs. Thus the poet's effort of writerly comprehension is not pragmatic, though it is muscular; not history minded, though it eschews visions of eternity; not self-aggrandizing, though it partakes of vastness. To such an artist — Dickinson, of course, being the best example — endlessness, though a human idea, refuses deployment for human ends. Infinity elicits from a writer a response unrecognizable as action, an instance of tremendous anaerobic effort that has nothing to do with happenstance.

Lyric infinitude as conceived here, thoroughgoingly unpragmatic, forces cultural criticism (not unwillingly) into an aesthetic mode. Philosophical, theological, and even ecological frameworks have a role as well, but the following study would be incomprehensible to a reader without a sense of the predominant importance of beauty. Happily, Emersonian philosophy is based on a sensory experience accessible equally to our own era as to earlier ones. Whatever quality of continence America no longer possesses, it is still insular: at a remove from its wells, it still has shores, and limits, to contemplate. The superimposed feelings of expansiveness and diminution — the shoreline experience — can inform our reading of these poems just as they underlay the writing of them. To be sure, awareness of history's differences is the footing for all intelligent reading; but solidarity is reading's lifeblood. Emerson asked, "Why should not we also enjoy an original relation to Nature?" The beaches afford to us the same vantage that they have afforded to poets. Why should not we also stand at the brink of infinity, while sand works its way up over our toes?

Acknowledgments

The scholarship underlying this book was supported materially by Harvard University and by Fellowships in the Humanities from the Mellon Foundation (1996) and the Whiting Foundation (2002).

Gratitude is due for Elisa New's mentorship across the spectrum of wisdom, extreme intelligence, and whimsy; Katie Peterson's unsurpassable skill at conversation, books, and love; Vikram Savkar's vigor, rigor, and patient devotion; Lawrence Buell's genius at bibliography; Peter Sacks's colossally sensitive reading; and the teacherly examples of Robert Haaser, Robert Hollander, Michael Wood, T. P. Roche, Jesse Matz, Douglas Mao, Helen Vendler, Jim Engell, Lynn Festa, Oren Izenberg, and (with special gratitude for a 1993 course of lectures in Princeton's religion department) Cornel West. I hope, too, that I have learned enough from the essay writers I admire that my work can show some flickers of the ardency of its igniting flame: the desire to emulate, all at once, my teachers and fellow students.

A version of chapter 1 appeared in *Raritan* (Winter 2003). A version of chapter 4 appeared in *ESQ: A Journal of the American Renaissance* 51, no. 4 (2005).

recorded — only — "], 446 ["This was a Poet — It is That"], 969 ["Escaping backward to perceive"], 910 ["Finding is the first Act"], 1287 ["Power is a familiar growth — "], 99 ["Low at my problem bending"], 124 ["Safe in their Alabaster Chambers"], 320 ["There's a certain Slant of light"], 363 ["I know a place where Summer strives"], 601 ["When Bells stop ringing — Church — begins — "], 673 ["I saw no Way — The Heavens were stitched — "], 860 ["No Notice gave She, but a Change — "], 817 ["This Consciousness that is aware"], 772 ["Essential Oils — are wrung — "], and 340 ["And then a Plank in Reason, broke,"] from *The Poems of Emily Dickinson*, Variorum Edition, edited by Ralph W. Franklin. Copyright © 1951, 1955, 1979, 1983, 1998 by the President and Fellows of Harvard College. Reprinted with the permission of the Belknap Press of Harvard University Press and the Trustees of Amherst College.

Robert Frost, excerpts from "Neither Out Far Nor In Deep," "Bond and Free," "Once by the Pacific," "Good-By and Keep Cold," "Tree at My Window," "To Earthward," "The Star-Splitter," "Desert Places," "New Hampshire," "All Revelation," "A Star in a Stoneboat," "Mowing," "Stars," "Rose Pogonias," "A Hillside Thaw," "Brown's Descent," "The Last Mowing," and "After Apple-Picking" from *The Poetry of Robert Frost*, edited by Edward Connery Lathem. Copyright © 1916, 1936, 1942, 1944, 1951, 1956, 1958 by Robert Frost. Copyright © 1964, 1967, 1970, 1975 by Lesley Frost Ballantine. Copyright © 1916, 1923, 1928, 1930, 1939, 1947, 1969 by Henry Holt and Co., Inc. Reprinted with the permission of Henry Holt and Company, LLC and Jonathan Cape/ Random House UK Ltd.

James Merrill, excerpts from *The Changing Light at Sandover*. Copyright © 1996 by James Merrill. Excerpts from "Swimming by Night," "The Broken Home," "Syrinx," "A Downward Look," "Self-Portrait in Tyvek[(TM)] Windbreaker," "Overdue Pilgrimage to Nova Scotia," and "McKane's Falls" from *Collected Poems*. Copyright © 2001 by James Merrill. All reprinted with the permission of Alfred A. Knopf, a division of Random House, Inc.

At the Brink of Infinity

1 The Beachcomber's Horizon

Before Emerson's writings were ever about power, they were about knowledge. His ethics have been deplored equally for excessive idealism and for excessive pragmatism: his continued importance to readers results instead from the bold and jagged contours of his philosophy. No call to action stirs the reader of Emerson in the way his alterations of perspective do. He holds intellectual and aesthetic attention not because of his renown in the lecture halls of his age, or any powers of persuasion, but because of the special effort he undertakes to situate the human mind at the center of the natural world. All that extra effort is necessary because he makes the task so hard: rather than subjecting one to the other, he refuses to limit the potential either of the mind or of the world.[1] In many of the most striking passages of Emerson's prose, and in the most rigorous poetry of the following generations, boundlessly ambitious American knowledge confronts its own absurdity.

Infinite in its possibilities, and therefore both unchanging and unstable, the Emersonian imagination meets its match not inland, in the arena of temporal activity, but in the open horizon of the uninhabitable ocean. The result is an aesthetically intense double bind for American philosophical poetry. No finite space can correspond adequately to the depth of the human spirit, yet no human action can respond adequately to the vastness onto which the poet's eye opens.[2] On the beach, absolute ambition paralyzes both the Emersonian epistemologist and the Emersonian poet. Uncannily, a powerful imagination entangles helplessly with its external equivalent: a world without borders. The secret of Emerson's epistemology, then, is the problem this tangling represents to triumphalist, dynamic ideas of sensory knowledge. What is to be done when the world's vista coincides all too perfectly with the writer's view?

That problem gives rise to some of the most intense American poetry of the following generations. The four lyric poets examined here all read the bare ocean horizon with a complex double attitude of aspiration and subjection. In one instance, Robert Frost describes the sensation in an end-stopped trimeter that suggests the abortiveness of seaward longing. In "Neither Out Far Nor In Deep," he depicts a scene without any apparent societal context, severed both from inland variability and from the satisfactions of deep oblivion.

The people along the sand
All turn and look one way.
They turn their back on the land.
They look at the sea all day.

As long as it takes to pass
A ship keeps raising its hull;
The wetter ground like glass
Reflects a standing gull.

The land may vary more;
But wherever the truth may be —
The water comes ashore,
And the people look at the sea.

They cannot look out far.
They cannot look in deep.
But when was that ever a bar
To any watch they keep?

The inexhaustible fascination of what is fundamentally a dull tableau resembles the ongoing appeal of Emerson's philosophy. The multiple minds of Frost's poem, like the diverse readers every Emerson paragraph seems to anticipate, are absorbed with the vision of a space of pure possibility, outside of variation. Inevitably, they fail to probe that possibility in full. In turn, the performance of such failure — represented here by the catch in the breath at the word "bar," before Frost's awkwardly enjambed final line — supplies the principal beauty to a lineage of American poetry. The sensation of possibility should always create ambivalence, for the incomprehensibly boundless world is a recapitulation of the unknowable American self.

Emily Dickinson, Robert Frost, Elizabeth Bishop, and James Merrill constitute the central line of a distinct Emersonian tradition of the seascape.[3]

This does not mean that they are simply influenced by the essayist. Interpretive reciprocity, rather than unidirectional "influence," describes the proposed relation between Emerson and the writers of this school. He makes it possible to discern and understand their obsession with boundlessness, while their poems are crucial to any reader who would fully discern Emerson as a thinker of electric stasis (as well as an advocate of competence or a champion of newness). We know Emerson better when we read him retrospectively through succeeding poets, just as we know those poets better when we read them as Emersonians.[4]

In considering the difficult epistemological questions Emerson faced so directly, most recent attention has focused not on space but on temporality and action of the sort notably absent from "Neither Out Far Nor In Deep." The open visual world at the shore is the only fitting counterpart to the expansive imagination that turns toward it: in this it superficially resembles the frontier, the governing topos of U.S. narrative literature. Many critics have taken outdoor openness in those writings as a projection of acquisitive desire, and observed that it prepares the Emersonian writer to dominate the landscape. Other, more recent critics downplay the vastness of the frontier horizon to discern in Emerson the origins of a penchant for flexible engagement, at closer range, with the land. But infinity is rarely taken seriously, and literally, as a term describing narrative horizons. And few literary interpreters turn, as Emerson himself often did, toward the inalterable vista of the seascape.

To be sure, Emerson wrote many descriptions of a dynamic interface between mind and world. But in the static, "shoreline" Emersonian mode, certain questions freeze up the machinery of sensation and action: there are explosions in the cylinder, but the piston does not move. These questions are as old as philosophy, and renewed every time a writer tries to represent what she sees. Taken together, they ask what should count as knowledge of nature.

How are we changed in the instant of seeing the world? How is the world changed in the instant we see it? How much context do we need to know an object? Emerson's style doubles these difficulties by inviting us to apply them to textual understanding as well as to sensory knowledge. Thus a parallel set of questions is whispered in every Emerson paragraph: How are we changed as we read an essay? How does reading a sentence change the previous sentence? How does reading unify a text as it registers the distinctness of its parts? The point is not to maintain that these questions are in fact unanswerable, only to show how a certain sort of poetic imagination is founded on the apprehension of their intractability. The poets featured here are Emersonians without answers. The sensory terrain for their edgy questioning is the very edge of terrenity itself—a shoreline.

AN EPISTEMOLOGICAL question is always begged when we respond to it, since language is no more securely knowable than its objects. Unfortunately, the critic can name what a text does when she reads it only by writing another text. The poet, likewise, addresses subjective experience of the world by making an object—a thing that may be an enactment of the encounter, but is also, basically, only a souvenir of it. In recent years, a strain of criticism broadly called "pragmatic" has addressed these problems by showing how the two fundamental writerly activities, observing and writing, are comprised by a certain unity. Neither needs an epistemology of its own: sensation and *poesis* ("making") are mutually constitutive. In such criticism's coherent and effective version of the relation between (readerly) experience and writing, there is no categorical difference between engagement with objects and description of them, between doing something and recording it. Thus simply by experiencing their landscapes, confident and flexible American writers make something new: they build a human place within it.

With the help of this critical pragmatism and the authorial pragmatism it describes, readers might manage to find themselves at home in America's innovative literature. To use the familiar landscape metaphor, American literary homesteaders of the nineteenth and twentieth centuries developed an imaginative claim on their world that allowed for relinquishment of older, European connections. Writers and thinkers like Henry David Thoreau, Walt Whitman, William James, Gertrude Stein, William Carlos Williams, Wallace Stevens, and Stanley Cavell framed a shelter on Emerson's foundations. Their work named (and, in the same moment, built) a home in which American culture continues to dwell, one that American writing continues to renovate. In their supple imagining of the world, ready practicality is the watchword: Emerson is important for these writers because he represents life always on the verge of newness. As Emerson puts it, "I am ready to die out of nature and be born again into this new yet unapproachable America I have found in the West" ("Experience" III.259). Stanley Cavell interprets this readiness as optimism: "Emerson's writing is (an image or promise of, the constitution for) this new yet unapproachable America: . . . a rebirth of himself into it" (*Unapproachable* 91).

The experience of constantly being on the brink of something cannot always be contained pragmatically. Cavell goes on to say that "to find this new America is indeed (to be ready) to be born again, that is to say, suffer conversion; . . . and that seems to be a matter of *discontinuity*" (*Unapproachable* 92). Poets are not so comfortable using techniques of compromise like the parentheses that, in both of the preceding quotations, set off Cavell's mere readiness from the realization it awaits. More radically discontinuous than even a skeptical interpreter would guess, Dickinsonian poets after Emerson emphasize not the newness but the unapproachability of "this new yet unapproachable America." No matter how ready one is for a close encounter with the infinite, that confrontation always remains impossibly distant. The leap from one state to another, from alienation to knowing, is for these poets neither a single event nor an ongoing negotiation, but a constant aching impossibility. Approach is foreclosed whenever the horizon opens. That gap between extreme possibility and cognitive disability, moreover, corresponds to an abyss at the heart of writing itself.[5]

What might it mean for an Emersonian to find, and even claim, such an America — one that is itself an abyss, a pure space of possibility rather than an Edenic, inland promise? It would mean, on an elementary level, that her position on the brink cannot imply forthcoming action. (With a few exceptions, seafaring in American literature is no matter of self-reliance; it relies on coffinlike ships and social ties.) No storyline encompasses and makes sense of the lyric poet's sensory encounter.[6] Unless we purposely filter it out, we readily discern such a static, oceanic sensibility in Emerson's own writing. In fact, it emerges instantly, with a vengeance, even in the sentence about rebirth that Cavell cites, when emphasis is placed on the word "unapproachable" — the term that tends in most citations to pass unnoticed alongside "new," in the electric phrase "this new yet unapproachable America."

The word "America," because it refers both to the human-made nation and to the physical continent, serves as an especially apt emblem of a paradox fundamental to post-Kantian epistemology. Is the world something made, or something given — an idea, or a thing? The ocean setting intensifies that question to the utmost, testing the senses in a space where blankness both invites and frustrates the search for meaning. The shoreline poet highlights the strangeness of the mutually constitutive relation at the heart of knowledge: the interaction between the world's intrinsic features and the human sensation that registers them. The artist is both an observer of the landscape, with its boundless integrity, and a creator of that unified vista. As Emerson says in *Nature*, "Miller owns this field, Locke that. But there is a property in the horizon which no man has but he whose eye can integrate all the parts, that is, the poet" (I.9).[7] In a word, then, the Emersonian in nature invents what is already there: unity, the very thing that naming parcels up and banishes. Here, as Richard Poirier has observed in *A World Elsewhere*, this paradox of perception is solved with a superb pun: the "property" is both a feature of the landscape and an imposition upon it. Either eye or horizon can be read to endow the scene with the integrity of boundlessness. Such a solution works well when there are social reference points, the farms in the middle distance and the flexible word "property." But when that middle range of transactional language is omitted, the paradox of the writer's vision cannot be accommodated.[8] At the seascape, the unitary property of infinitude has no ground for interaction with the proprietary and partial vision of the socialized speaker.

To Emerson, both the horizon's unity and its starkness represent the nature of solitary thought itself: the essay "Experience" admits, "I know that the world I converse with in the city and in the farms, is not the world I think" (III.31). Like thought, lyric discourse is not conversation, and is not transactional in the way that the assignment of property is. In an encounter with the horizon, no Emersonian can be confident of a difference between the given and the made. She cannot be sure of the relation between things and thought. Indeed, horrifyingly, it may be that the vast and incomprehensible horizon of the ocean is precisely the world that the poet thinks. Such a congruence could not be the end of any story; it is the beginning of fresh and unworkable problems.

Writing in very different styles over a century and a half, these poets of the horizon — Emerson, Dickinson, Frost, Bishop, and Merrill — nonetheless share an important (and strangely ambiguous) characteristic: they have minds that do not know their own limits. That description, conventionally, describes a kind of imaginative power — but it also indicates a distressing ignorance. Anything is possible, but nothing can be delineated. To the writer who hopes to map a vast world, superimposing borders and contours on it, the inability to know limits means profound weakness as much as it means enormous possibility. Indeed, the ignorance of limits creates a tightly clenched relation between the opposite sensations of power and powerlessness. Their incongruity becomes a stark paradox, not merely an aspect of a narrative in which time might allow ambition to play itself out or be transformed. Asking ambitious Emersonian questions turns out to be the most passive of activities, and to feel the enormousness of one's vision is also to feel very small.

FOR NATURE WRITERS of this stripe, Emersonians obsessed with infinity, history is no canvas to work on. The very concept is generally undertheorized in their works. The blank horizon proffers them a spare beauty that takes the place of historiography, in a substitution that always appealed to Emerson himself. "God delights to isolate us every day, and hide from us the past and the future. We would look about us, but with grand politeness he draws down before us an impenetrable screen of purest sky, and another behind us of purest sky. 'You will not remember,' he seems to say, 'and you will not expect'" ("Experience" II.39). In the transition between the first sentence of this quotation and the second, temporal propositions are translated into spatial terms — a shift already anticipated in the "island" root of the word "isolate." In turning to the horizon as his emblem of wholeness, Emerson draws such a screen down as well, not as a negation or a mask but as a positive experience of blankness. To him, what *happens* in America is immaterial, compared to the primal fact of sublime experience in the landscape, the world's encircling unity.

Emerson himself rarely named his opposition to narrative meaning successfully — such a negative claim has little place in what is, in many ways, hortatory writing. Nonetheless that opposition informed his thought early on: in 1826, the year he began preaching, he wrote to his aunt, "It is one of the *feelings* of modern philosophy that it is wrong to regard ourselves in a historical light as we do, putting Time between God and us; and that it were fitter to account every moment of the existence of the Universe as a new Creation."[9] This instinctive aversion to temporality as a parameter of self-understanding is described properly not as a proposition (it would surely be indefensible) but as a feeling, an experience of the sort poetry embodies.

Without conceiving of herself as having a place in history, a writer is hard-pressed to know what her work should accomplish. It is a strange thing, after all, to be a nature writer, when you feel that "the simplest utterances are worthiest to be written, yet they are so cheap, and so things of course, that in the infinite riches of the soul, it is like gathering a few pebbles off the ground, or bottling a little air in a phial, when the whole earth and the whole atmosphere are ours" (Emerson, "The Over-Soul" II.172). As the contrast of "phial" and "atmosphere" in this passage suggests, the beachcomber's brooding double awareness pivots about the twinned experience of opposite size-extremes. Infinite reach and tiny grasp are simultaneous rather than consecutive.

In disappointing passages that mirror the anticlimactic endings of his lyrics, Emerson sometimes chooses a sentimental mode to resolve the sensory paradox at the center of his work. He sometimes tries to put limits on the challenge that open sensation poses to the bounds of temporality (what he calls "the kingdom of known cause and effect"): "How easily . . . we might keep forever these beautiful limits. . . . But ah! presently comes a day, or is it only a half-hour, with its angel-whispering — which discomfits the conclusions of nations and of years!" ("Experience" II.35). This is the easy version of limitlessness, which places it in a storyline and gives it a clear temporal endpoint: the next day, reassuringly, cause and effect are back to normal. More ingenuously discomfited in other places in his prose, Emerson works to avoid shortcuts like the phrase "angel-whispering" in this passage.

A lineage of lyric expressions following on Emerson's writing addresses the matter more rigorously, keeping faith with the experience of vertigo that limitlessness creates in a writer. One particularly difficult Dickinson poem, "Time feels so vast," offers a powerful antidote to the genteel transcendentalist version of sublime sensation. The disruption of limits has repercussions more significant than an aphorism can contain. For Dickinson, no special day or half hour reminds the poet that time's circumferential limits are not all-inclusive. She refuses to write occasional poetry (even in her letters). Instead, she senses directly, and inconveniently, the presence of boundless invariability.

> Time feels so vast that were it not
> For an Eternity —
> I fear me this Circumference
> Engross my Finity —
>
> To His exclusion, who prepare
> By Processes of Size
> For the Stupendous Vision
> Of his Diameters — (858)

The central beauty of this poem is the phrase "Processes of Size" — a carefully crafted oxymoron. Of course the raw concept of "Size" neither engenders nor participates in any "process": it is an abstraction interlocked with the idea of movement. Jammed into the cogs of the wheeling universe, the word "Size" in this poem makes narrative impossible.

The donnée of this Dickinson poem is the category of eternity — usually the destination rather than the point of departure for religious and Romantic poetry. Dickinson's first stanza expresses gratitude for what she considers an obvious pressure exerted on time by eternity. If not for this pressure, she says, temporality would seem to be the only conceptual frame possible. Uncorrected, the lens of time would falsely magnify ("Engross") both itself and the finite speaker, who then could know her situation fully. But the unsituated proceedings of this poem, the works of the awesome other whom time excludes, happen instantaneously and never: thus Dickinson names "His" activity in the infinitive, using the ungrammatical word "prepare." To be sure, the spirit of manifestation here somehow proceeds from aspects of the divine. But that procession is a tableau rather than an occasion, no day or half hour but a ritual stopping of the clocks. ("Rudiments," the variant given at the bottom of Dickinson's manuscript page, shares the ambiguity of the word "Processes," since it invokes substantive elements as much as anticipatory maneuvers.)

It is difficult to decouple theological poetry and Christian historiography. This poem's beauty stems primarily from the strange verbal choices involved in the effort to do so. Language's incapacity to encompass atemporality leads to mismatches of verb with verb and category with category. The virgules early in the poem, associated with the word "Finity" and the poet's smallness, are reprised by the small dash at the poem's end, which is supposed to be associated with God's eternity. Contained in circumferences, the poet can only indicate, and can never represent, the absolute perspective that all circumference of any particular size excludes. Thus the bisecting "Diameters" of the absolute do not alter, but merely measure, the world and the mind. They cut across, but do not burst, the concentric "circles" Emerson describes in his essay about the confining scope of knowledge. But the diameters, in making contact between a centering self and its circumference, also slice through both self and world and disrupt vastness with the imposition of a totalizing measurement.

Grasped by the poet's mind, the redemptive story of Revelation seizes up here into a single moment of sensation, a tableau rather than an event — static, cold, and implacably geometric. God's lines of power are imposed on her without recourse to the language of events. As the pure vastness of size answers the mere grossness of time, fulfillment and delay are unified absurdly in the ceaselessness of the infinitive verb "prepare." The poem, then, encounters its prospects in a moment that contains both stupefied longing and potent invocation. The speaker is starkly confined by her finitude just as she surmounts it. And such spatial tableaux tend to offer a glimmer of representational success. The poet's final mark, the crossbar for the "t" in the word "Diameters," a line that in the manuscript floats free of the word itself, fails to name those lines coherently. But it also represents them, with vigor and panache. Boldly substantive, unlike the small transitional dashes of the poem's sequential propositions, this stroke is an image of the diametric slice the poet herself superimposes on the world of objects, spanning all the truth but making it a slant.

THERE ARE PRECEDENTS for the celebrated Emersonian encounter with the sublime, but most of the roughly contemporary examples, from European Romanticism, are less extreme and more sensible. When Wordsworth, for example, regards the view over land to the sea from Mt. Snowdon, a comfortable buffer of beauty separates him from nature's open-ended power.

> The Moon hung naked in a firmament
> Of azure without cloud, and at my feet
> Rested a silent sea of hoary mist.
> A hundred hills their dusky backs upheaved
> All over this still ocean; and beyond,
> Far, far beyond, the solid vapours stretched,
> In headlands, tongues, and promontory shapes,
> Into the main Atlantic . . .
> There I beheld the emblem of a mind
> That feeds upon infinity, that broods
> Over the dark abyss, intent to hear
> Its voices issuing forth to silent light
> In one continuous stream; a mind sustained
> By recognitions of transcendent power,
> In sense conducting to ideal form . . . (*Prelude 1850*, Book XIV, l.40 – 77)

In these last lines, the power of the scene infuses the intellect that perceived that scene — by becoming a metaphor for it. The environment serves the human purpose of self-understanding, and the mind interlocks with nature, as Romantic idealism demanded (having absorbed Kant's insight about the interdependence of the two). But one of them is subjugated to the other. As a result, there are linguistic and physical cushions at their points of contact: images of eating, brooding, and voice, along with the Welsh landscape presenting itself reassuringly, like a herd of friendly sea lions, between mountain and shore. Meanwhile, the moon's luminary oversight protects the writer from the sense of uncontrolled solitude that Emerson recommended and Dickinson inhabited. (In like fashion, even Keats's Cortes, also astride a mountain at a distance from his awesome ocean, is defined not by what he sees but by his own "wild surmise," a human achievement commensurate with that of Homer.) The British Romantics' ocean presents no questions, just particular human answers, furnished with sublimity's European accoutrements. This is the same generic upholstery that Emerson urged his auditors to cast away — for he believed that they could.

The appropriate precedent for Emersonian poetry of nature is found not in the European Romantics, whose philosophy Emerson adapted, but in the transplanted Puritans, whose sensory imaginations he inherited. The eyesight of the poet in this heritage has the same athletic passivity as the soul of the Puritan: a character of paralyzed awe that somehow fires the imagination while insisting on the futility of its cognitive task. Taking on some of the agency formerly assigned to God, but also highly acquiescent to the world, the poet builds her own small turret over the abyss. The poet herself occupies both of the roles that Jonathan Edwards divided between the all-powerful being — "The God that holds [us] over the pit of hell, much as one holds a spider, or some loathsome insect over the fire"[10] — and the suspended human in God's hands: "Your own care and prudence, and best contrivance, and all your righteousness, would have no more influence to uphold you and keep you out of hell, than a spider's web would have to stop a falling rock" (479). Such metaphors were the Puritan jeremiah's way of expressing the weakness of humanity over against the infinite; but explicitly for Emerson (as implicitly for Edwards), the metaphor of height and suspension also entails a sensation of power.

In the Puritan imagination, the opposed categories of power and powerlessness had been linked productively, in communal historiography:[11] in the face of eternity, in that worldview, historical deeds were both highly significant and totally inconsequential. As this paradox was flexed in Puritan society, the possibility of sempiternal life was infused into each deed and sensation. Incommensurable Emersonian knowledge, though, dwells in infinite space rather than infinite time. As a result, impossible size replaces possible futurity as the yardstick of knowledge. In a spatial rather than historical imagination, the human being lacks all access to her only stable reference point, the infinite horizon. The individual's godforsaken body, all surface, stands exposed under a firmament without features or limits. In the boundless arena a person cannot occupy, the arena her eye takes in instantaneously, failure and success are the same experience.

THE EPISTEMOLOGY that presides at the brink of infinity is very different from any effective U.S. hermeneutics of action. One good way to understand the shoreline experience is by contrasting it with its best inland counterpart: Emerson's protopragmatism.[12] In the pragmatic inland account of the perceiving mind, a story of engagement makes worthwhile action possible, without merely enabling ignorant domination of the landscape. As this story has it, the central tenet of Emersonian knowledge is a simple one: the world, although in essence a tremendous unity, can be known as we encounter it piecemeal. Each small circle of comprehension is an emblem of the great circle of the horizon. Every part is adequate to teach us about the whole: this is a classic tenet of empiricism that Emerson was the first to test in the crucible of language. Since the part and the whole are interdependent, every piece of his writing emphasizes the importance of both. That principle, in turn, accounts for the distinctive style of Emerson's essays: he seeks to accustom his reader to the awkward but crucial leaps involved in knowledge's transmission, the leaps from world to mind, from sentence to sentence, and (fundamentally) from part to whole and back again. In these "transitional" leaps, critics say, Emersonian power is born. We feel it reading, every time we encounter a surprising rhetorical gap between a pair of sentences, and he felt it as he chose the words that would span deeper, conceptual abysses. In the successful version of Emerson's knowledge, both reading and writing are athletic; like a gymnast of thought, he is aware of every piece of the apparatus, and touches them all in rapid, even blindingly fast sequence.

Thus in the dynamic, pragmatic readings of the past few decades, Emerson and his reader together make things work. The fellow-feeling between writer and critic is appropriate, since Emerson considers himself just a reader of the world. Even when he writes about writing, he describes it as an act of reading—as if making a text about the world were just a matter of following nature's own recipe.

> Nature will be reported. All things are engaged in writing their history. The planet, the pebble, goes attended by its shadow. The rolling rock leaves its scratches on the mountain; the river its channel in the soil; the animal its bones in the stratum; the fern and leaf its modest epitaph in the coal. The falling drop makes its sculpture in the sand or the stone. Not a foot steps into the snow, or along the ground, but prints in characters more or less lasting a map of its march.[13]

Human remarking on nature, in this passage, is of a piece with nature's own marking of itself, and textuality is as automatic as gravity. In the compelling flow of these sentences, the essayist accordingly asks us to forget that he is there, and simply to read along with him. It is hard to imagine a sentiment farther from Dickinson's apprehension of eternity, her inscribing centrality at a distance from time's objects.

The theory of the writing process as itself a kind of successful knowing becomes still richer and more complicated under close scrutiny. Even in sentences where writerly power is both well hidden and well exercised, the complexity of knowing—even of simply seeing—is a vital principle. Human writerliness informs even simple observation, for knowledge is not only an experience but also an act of inscribing the world. What Emerson knows of nature is itself inflected by the human mind: thus it should be no surprise that in the subtly ambiguous passage quoted above, linguistic workings are identified with natural forces like gravity, and vice versa. Flexible puns entwine human agency and the agency of nature. For example, the assertion that nature has a "will" is counterbalanced by the passive quality of what it wills: the world would like "to be reported," which requires human initiative. In the same way, the "engagement" of all things "in writing" might be their investment *in* their own activity of writing, or their sensory engagement *by* the human who writes.

Thus, although the gist of this passage is that nature writes itself, Emerson does not sublimate the human act of writing—the deeds of art, or of mere mapping. For him, suppression of the human imagination would mean a world without cognitive order, and a world to which we are incidental. The small puns here reflect a vital Emersonian truth: the human mind makes the world what it is. The writer's sentences partake dynamically of the world that she reads. In the same way, the rolling rock inscribes on the world just the natural history that nature as a whole would choose to tell; in the same way, the critic analyzes a single quotation to summarize many volumes of Emersonian prose. The part and the whole are engaged in each other. This mutuality is America's best sort of answer to crucial cognitive questions about the relations between self and world, and between fact and context.[14] In the mainstream tradition of addressing Emerson's cognitive concerns, sociable poets like Whitman, pragmatic poets like Stevens, and novelists of many stripes used this Emersonian mechanism. Actuated by the flexibility of linguistic objects, such dynamic relation between part and whole is (the story goes) our most important cognitive inheritance from Emerson.

The student's question about Emerson's prose, though, is how this mutual work of mind and world functions in actual cognitive deeds, in a landscape. What do the parts of nature say to Emerson when they speak for the world as a whole? We may scan his strongest work for "close readings" of nature, but we will be disappointed. Henry David Thoreau is instead the exemplary practitioner of such reading and writing of the world: in *Walden*, he creates fresh knowledge through a dynamic consideration of nature as a whole, with many of its parts examined closely.[15] Likewise some of the best deployments of pragmatic Emersonianism are to be found in American literary criticism, in which a text is powerfully reported through ambiguous but productive tensions between part and whole, the critic's excerpt and the author's vision.[16]

Most sessions of reading Emerson's prose, though, yield the same awkward discovery: though he may recommend them, he actually occupies neither of these successful and dynamic modes of knowledge. In the essays, his attention to particular features either of nature or of human stories is unsustained, even paltry — in the lines cited earlier, for example, the rock and the footprint are purely generic tokens. Emerson's neglect of particulars still vexes our reading of him, and even if we no longer simply call him a transcendentalist, his transcendent urges must be faithfully reported. For example, the paragraph immediately after the sentences about nature's self-marking insists on human transcendence, radically undermining their meaning: "In nature this self-registration is incessant, and the narrative is the print of the seal. It neither exceeds nor comes short of the fact. But nature strives upward; and, in man, the report is something more than the print of the seal" ("Montaigne" IV.151). This "something more" about human writerliness — and thus human knowledge — constitutes the unfortunate difference between Emerson's epis-

temology and Thoreauvian pragmatism. As the last two clauses suggest paradoxically, that troublesome "something" is found equally in humanity and
in nature — which is to say, everywhere. This "striving upward" threatens to
render meaningless all the previous paragraph's celebration of earthy writing
driven by gravity.

Even worse, this claim — that the transcendent unity a human mind imposes on the world undermines, rather than guarantees, the status and integrity of each object — disrupts a central tenet of the empiricist Emerson
described above. After all, the point of a successful pragmatic hermeneutics
is that part and whole participate in each other: each step can be read as the
map of the march, each scratch of the pen encapsulates the story of a self who
gathers no moss. Such complex pragmatic readerliness characterizes the Emerson well won for modern America in recent decades; it seems retrograde to
question the healthy Emersonian symbiosis of part and whole by insisting on
the special status of vastness in his philosophy. Nonetheless, that spoiling element in the Emersonian hermeneutic is not an incidental one. Limitlessness,
in fact, is to Emerson the defining feature of nature's unity.

The oceanic character of this unity, its very blankness, is a faithful image
of Emerson's philosophy. The whole that he craves, the fullness that his mind
reads into the world, is absolute — an imaginative freedom without limits.[17]
The pragmatist, to be sure, would feel no such absolute need for exhaustive-
ness, and would be pleased to make her way to each object in turn while neglecting the all. But Emerson himself most often chooses as the instrument of
knowledge not the exploring hands and feet but the infinitely receptive eye, its
wide aperture capable of extreme reach without direct grasp. The universality
we deplore in Emerson is not a proposition for him but a fact of ocular experience, which is defined by nearly immediate sensory awe: "In every landscape,
the point of astonishment is the meeting of the sky and the earth, and that is
seen from the first hillock as well as from the top of the Alleghanies [sic]. . . .
There is nothing so wonderful in any particular landscape, as the necessity of
being beautiful under which every landscape lies" ("Nature" III.103).

One way of appreciating Emerson's genius is to note how he creates such
direct relations between "wonder" and "necessity." The essence of the phenomenon is encapsulated in the phrase "point of astonishment": for Emerson,
we are not adequate to the primal fact about any vista in nature. Infinity is
the first fact, the feature that we make ourselves as we read the line of sky and
earth: "The eye is the first circle; the horizon which it forms is the second." The

two-inch capsule of nerves and aqueous humor, drawing the world into itself, is here brought into immediate relation with the opposite figure, the horizon, opening ever outward. The complexity of this inside-out interaction vexes Emerson's knowledge. Juxtaposing extremes of scale — eye and horizon — this handling of size differs fundamentally from the successful pragmatic negotiation with space and representation. In a pragmatic reading of nature, as in most successful literary-critical technique, the "map of its march" is simply scaled to the size of the footprint, the footprint scaled to the size of the land. The two are superimposed: if they correspond, we are pleased by aesthetic unity; if they contradict, we are equally pleased by irony or incongruity. The image of the horizon (often in Emerson, as too few critics have remarked, an ocean horizon) challenges this scheme's core assumptions. What if the walk is not merely improvisatory, but endless, so that no map will contain it? What if the material of the world is too fluid to hold our prints? No journey can be undertaken in such a medium; no home can be built from such materials. As Emerson puts it in "Experience," our idea of knowledge arrives here "Not at a wall" (to be scaled), "but at interminable oceans" (III.42). The ocean, in fact, is the vista Emerson reads more often than any particular inland terrain, and it is unmarked — unreadable.

Such trouble arises because of the pressing epistemological problem that underlies the celebrated Emerson project of linking mundanity and transcendence. The problem can be sensed in the sentence about the meeting of earth and sky, where Emerson creates a strange chime between the phrases "any landscape" and "every landscape." The issue of "any" and "every" — of how examples relate to ideas, and how instances relate to contexts — informs the central effort of the crucial Emerson poem analyzed below, "Each and All." Within a pragmatist's horizon, every part should reflect the whole; but at the shoreline, where horizon perfectly matches the idea of horizon, the vastness dwarfs any particular clue to its nature that we might comprehend. This troubling incommensurability presents a radical threat to this nature poem in which we might hope to see the pragmatic Emerson hermeneutic in action. The title's ambitious linking of part and whole (rendered as interdependence, as in the line "All are needed by each one") might be expected here to animate American knowledge in methodical descriptions that interact dynamically with universal truths. Instead, in the poem's central episode, the hermeneutic fails miserably in the face of unapproachable openness — before the quintessential, indispensable Emersonian "point of astonishment," the horizon. In the heritage of incommensurability, the American poets to follow Emerson will have to address a radical mismatch: the disjunction between the poet's mind and the boundless possibility onto which it opens.[18]

TO BE SURE, American poets of the infinite do not always consider it unapproachable, as Emerson did. Emerson's contemporary Oliver Wendell Holmes Sr., for example, lays claim to infinite scope through a simple act of interpretation. In "The Chambered Nautilus" (1857), he reads a part of nature, the spiral shell of the titled animal, as offering a cognitive vantage on the whole.

> Still, as the spiral grew,
> He left the past year's dwelling for the new,
> Stole with soft step its shining archway through,
> Built up its idle door,
> Stretched in his last-found home, and knew the old no more.
>
> Thanks for the heavenly message brought by thee,
> Child of the wandering sea,
> Cast from her lap, forlorn!
> . . . .
> While on mine ear it rings,
> Through the deep caves of thought I hear a voice that sings:
> . . . .
> "Let each new temple, nobler than the last,
> Shut thee from heaven with a dome more vast,
> Till thou at length art free,
> Leaving thine outgrown shell by life's unresting sea!"[19]

Paradoxically, the mollusk leaves us the shell as a sign of its ability to escape the shell: its enclosure is the sign of its freedom. Like Walter Benjamin's "allegory" (although less obviously melancholic), the shell embodies a concept opposite to the one it expresses. Eventually in Holmes's storyline, absolute wholeness, a sphere without a boundary, intervenes in the brooder's meditation on partiality and shelter. For Holmes, predictably, this means that the open-edged circle of freedom replaces the spiral, with its gradually expanding scope. Thus the poem's final vantage on nature is a boundless heaven — an openness somehow conceived with the help of the radically bounded shell.

The abrupt transition from the closed shell to its message of open space enables another shift of categories, from liberation to salvation, to give the poem its clichéd religious conclusion.

Holmes stakes the integrity of his interpretive endeavor on the physical integrity of the seashell. In the mollusk's construction of the shell, a large enclosure is repeatedly soldered onto a smaller one; by analogy, Holmes concludes that the infinite freedom of heaven can be soldered onto the finite earth, bringing all space — even spatiality itself — under the purview of the inquiring human. Whereas Emerson's essay "Circles" shows from outside how every new structure of knowledge is ripe for obsolescence and shrinking, "The Chambered Nautilus" celebrates, as if from within, ever-better structures of containment, bigger houses and new temples. In the last stanza, though, it lays claim to boundlessness, performing a final, quite different transition — out of the very category of containment. Holmes's accretion of chambers upon chambers builds momentum somehow, to transcend all chambers, and achieve absolute "freedom." As if to question this leap, though, unknowable space reasserts its power in the last line: the poem concludes with the image of the "unresting sea," the abysmal brine that is the true resting place of the dead and denuded nautilus.

"The Chambered Nautilus," then, as a cognitive act, asserts the possibility of a smooth progress from earthly clues of freedom — the incrementally larger new spaces in which the nautilus "stretches" out comfortably every few weeks — to absolute freedom, a stable heaven. There is no need to refer to Emerson's theology ("Every thought is a prison; every heaven is also a prison" ["Intellect" III.19]) to show that this readerly maneuver would not appeal to him. Emersonian circles of knowledge do not join with each other, in a series of transitions, to form a spiral like the one that enables and records the nautilus's progress. In fact, they destroy each other: "Each thought [forms] itself into a circular wave of circumstance. . . . But the soul . . . bursts over that boundary on all sides and expands another orbit on the great deep, which also runs up into a high wave" and so on ("Circles" II.180 – 181). No fossil is left behind in this liquid process to teach humanity. Human knowledge, then, though it may be well suited to read the shell on shore, must attempt a focus on the "great deep" — the unresting sea, and its ultimate carapace of open sky. Emerson's encounters with that sea earned him Holmes's appraisal as a writer of "over-statement," often "fearfully near the abyss of the ridiculous";[20] but if we take Emerson's claims on infinitude seriously, we must conclude that the turn to nature is for him not a recommendation of natural history or even work. It is a difficult turn toward unresting vastness. His extreme philosophy constantly invokes this infinite space but, axiomatically, cannot contain it.

Like the speaker of "The Chambered Nautilus," the speaker of "Each and All" chooses the integral seashell as his point of access to nature's boundless unity; Emerson's poem, though, is about the absolute failure of Holmesean knowledge. (Not only Oliver Wendell, the inductive reader of shells, but also Sherlock, the deductive reader of footprints, is challenged here, as Emerson prefers to highlight the impossible rather than the improbable.) The inspecting mind makes the shell a symbol, but by that very act negates the shell's participation in the all: astonishingly, then, *no* part of nature partakes of the whole's perfection. The episode begins promisingly enough, as Emerson's speaker performs the deed of fetching the shell and bringing it inside that must have preceded Holmes's naturalist inspection of the object.

> The delicate shells lay on the shore;
> The bubbles of the latest wave
> Fresh pearl to their enamel gave;
> And the bellowing of the savage sea
> Greeted their safe escape to me.
> I wiped away the weeds and foam,
> I fetched my sea-born treasures home;
> But the poor, unsightly, noisome things
> Had left their beauty on the shore,
> With the sun, and the sand, and the wild uproar.[21]

Indicating the shore's beauty but no longer of it, the shells are failed symbols of the speaker's experience of wholeness. The shell's integrity, which for Holmes made it readable as a clue to nature's progress toward freedom, for Emerson renders it stiff and ugly — an eyesore on his mantel (despite its liberation from the incidental, ugly "weeds and foam" of the beach). The collected shell is totally alien to the context of iridescent flux in which he found it — the very context of which it was meant to be a lasting emblem. The Emersonian naturalist's rigorous sampling of the world is foiled by the rigor mortis it creates in its object.

With its particular desire to account for itself, the lyric is the proper mode for working on, if not solving, the gap between experience and representation. Unfortunately, instead of rising to the challenge of the shells in "Each and All" and reasserting humanity's writerly mutuality with nature, Emerson offers a weak compromise: leaving the shells at home, his speaker glumly ventures out to the river — giving up on a version of nature as absolute and demanding as the seashore, and calling beauty "childhood's cheat." In response to the speaker's new artistic indifference — his resolution not to write the whole — nature offers up in consolation an inland experience of wholesome parts:

> As I spoke, beneath my feet
> The ground-pine curled its pretty wreath,
> Running over the club-moss burrs;
> I inhaled the violet's breath . . .
> Again I saw, again I heard,
> The rolling river, the morning bird; —
> Beauty through my senses stole;
> I yielded myself to the perfect whole.

Although they are not usually the reasons given, excellent reasons exist for the critical consensus that these concluding lines, in *this* poem, are unsatisfactory. The end of the poem cuts off speech just before the crucial moment, the transition from experience to knowledge with which Emerson's speaker has been struggling. The shells fetched home profoundly failed to contain their shoreline context — and yet in these last lines the trees and birds, fetched into verse, are said to contain the landscape. Incredibly, Emerson seems to have forgotten that the problem of the poem was never in passively having experiences of wholeness, but in claiming them: that is, in preserving them as objects of human ornament, textual or otherwise. In its final moments, "Each and All" forgets its own topic, the difficult transition between the wholeness of experience and the partiality of text.[22] This breakdown of attention, and the poem's weak ending, are caused by a rudimentary form of the observant American hermeneutic, which looks at objects as clues to their contexts. This faux resolution is born out of the capable piecemeal description that precedes the final line, a catalog of inland objects read in order, from ground's wreath to the "dome more vast" of sky, in a Holmesean progress. Such descriptive listing almost never occurs in the consistently electric prose; the essays more often invoke singular encounters with the "savage sea," the sea that still bellows offstage as the curtain drops on "Each and All."

Not because he avoids the parts of nature, then, but because he avoids the whole, Emerson the poet abdicates the task he set for American poetry in

"Each and All." At the close, a list of nature's parts stands in for the incommensurate "perfect Whole" surrounding them — even though that substitution's failure was the poem's central premise. In acknowledging the shells' failure of signification, we can now see, Emerson set himself an impossible cognitive problem. He chose that impossibility because he knew, in his many honest moments, that the workable cognitive dialectic between part and whole (that is, "Each" and "All") cannot accommodate the horizon's transcendence of size itself. Pragmatism has no handle on the limitlessness of experience Emerson demands of his Romantic whole. Any token of nature may speak to the scholar, but Emerson's "All," the absolute, mentally pure distance of the sea, corresponds to nothing smaller, nothing that can be studied in camera. Its restless swirl, unbounded like humanity's own potential, is incommensurate with anything we know.

Yet it is precisely the oceanic horizon's vastness that Emerson insists upon as the key to American imaginative freedom. Emerson sets fundamental cognitive tasks for the American poet, and the essays' concern with the interrelation of part and whole directly influences his idea of poetry's task. The writer of American nature that Emerson calls for in "The Poet" is not just large; she "Traverses the whole scale of experience" (III.5). Since Emerson's notion of experience requires an infinite "All," poetic representations in his tradition must face in some way the problem of incommensurability. Other poets often answer the challenge of Emerson's vaunted infinitude with lyric performances more rigorous — both more honest and more inflexible — than he himself could muster in verse. Their compact writings, in a way, pay homage to the struggle he sustained over thousands of pages of prose — the struggle to keep faith consistently with an impossible idea of what knowledge is.

These poets, Dickinson first among them, undergo and enact in poetry the rigors of the essays' least bearable insight. When infinity is involved (Emerson's ocean instead of Thoreau's lake or even Thomas Cole's mountains), subject and object stand irrevocably apart: nothing can mediate between the human scale and the writer's horizons of knowledge. Infinity may be the primal human prospect; but in encounter with infinite space, writing knows only its own failure, and can only gather souvenirs like the seashells. Dutifully, the four poets featured in this book set about this task, keeping their eyes on the horizon and keeping sharp the awareness of incommensurability that Holmes lacked. These later poets know that they could not "fetch their sea-born treasures home," either to a well-known shelter or to a domesticated heaven. As soon as the treasures of infinitude are grasped — even if only by an eye — they are already impoverished. It is a poverty that Emerson both deplores and celebrates: "We cannot say too little of our constitutional necessity of seeing things under private aspects, or saturated with our humors. . . . We must hold hard to this poverty, however scandalous, and by more vigorous self-recoveries, after the sallies of action, possess our axis more firmly. The life of truth is cold" ("Experience" III.46). Preserving the shells of his isolated experience, the beachcomber does not feel in them the warmth of the ocean-side walk they ornamented. He clutches them instead in their unsightliness, blindly, with the same cold grip that the horizon took upon him.

2　An Everywhere of Silver

Emersonian philosophy often captures the attention of literary criticism because it is, secretly, all about words. The operation of Emerson's sentences creates a drama more compelling than anything he describes outside the library. One of the highest compliments he seems able to pay to sensory engagement in the outdoor world is to call it literary: "Not a foot steps into the snow or along the ground, but prints, in characters more or less lasting, a map of its march."[1] Such writerly reference points for Emerson's work, its essential bookishness, ought to disqualify him from inspiring poets of sensation — especially modernist poets who have absorbed William Carlos Williams's dictum "No ideas but in things." Often, indeed, Emerson's things — like the seashell of "Each and All" — are held at a distance: "An innavigable sea washes with silent waves between us and the things we aim at" ("Experience" III.29). Frequently ignoring the footprint in favor of abstract, silent seas of alienation, Emerson can seem an airy, old-fashioned thinker whose poetics are no more useful to later poets than his poems are. It is the task of this chapter to reclaim true sensation as an Emersonian feature of art, and to find it precisely in that very image of alienation — the sea that dwarfs the beach-walker. The ocean horizon bears a human aspect (albeit a cold one): it is imprinted by the senses just as much as the sand is by the writer's foot.

Encounter with nature need not mean tight proximity between human desiring and sensory facts. When the human footprint is placed in the foreground of an Emersonian horizon, it no longer suggests a harmony between world and poetic work, but an absolute contrast, a relation of incommensurability that pragmatism cannot govern. And yet the unity of the horizon proceeds from the nature of the eye itself: "The eye is the first circle; the horizon which it forms is the second" ("Circles" II.179); "The health of the eye seems to demand a horizon" (*Nature* I.13). Again and again in the essays, the link between eye and horizon suggests that Emerson is less interested in the marks made on the world by touch than in the mark made by vision. It is as natural for the eye to create infinity in its object as it is for the foot to map itself in the sand. The eye's mark, in the tradition of idealism, is wholeness: idealist vision imposes conceptual unity on a world of parts. Thus the concavity of the (infinitely distant) firmament corresponds perfectly to the (infinitely receptive) convexity of the eye.

The eye-print, however, unlike the footprint, has a kind of scope that vexes its own source. The matching of firmament and eyeball breaks down when the extremity of size asserts itself. In one Emersonian story of knowledge, the eye forms the horizon, but another story reverses the sequence: "Men seem to have learned of the horizon the art of perpetual retreating and reference" ("Experience" III.29). Infinity is not just made by the human gaze; it also imposes itself upon human cognition. In the horizon is the sign of every look's inadequacy: space opens out indifferently, not seeming to require its perceiver. This difficulty with infinite (as opposed to merely continental) space is not a critique of Emersonian philosophy. The issue is of crucial concern to Emerson himself, a fact that becomes apparent when the category of size is foregrounded in key passages in Emerson — not only the late Emerson of "Experience" but also the more buoyant early Emerson of *Nature*.

The tininess of the head and the eye in the locus classicus, the "transparent eye-ball" passage, contrasts starkly with the absolute vastness into which nature introduces the senses:

> Standing on the bare ground — my head bathed by the blithe air and uplifted into infinite space — all mean egotism vanishes. I become a transparent eye-ball; I am nothing; I see all; the currents of the Universal Being circulate through me; I am part or parcel of God. . . . In the tranquil landscape, and especially in the distant line of the horizon, man beholds somewhat as beautiful as his own nature. (*Nature* I.10)

The terms of size in this passage carry out an ongoing and uncomfortable dialectic of largeness and smallness — between the head's consoling bath near earth and its subjection to the yank upward; and, in the central list of clauses, between the smallness of "eye-ball"/"nothing" and the largeness of "all"/"Universal." The final sentence of the paragraph draws its imaginative strength from the same oscillation: the word "in" seems at first to refer to the location of the self (securely placed within the landscape), but it turns out to be just describing the location of the beauty the self discerns. Beauty is found not alongside humanity, "within" the landscape, but "in" the horizon named by its distance from the human.

Infinite space is claimed here — but it is claimed by an infinitesimal self, reduced not only to liberating anonymity but to the "nothingness" of the horizon turned inside out, the punctiform "eye-ball." The same emphasis on distance, a key term in Emersonian knowledge, is crucial also to the orphic poet's description of nature's human origins later in Emerson's first extended essay. Once coextensive with humanity, nature is now a "Huge shell" (with humanity shrunken within it) that corresponds to the human "From far and on high" (*Nature* I.42). This distance, the distance of the firmament itself, is constantly reinvoked in Emerson, and such a gap between self and shell, unlike that between foot and footprint, is never bridged except by the longing and encapsulated eye.

Critics often neglect the spatial contrasts that give passages like this one their energy; this is true whether those readings decry or debunk Emerson's gigantism. For the recent Americanist critics who can be gathered under the heading of "pragmatism," an imprinting, tactile immediacy affirms and exercises human suppleness in a way that experience of the sea cannot. Sensory experience impresses truth on the human, and exacts it from his work.[2] The dynamic mediation at the heart of these readings gives poetry a more humane mode, chastening without eliminating its ambition as it brings it into experience. The best of ideological criticism, too, makes note of the way humble reality disciplines and reactivates the dominant imagination.

If size is regarded as a tool rather than a category of experience, largeness of vision, the eyeball without boundaries, becomes mere shorthand for Emersonian dominance of the landscape. Openness sometimes seems like an arrival point, a solution to Emersonian compositional problems; yet in truth those problems are just beginning when the writer steps outside. The vexations of outdoor experience seem like a mistake, one that an industry in criticism has set out to correct. Myra Jehlen, for example, takes it as axiomatic to her powerful pragmatic mode that Emerson's "transparent eye-ball" passage is effectively identical to Thoreau's similarly famous celebration of cognitive burrowing: "I think that the richest vein is somewhere hereabouts; so by the divining rod and thin rising vapors I judge; and here I will begin to mine" (Thoreau 351). The metaphors' inherent differences are regarded as a synthesis in embryo, to be realized in history and discerned by the critic. "Not blind like a mole but become 'a transparent eye-ball,' not pressed about by actual soil but abstracted into the most insubstantial spirituality, . . . Emerson is nonetheless located in a nature that he explicitly possesses as (spiritual) property. Incarnation (the assumption of the continental body) is for him also the basic condition for transcendence" (Jehlen 11). The question raised by this reading is what constitutes an essential difference, if as Jehlen maintains there is no essential difference between Emerson's description and Thoreau's. It is the difference between up and down, between the heritage of Plato and that of Aristotle — between the absolute infinitude made by the eye and the gritty specificity the hands and feet know. It is, moreover, this very difference of scope that all agree is the distinguishing feature of Emersonian knowledge.

Somehow, according to the conventional wisdom, world and mind must meet in the middle, whether to chasten ideology or to empower observation. That productive drive toward equipoise of eye and object is the newly agreed upon legacy of Emersonian epistemology that this chapter means to examine and qualify. Pragmatic and ideological readings both focus (the one with admiration, the other with suspicion) on the narrative of harmonious interlocking of self and world. In this lyric tradition, though, self and world are often held apart by a magnetism of absolute difference — even as the magnetism of Emerson's naturalistic idealism holds them in encounter and makes them mutually dependent. In Emerson's philosophy and variously in the work of several poets who follow him, a fundamental asymmetry disrupts pragmatic relation between human action in the world and the world's presence to the human. This asymmetry is the problem of infinity, a problem not only figured but also experienced as unlimited horizontal space. It is not just the mind or the language faculty that encounters this problem; it is faced by the body afoot.

The primary disruption to the idealist's vision of outdoor space is also its fundamental category, size. When there are no limits to demarcate a tableau and give it scale, any centering presence can be rendered insignificantly small. There are no elements to mediate between pure, punctiform foreground and featureless background. What, then, is the perceiving mind called upon to do? What is there to know? The answer is unpragmatic: all or nothing; or, all and nothing. These are the terms insisted upon by the "transparent eye-ball" passage's linking of horizon and aqueous drop, with no middle ground offered. When the human spirit refuses containment, the continent no longer serves its purpose.

It is because of land's finitude that Emerson is "uplifted" from the ground in the "transparent eye-ball" passage — flight is a crude metaphor for the erasure of middle ground. In another place, in his journals, he castigates Americans for "self-distrust — a fear to launch away into the deep, which they might freely and safely do. It is as if the dolphins should float on rafts, or creep and squirm along the shore" (quoted in S. Whicher 47). The shoreline version of cognitive freedom is much to be preferred to the clichés of flight and ether, and not only because the dolphins are a welcome update to British Romanticism's skylarks and nightingales. In the encounter with water, one is vigorously reminded of the medium's alien quality. Seawater's inhospitality emblematizes the fact that the finitude of the continentally bound perceiver can never be in equipoise with the infinitude of her vision. They are inevitably, axiomatically, at odds. Yet Emerson tries to insist on the total freedom and safety humanity should feel in this outer world. He chooses the unworkable sea, not the beckoning frontier, as the figure for perception's destiny.

EMERSON'S INITIAL description in "Experience" of the mind's power in natural space is fanciful, rather than imaginative. It adopts and combines clichés of American expansionism and English pastoralism: "By [my] persisting to read or to think, this region gives further sign of itself, as it were in flashes of light, . . . as if the clouds that covered it parted at intervals and showed the approaching traveller the inland mountains, with the tranquil eternal meadows spread at their base, whereon flocks graze and shepherds pipe and dance" (III.41). Mere topographic description, of clouds and mountains, leads almost immediately to tokens of other, English Arcadias. Narrative negotiation of the landscape, a pilgrimage to the West, is the dominant metaphor — but at the same time the clichés suggest that no claim of originary knowledge is being made. And what is worse, having described the pastoral destination, Emerson immediately admonishes himself that his description is inadequate: "But every insight from this realm of thought is felt as initial, and promises a sequel" ("Experience" III.41).

There is always more to know — and this means frustration as well as thrill. The dynamic of endless surmounting creates more ambivalence in Emerson than has yet been remarked. The trope of ever-unfolding knowledge from the essay "Circles," for example, signifies not only power (as many critics have observed) but also constant redisappointment. In claiming infinitude, and seeking freedom from old literary conventions, human power is indeed always moving forward — but never arriving. Narrative disappoints itself, every insight becoming instantly only "initial." The only temporal solution to this problem is a fresh break and a new start, a conversion that Emerson tries to name in the following sentence: "I am ready to die out of nature and be born again into this new yet unapproachable America I have found in the West" ("Experience" III.41).[3]

In this formula, the cultural limitation of cliché and convention is escaped, but the price of this freedom from old images, the "walls" other hands have built and the mountains that "were there already," is an uninhabitable structurelessness. There is a point of arrival in this most stringent of Emerson's geographical visions — but it is a brink rather than a dwelling place: "Suffice it for the joy of the universe that we have not arrived at a wall, but at interminable oceans" ("Experience" III.42).

Teleology and process give way in this sentence to pure, inhospitable ontology, not only crossing frontiers but dreaming of a passage "out of nature." The region of the American absolute is not inland after all, but beyond travel: the space of freedom is an ocean rather than a promised land to be occupied. An entirely different American paradigm is the consequence — the poetics of unapproachability rather than the narrative mode of romance.

In the best of Emerson's prose, then, the paradoxical simultaneity of knowledge and absolute distance characterizes the solitary eye, which claims the horizon that it cannot approach and divorces experience from process. Knowing even more intimately than Emerson does the unapproachability of vastness, Emily Dickinson writes smallness not only as a fact of the eye but also as one of the body. While Emerson discerns that people "Stand on the brink of the ocean of thought and power, but ... never take the single step that would bring them there" ("Experience" III.37), Dickinson describes what that stasis feels like, and enacts it verbally. She knows, too, that that decisive step will come not through her own will, but through the breaking of a "Plank in Reason" (see 340) — an inexplicable transition, a death out of nature into inhumanity. The most absolute of her protagonists' experiences challenge the ground on which they stand: this is a linguistic challenge, to be sure, but more fundamentally it is an extension of natural metaphor beyond its useful limits.

The poem "It was not Death" represents Dickinson's investment in nearly speechless sensation, rather than aporetic abstraction. Ineffable and stupefying though her speaker's experience is, it finds an adequate metaphor in the vista of ocean. When experience involves infinity, of course, it is easily mistaken for speculative philosophy or mere linguistics.[4] The sea trope tempers this assertion by presenting scenes in which concerns that seem purely linguistic are staged faithfully in a natural landscape — an object terrain empty of objects. Sensation can sometimes be abstract all by itself.

At the close of "It was not Death," for example, after an extended denial of the adequacy of sensuous terms for the speaker's uncanny experience, linguistic ingenuity seems indeed to be all that is left:

> As if my life were shaven,
> and fitted to a frame,
> and could not breathe without a key,
> And 'twas like Midnight, some,
>
> When everything that ticked — has stopped —
> And Space stares all around . . . (355)

Until the invocation of staring "Space," the poem comprises not descriptions, but propositions — or, more precisely, proposals — of analogies that might be adequate to its subject matter. Sealing off its protagonist and freezing her, and systematically rejecting metaphors for its subject matter, the poem is headed toward what Emily Budick calls "[a] sphere that is not even to be conceptualized in relation to geography or its absence" (210). The speaker occupies a "frame," a representational space rather than a sensory one. But just at the point of primordial abstraction, the words "Chaos" and "Stopless," sensation is reasserted. The metaphor that comes closest to being satisfactory turns out to be the ocean — and it satisfies precisely because of its sensuous poverty.

> But most, like Chaos — Stopless — Cool —
> Without a Chance, or Spar —
> Or even a Report of Land —
> To justify — Despair. (355)

The word "Cool" at first seems designed to mediate "not Cold" and "not Fire" from the first stanza, but its most important effect is to return us to the body in natural space. After a last effort at unsituated meaning ("Chance"), the dominant metaphor of vastness in the American tradition asserts both oceanic feeling and metaphoricity itself. In its visibility it defeats the bodilessness of pure language.

It is important to remember, despite the final metaphor of body, that this text is about an experience of nothingness. As New writes, "The ultimate door against which Dickinson leans is the door of the Void" (*Regenerate Lyric* 152); hence the theme of this poem is not only the "frame" that keeps the speaker in place, not only the words that refuse to match her experience, but also simply the experience itself, the sensation of unstinting vastness. That sensation, static but still outdoing propositions, finds its adequate metaphor in the unrelenting sea. Thus the poem succeeds only because it gives up its insistence on transparency, and refuses abstraction from the body (just as Emerson's transparency captures the imagination only because it is encapsulated in an eyeball). Though neither a "Spar" nor "Despair" should be stationed in the depicted scene — they are mentioned in the negative — the poem clings to both. The flotsam of recognizable human emotion bobs to the surface, and it becomes the poem's message. The image of the speaker adrift and despairing, rather than drowned (or absent) and numb, gives the poem imaginative strength even as it undermines its more radical linguistic claims to abstraction. The visual experience of void matches up with the idea of Void, but that image only functions when something solid is in the foreground.

The match, indeed, is not perfect — it is the difference between spar and no spar, a self that feels itself to be not there and the nothing that is, between Emerson's "Each" and Emerson's "All." It is a mismatch of extravagance, featuring an excess that Dickinson probes routinely in consciously bizarre metaphors, in passages like her description of the distance between two lovers:

You there — I — here —
With just the door ajar
That Oceans are (706)

In leaning on that "door of the Void," though, Dickinson does not simply exercise her intellectual muscles. She also registers the sensation of infinitude on her finite flesh. The importance of lines like these is not just the effect they have on language but the underdetermined shiver of strangeness that that linguistic oddity creates in the reader. This effect is lyric's advantage over the essay; it corresponds, moreover, to the power of kinesthetics in nature as opposed to that of vision alone. In asserting the importance of the poem to be experiential as well as rhetorical (see New, *Line's Eye* 203), this reading suggests that Dickinson's verbal strength is drawn from deeper streams than Emerson's.

IF DICKINSON IS a better poet than Emerson, though, it is because she is a better Emersonian. In Emerson's most sustained handling of infinite space, in "Experience," freedom from cultural boundaries locates him on the shore of "vast-flowing vigor": "Suffice it for the joy of the universe that we have not arrived at a wall, but at interminable oceans. Our life seems not present so much as prospective. . . . So, in particulars, our greatness is always in a tendency or a direction, not in an action" (III.42). That direction, of course, would be outward, and the impossible action called for is the stopless tracing of ever-larger realms of knowledge even after human footing is left behind. Such is the demand of the essay "Circles," in which incommensurability of size is embraced directly ("I am God in nature; I am a weed by the wall" [II.182]). Disappointingly, though, in "Experience," Emerson turns away from the seascape and is soon speaking not of outward cognitive effort, transcendences of size, but of a campaign to achieve greatness in linear history — "Onward and onward!"[5] Backpedaling from those "interminable oceans," he lapses out of sensory philosophy into a dream of the future, in which skepticisms (merely "limitations of the affirmative statement") can have "Affirmations made outside of them, and out of unbeliefs a new creed shall be formed" ("Experience" III.43).[6] In invoking the construction of affirmations, Emerson overlooks the limitation that he has just named: he forgets that outside of firm ground there is no place for building to begin. The oceans of the passage's central sentence thus undermine its subsequent efforts to found a workable creed. The writer tries to ignore the irreconcilability of "firmness" and miasma (properties respectively of "a wall" and "interminable oceans") and obscures the presence at hand of negative, oceanic space. The turn away from the absolute here, toward inland activity, does not perform tragedy, but ameliorates it, coaxing the aspiring self back away from its shoreline arrival point.

Responding in turn to this self-soothing diversion, Emerson corrects himself in the essay's next paragraph, and introduces his most strongly self-aware formula: "It is very unhappy, but too late to be helped, the discovery we have made that we exist. That discovery is called the Fall of Man. . . . We have learned that we do not see directly, but mediately" ("Experience" III.43). The reintroduction of the human into the scene reverses the previous paragraph's claim of immediacy: arrival at oceans of vigor is once again acknowledged to be different from unity with them. Irresolution is the effect of the Emersonian excursion. When oceanic power is named directly as a human experience, a phenomenon of the senses, Emerson is out of his depth. His continence of description is inadequate to his vision.

Dickinson's rendering of personal history answers more vigorously the questions of knowledge and self-location left open in "Experience." As in "It was not Death," her uncertain power often locates itself in a bare American landscape, with no prospect of motion; often, too, it reaches without flinching into the boundless water toward which Emerson can only gesture at the climax of his efforts. Her imagination, knowing impossibility and facing it without the retrenching recalibrations to which Emerson sometimes succumbs, brings us beyond the limits of Emerson's essayistic capacity. Her responses to ocean, though still philosophical, theological, and experiential, are synchronic answers partaking of a simultaneity that cannot be evoked even by Emerson's most atomistic and paradoxical sentences (such as the bifurcated formula "I am nothing; I see all").

In Dickinson's most thorough poem of landscape and cosmology, the first two stanzas outline the Emersonian problems of featureless landscape at the shoreline, with a similar interest in the possibilities of the West. Like the strict visual philosopher of *Nature* and "Experience," though, Dickinson returns from narrative and the future it opens to arrive at lyric self-awareness of "the Term between."

> Behind Me — dips Eternity —
> Before Me — Immortality —
> Myself — the Term between —
> Death but the Drift of Eastern Gray,
> Dissolving into Dawn away,
> Before the West begin —
>
> 'Tis Kingdoms — afterward — they say —
> In perfect — pauseless Monarchy —
> Whose Prince — is Son of None —
> Himself — His Dateless Dynasty —
> Himself — Himself diversify
> In Duplicate divine — (743)

The temporal frame of knowledge is here rendered directly into spatial terms: with the word "Drift" (itself adrift between noun and verb), the chronological passage into death is depicted as a slice of sky. With the words " 'Tis Kingdoms — afterward," the afterlife, too, is rendered into space, as an elsewhere-life. And spatiality is assigned all the grandeur that America assigns to the term "West." At the same time, though, the land that a power-oriented pioneer mentality would claim as its own pure possibility is assigned to a feudal owner, a "Prince." Whoever he is, he is not the (female) poet, and in his rugged, oddly Trinitarian individualism there is no room for relationship ("Himself — Himself diversify"). The loneliness is geographic as well as theological: Dickinson is drawing a map of the "Dateless" world in which motion is impossible, and it is for the poet only to survey the distance from a fixed spot. To budge from that spot would be to plummet through time and into timelessness — into the "Dips" of eternity or immortality.

Geography is a topic of this poem rather than just a metaphor. The West Dickinson invokes is an American West, registering not only sunset but also dreams of new power. For her, it is a realm of possibility to which access is impossible, like Emerson's "new yet unapproachable America that I have found in the West." Here impossibility of achievement is a matter of class ("Kingdoms"), gender ("Son"), individual sin ("they say"), and language ("Term between") — a tetrafecta of master tropes, all governed by the poem's spatial metaphor. The "Term between," Dickinson herself, is spoken into a space whose linearity traps her (backward is inexplicability, forward is patriarchal timelessness) even as a void opens beneath her feet. This double bind — theological confinement and the predawn darkness of pure space — awaits a simultaneous expression that also does justice to the individual's sense of herself. Having stationed the horizons both of finitude and of infinitude, of politico-theological structure and of absolute idea, the speaker turns in the final stanza to imagine the possibility that she should be adequate either to deserve or to defy these titanic arrangements. Like all good ocean-poems, this one turns ultimately to consider the status of the embodied perceiver within the poem.

In the first two lines of the last stanza, a final effort to introduce the temporal and logical ("then") gives way to a focus on the body in space ("between"). The poet looks offshore to find herself.

'Tis Miracle before Me — then —
'Tis Miracle behind — between —
A Crescent in the Sea —

With Midnight to the North of Her —
And Midnight to the South of Her —
And Maelstrom — in the Sky — (743)

In this omnibus poem of alienation and power in the landscape, Dickinson solves her panoply of cultural and ontological problems by an effort at dissolution rather than affirmation. In placing herself east of America, moreover, stepping back from the vista of western possibility, she implicitly opts for a featureless eternity ("behind" her) rather than the future immortality charged with culturally overdetermined power. Dickinson's speaker has no diachronic options to make synthesis possible: she operates under a Kierkegaardian hermeneutic of "either/or," in which each realm retains its appeal, but neither is acceptable. Stepping back off the firm land of the American "Prince," this speaker shows that her efforts are sensory, not historical; absolute, not pragmatic. She longs to make a claim on the pure possibility that Emerson gestures toward, not to storm or guard the walls (present or future) of myth, walls that might comfortably encompass skepticism and belief together. Spatial figuration of the self, rather than of its constructs, then saves the poem from excessive world-historical maundering about the difficulties of heaven and the bareness of earth.

In the final lines, Dickinson's speaker names herself in terms of verbal power, as a growth — a crescence. In the processualism of the word "Crescent," formed from the Latin participle "growing," she makes herself more dynamic than flotsam, emerging to dominate the landscape, forming of a sector of it a rise above its flatness. She is not choosing to be a dissenter, moving on a vector against (and therefore assimilable into) the east-to-west arrows of social progress and Christian world history.[7] Her orientation is at right angles to those histories: north, south, and up. All three orientations are brought into the realm of the visible by Dickinson's dynamic confrontation with the ocean.

This swelling visionary power, however, is confronted and profoundly altered by the fact that "Crescent" is also a brittle noun, pale and distant.[8] Reflected "in the Sea," the waxing or waning moon is a reminder of the transience of light and tide, but also insists stonily on the specific location even of the dynamic self — a "Her" boxed in at all points of the compass. Through a simple choice of perspective (the perspective of the poem is downward toward the "Dip" and the reflected "Crescent," rather than up at the sky), the moon is denied the chance to preside over the scene, and placed instead precariously in a tiny patch of water. Thus the scene, featuring a diminished thing adrift, maintains a tiny scope even as it offers an impossibly broad vision of the "Maelstrom," and a self expanding by her vision. Threatened by "Miracle," "Midnight," and "Maelstrom," and (paradoxically) confined by open largeness in all directions, the speaker chooses a "Term between" to describe her uncertain size.

The endangered brittleness of the lyric self and its presiding and expansive power are named simultaneously in the ambiguous word "Crescent." This ambiguity, sharper than a simple uncertainty about a pioneer's destination, hinges on the human perceiver's relation to nature's liquidity. Is it possible to dissolve into nature's flow while retaining volition, becoming a wave that can crash defiantly into the Christian continent before relaxing into oblivion? Or is an overmatched self more likely to look glumly down at her reflection, standing outside the surge (and ultimately toppling forward into the dawning of someone else's West)? In the first version, the self is participial, existing strongly in the crescendo of the moment while submitting in a larger sense to the flood; in the second, it is nominal, an object — a cold body in space, overwhelmed and paralyzed by vastness. In Dickinson's poetics, neither scenario can be neglected. Her project, in one aspect, expresses the intense and abiding sharpness of these ambiguities. In an instance of the compression only the lyric can manage, though, the doublenesses of her rigorous epistemology are here all packed into the single word "Crescent."

OCEANIC POWER excites poetry of Being. At the same time, and for the same reason, it presents a danger to the beings who encounter it. In a tiny poem naming that vast power, Dickinson calls ocean

> An Everywhere of Silver
> With Ropes of Sand
> To keep it from effacing
> The Track called Land. (931)

The Emersonian attention to this "Everywhere" characterizes the poetics here being described, and distinguishes it from the narrative theory of the "Elsewhere" developed by Richard Poirier. Since it is an "Everywhere," however, it offers no focal point except the centering self, who finds it impossible to avoid either confining solipsism or total dissolution. The writing of poetry in such a scheme is, as Frost puts it, "The impossible undertaking we undertake" (quoted in New, *Regenerate Lyric* 42). The "rope of sand" in this Dickinson poem is an emblem of the futility of human device, but the rhythmic strength of the land's nouns suggests that somehow in the act of writing effacement can be prevented, and a "track" or trace of poetic self-assertion preserved. Indeed, land (unlike sea) is here identical with the uses to which it is put — it is the realm of pragmatist footprints. This tracking, imprinting the self on earth, may be absolutely undermining to the primary vision of Dickinson's poetry, and that vision may threaten absolutely to efface her writing energy; yet for poets who stand a little farther from the water, other poetic outcomes are possible.

"Everywhere," absolute freedom, is an unavoidable topos to the self-liberating American writer unwilling to compromise. Its glittering attraction is irresistible to American poets who crave release from the beaten track. While Dickinson, with her unaccommodated body, sometimes lacks the equipment (or the will) to protect the paths of language from effacement by vastness, later poets look to the media of human engagement with the environment. Uncannily and consistently, though, human deeds and demarcations take on a different aspect when they are placed in the presence of absolute vastness. Sensory presence is distorted by an absence at hand, the vertiginous openness that corresponds perfectly — albeit inside out — to the clear eye that beholds it. The poem itself, likewise, and for the same reasons, is estranged.

At the brink, the lyric self staves off vertigo in a variety of ways, almost successfully. Careful reading shows, however, what strange rhetorical choices become necessary under Emerson's insistence on ocean horizon as the archetypal object of human knowledge. In choosing infinity as her backdrop, the Emersonian poet has committed to a consideration of Emersonian cognitive difficulty. She must occupy an ideal space, and at the same time give it body (in ways that Emerson could not). The beach, then, is the key scenario in this tradition of American poetry, the tableau in which philosophical extremity and sensuous experience intersect. The experience of a shoreline space offers, oxymoronically, experience of abstraction. To make real the power of human thought, then, the writer must make a mark on blankness, even while celebrating its openness. In a way, after all, the point of Emersonian philosophy is that "The blank, that we see when we look at nature, is in our own eye" (*Nature* I.44). At the brink a poet asserts pure visuality by acknowledging the idiosyncrasy of her individual sight.

IN "BOND AND FREE," the most explicit poem of imaginative freedom of the twentieth century, Robert Frost brings into the same space the tactile receptivity of pragmatic knowledge and the visionary power of transcendence. Flippantly, he names these entities "Love" and "Thought"; still more flippantly, they are gendered female and male.

Love has earth to which she clings
With hills and circling arms about —
Wall within wall to shut fear out.
But Thought has need of no such things,
For Thought has a pair of dauntless wings.

Like the freedom of Emerson's poet, Thought's freedom is figured as a freedom from gravity; like Emerson, though, Frost knows that this version of boundlessness is hackneyed: when Emerson describes meeting "This winged man, who will carry me into the heavens" ("The Poet" III.6), the joke is obviously on him. Here, likewise, the reader is offered a weak caricature of abstraction's power: a thin broth of astronomical cliché instead of any earnest description of the "gains" that make freedom worthwhile: "Thought cleaves the interstellar gloom / And sits in Sirius' disc all night . . . // His gains in heaven are what they are." There is ambivalence in this joke, though, as in Emerson's, for "Thought" is a real topic here: the final naming of Thought's "gains" partakes equally of begrudging acknowledgment and biblical force — the gains that "are what they are" being at once dismissed offhandedly, as dilute experiences of mere space, and subtly affirmed to be encounters with God, who defines himself by that tautology (Exodus 3:14). This ambiguity of sense corresponds to a rhythmic ambiguity about the placement of the line's only anapest — the two ways of scanning the words match the two ways of meaning them.

Thought, it seems obvious, has the best of both worlds, returning to "An earthly room" when ambition becomes unsafe. This cyclical and compensatory work is, in some versions, the Emersonian ideal of human productivity. It is congruent with Emerson's notion of mutually sustaining cycles of excursions and retrenchment: "The intellectual and the active powers seem to succeed each other, and the exclusive activity of the one, generates the exclusive activity of the other. There is something unfriendly in each to the other, but . . . each prepares and will be followed by the other" (*Nature* I.16). Of course, such diachronic schemes can all too easily disguise asymmetries of power. The lightness of tone here belies the difficult imaginative issues that Frost touches on in this poem: among them, the consignment of the feminine to docility or captivity; the airy surmounting in the masculine *via negativa*; the general indifference of the free toward the bound; the anxious violence implied in the need for protective "arms" against "fear" and even the Icarean danger evoked in the "burning on every plume" that drives Thought home at dawn.

"Bond and Free" makes use of a conventionally gendered opposition of airy exploration versus stable attention to the earth: "There is something unfriendly in each to the other." Indeed, unfriendliness is the crucial fact in the *ménage* of Love and Thought in this poem; but here, unlike in the temporal cycles Emerson describes, the key is not that the two follow each other (or, of course, that their marriage is a happy one) but that their experiences are in some way identical. This is why, albeit with a strange sort of distanced skepticism, Frost writes that "some say" Love and Thought have the same possessions of knowledge.

> [Thought's] gains in heaven are what they are.
> Yet some say Love by being thrall
> And simply staying possesses all
> In several beauty that Thought fares far
> To find fused in another star.

An untrustworthy "some" may say this as a conservative mystification of inherently patriarchal abstraction; or perhaps "some say" it because it is folk wisdom that runs too deep for proof. Of course, those alternatives are at root the same; but the crucial lyric fact that ideological readings might miss is that they lead to different aural experiences of the line. On the page, nicely mystified, these possibilities foster a feeling of suspension.

As adroit as these last lines are, they cannot resolve the thematic problem so easily, with the mere assertion of unity between dwelling and excursion: there is too vast a difference between the "earth" of the first line and the "[other] star" of the final line, between the "wall within wall" of Emersonian circles (progressing inward instead of outward) and the unrimmed "disc" of Sirius. The true heart of the poem, where we should look for a stabilizing lyric presence, is in the second stanza, where the only appearance of an "I" gives the poem an imaginative core in an act of Emersonian encounter with nature.

> On snow and sand and turf, I see
> Where Love has left a printed trace

With straining in the world's embrace.
And such is Love and glad to be.
But Thought has shaken his ankles free.

As Emerson says of the work of knowledge in nature (using economic metaphors), "the ground is full of memoranda and signatures" ("Montaigne"
IV.151). Here, though, writing is not part of a world of commerce (that realm
is left to Thought, which seeks "gains" in expedition) but a performative task,
its marks made "with" rather than "by" human action. It is not the exclusive
realm of the male, "plumed" with adventurous wing; it is informed also by the
immediate facts of closer interaction with earth. Such traces, convex molds of
the bodies that create them, may not reliably "be" what they "are," like the tau-
tologous (or profound) findings of abstraction — but they are directly visible
to the lyric speaker in nature. Earth is the page on which desire is immediately
imprinted (Thought may have the pens, but he writes only by "cleaving" and
"retracing").

Yet alienation, sexual and linguistic, is indeed the position in which this
speaker finds himself in the second stanza. His experience of Love is not of its
presence to the world (or the world's embrace of it) but of its absence. Engagement with the world becomes knowable only when it "has left" a trace — that
is, only when it has left. Love's "straining" muscularity, then, is not only the
strain of pleasure or of productive labor but also a scramble to escape.[9] It entails
absence as well as total union with the world. Even in viewing Love's "printed
trace," as Emerson puts it in "Experience," "An innavigable sea washes with
silent waves between us and the things we aim at" (III.29). The human super-
fluity of mind, the restlessness of thought, is fundamental even to the plainest
version of experience, a walk on the sand.

When the work of knowing produces printed knowledge, then, it takes
only two shapes: the distance in which closeness makes access impossible ("To
find fused in another star"), and the closeness in which distance makes access
impossible ("On snow and sand and turf," the speaker *sees* rather than *feels* the
mark of Love). The paradoxes are charged in their metaphoric versions with
experiential power. The interstellar distances that Frost cannot resist invoking often interface less benignly with the earth on which humanity imprints
its desire. A third possible voice in response to vastness — besides Dickinsonian stiffness and the split personality of "Bond and Free" — endeavors in vast
space simply to accede to its own erasure. Thus in "Once by the Pacific," where

the surge of ocean threatens to overwhelm the shore, which "Looked as if / It were lucky in being backed by cliff, / The cliff in being backed by continent," titanic forces are arrayed on either side of the shoreline. A vengeful God is offshore, and counterpoised to God is the American soil that should ratify identity itself. Without an embodied lyric speaker in between, though, less seems to be at stake here than in the bedraggled persona clinging to a spar of language in Dickinson, or even in the fanciful multiple personifications of "Bond and Free." The vanishing of the continent is a possibility that can be entertained, but the body that would undergo such a flood, and senses its rhythm, is sublimated into the solid cliff and into the powerful waves that look inland at their prey. The speaker allows that "There would be more than ocean-water broken," but does not acknowledge the breaking of the human. Indeed, in merely claiming vaguely that humanity is "something more" than ocean water, Frost recapitulates the least rigorous form of transcendentalism. Without the counterweight of "simply staying" Love, the eye facing ocean is an instrument only of Thought, and forgets itself.

THE EMERSONIAN BODY at the ocean, then, may be compressed into tininess, split along gender lines, or (least interestingly) made to disappear. A fourth alternative is worked through in the poetry of Elizabeth Bishop, where the perceiving presence is allegorized into animals and objects. In "Sandpiper," an early *ars poetica*, the intense pressure along the front of land and sea squeezes the bird persona laterally — so that it runs along the waterline — and forces its attention downward. Unlike Love in "Bond and Free," the sandpiper leaves the sand unmarked — for the prosaic reason that the waves erase his track: "As he runs, / he stares at the dragging grains" between his toes. Numbly, the sandpiper registers the oblivion that works concurrently with his movements, erasing his work, as he exercises himself to find or possess "something, something, something." This endless movement is given imaginative power not by its Beckettian eternal quality, and still less by that vague "something," but by two unspoken physical facts: the sandpiper's unused wings (hardly "dauntless" like those of Thought but still present) and the ocean.

If not for the possibility of total openness, the poetics of "Sandpiper," intent on the sand itself, would be reducible to a single Moorean phrase from its second stanza: "(No detail too small)."[10] In such a poetics, there are no ideas but in things, and no ideas bigger than the things we can observe methodically. But infinite space — registered as it were in the poem's peripheral vision — alters the meaning of the poem fundamentally. A strange moment of self-interruption begins this transformation. The "detail" referred to in the parenthetical comment "No detail too small" — a detail included only because the speaker reminds herself that all details are worthwhile — is the hardly incidental fact that the water between the bird's toes is ocean, "the Atlantic." The tremendous mismatch between ocean space and the square inch between a sandpiper's toes, and the sudden inversion of the two in importance (so that the fact of the Atlantic becomes trivial, only worth mentioning when "no detail [is] too small"), typifies this poetics' intense interest in incommensurable spaces.

Incommensurability issues forth in the oddly false casualness with which the ocean is mentioned. The poet's attention is drawn seaward, and the sandpiper is an instrument for resisting that strange gravity. "The roaring alongside he takes for granted; / and that every so often the world is bound to shake." As in "Once by the Pacific," the threat represented by tidal power is a radical one, shaking the poem's world. The ocean and its avoidance are essential to this imaginative act.[11] If it were set by a river, "Sandpiper" would lose its effect: it would be about grains of sand only, rather than naming a state of mind before the infinite. By its straining effort to fend off the oceanic — and, concomitantly, by the sandpiper's own panicky motion athwart the tide — Bishop's bird-poem infects its last two lines with unease.

The climactic leap in this poem is almost as bizarre as the leap in scale from "(No detail too small)" to "Atlantic":

Poor bird, he is obsessed!
The millions of grains are black, white, tan, and gray,
    mixed with quartz grains, rose and amethyst.

This ending's eerily calm catalog of sand and its qualities not only asserts the tiny (and the variegated) as the proper subject for poetry. It enacts the horrible incongruity between the world's obsessing vastness and the smallness of knowledgeable language. However authoritative this list of grains may be, with its reassuring quantification of the grains, the roaring alongside the frame of the poem continues unabated, and destabilizes even this final sentence. There are traces of willful self-discipline in the lyric voice here, the same restraint that led to the choice of the bird conceit in the first place. The eerie calm imposed across the last two lines may indicate authoritative, human sand-

science or the bird's own obsessive "controlled panic." Neither oblique physical movement (without a sidelong glance) nor abrupt tonal oscillation (without a centering emotion) suffices to ease the tensions of this shoreline space.

Yet there is a visionary moment in "Sandpiper," even though the bird is focused downward rather than outward: immediately after the world is said to be a "mist," frustrating vision entirely, comes a single line of real calm: "The world is minute and vast and clear." Qualitative knowledge of this sort does not resemble the merely heaped facts of the final two lines. This line presents the possibility that the space between the bird's toes may be sublime after all, and the Atlantic truly just a detail next to the clear and comprehensible vastness of the world in an inch-wide expanse of sand properly seen. But an important question remains: Bishop's speaker says that the clarity of the world in this moment of vision results from the fact that "The tide is higher or lower" — but "he couldn't tell you which." It is not certain whether such vision relies on the receding of fluid otherness or on its cleansing sweep before the eyes. In the poem's last words, though, stiff nouns impose themselves against the dynamism of a questioning self: the participle "obsessed" is rhymed awkwardly with the faceted noun "amethyst." In the presence of oceanic fluidity, cognition gains no traction — or gets far too much, and jams its mechanism with the gritty particularity of its tiny objects.

SOLID STRUCTURES occasionally provide useful vantage on infinity. This is true, for example, in Frost's first collected poem, "Into My Own," where the forest stretches "to the brink of doom" as a calm and shady counterpoint to the "road where slow wheel pours the sand." But the forest, unlike the ocean, offers no horizon and can be met with far more geniality than the ocean. In Bishop's "Seascape," visual power and a certain cranky isolation enkindle the strongest personality depicted in these poets' confrontations with the infinite. But first there is acknowledgment of the way that natural vistas, like Frost's limitless forest, can be projections of human desire.

> This celestial seascape, with white herons got up as angels,
> flying as high as they want and as far as they want sidewise
> . . . .
> this cartoon by Raphael for a tapestry for a Pope:
> it does look like heaven.

This space, however, is inaccessible both to human exploration and to human naming. Aimed forebodingly into empty space as a reminder of the continent's firmness, the lighthouse's beam is at once a mode of sight and a mode of speech: the metaphor blends the dynamism and the passivity of poetic vision perfectly.

> But a skeletal lighthouse standing there
> in black and white clerical dress,
> who lives on his nerves, thinks he knows better.
> He thinks that hell rages below his iron feet,
> that that is why the shallow water is so warm,
> and he knows heaven is not like this.
> Heaven is not like flying or swimming,
> but has something to do with blackness and a strong glare
> and when it gets dark he will think of something
> strongly worded to say on the subject.

Rejecting the clichés of "heaven" that accompany American talk of whimsical freedom like the herons', the lighthouse with its cranky glare insists on an eschatology at once firmer and more open — a self more anchored, and space infinitely less suffused with consoling particulars than the opening lines of this poem. The "glare" embodies both the strength of that anchored self and the absence of objects on which it could shine; in similar fashion, it reveals both the conversational force of the cranky lighthouse's gaze and its sputtering (daytime) inability to come up with something specifically (and strongly) "worded" enough for the occasion. Out of its element, as the winged sandpiper is at the conjunction of sea and land, the lighthouse in daytime embodies tremendous strength undeployable, a vessel that can never pull up anchor.

In a similar poem of shoreline structure and oceanic experience, James Merrill seeks to use the localizing strength of such a house on shore to sustain a Dickinsonian foray into the sea. The poem recapitulates several of the tropes seen so far, and ultimately offers a single image that holds many of their elements together. "Swimming by Night" begins with an acknowledgment of social scenes like the one Bishop's lighthouse mars with its glaring defiance. Like Dickinson's poems of solitary encounter with ocean, though, it meditates on isolation and dangerous immersion.

A light going out in the forehead
Of the house by the ocean,
Into warm black its feints of diamond fade.
Without clothes, without caution

Plunging past gravity —
Wait! Where before
Had been floating nothing, is a gradual body
Half remembered, astral with phosphor,

Yours, . . .

The rediscovery of the body, which is "gradual" because it usually moves in "steps" rather than fluidly, localizes the poem's imaginative scene in a strangely dislocated torso (it is only "half re-membered" because its legs are out of sight). Meanwhile, the luminescence of the swimmer gives his flesh an unwonted expressive power, like that of Bishop's lighthouse. Both of the powers attached to the body in the second stanza, though, stem from the house that first locates and then does the lighting for the scene. The house is the provider both of light and of the conspicuous, pleasant darkness that results from that light "going out." The swimmer's glowing body is a pale answer to the house's socialized warmth, and returns to the house inexorably: this "Weak lamp," with its expressive "Glimmerings," is half-rhymed with its own later "Limp / Heavily over stones to bed." The light from within, though, even if it is only stored up from the social setting indoors (it is fed by "the evening's alcohol"), sustains a moment of intense experience. Rejected outright by Bishop's lighthouse, the freedom of swimming here is sustained for some span by the lingering chemistries of the beach house.

In its deployment of a temporal as well as a spatial limit — the swimmer is free from gravity in the chilly water until the glow of earlier sociability wears off — this poem is unlike the others examined in this chapter. Contained by that narrative as well as by the orienting house on shore and the inadequate body, the speaker nonetheless breaks free of all three influences in the last few lines, centering the poem not on its storyline but on the shoreline where ocean has its end in land. The moment of wave-break — counterpart to Dickinson's "Crescent" moment of wave-growth — places "Swimming by Night" firmly in a tradition of instantaneous poems of ocean space.

You wear your master's robe
One last time, the far break
Of waves, their length and sparkle, the spinning globe
You wear, and the tear running down his cheek.

This stanza is a suitable one with which to conclude this chapter's discussion of tone: with its subtle markings of portent, especially the phrase "One last time," this conclusion translates the darkness of the poem's setting onto its meaning. Once the light in the house window has gone out, the surrounding space is dark and foreboding—everything is empty between glowing "stars" and "astral" body. Death by drowning is an implicit topic. That dangerous threshold space between self and stars, though, becomes temporarily insignificant as smallness and largeness coincide. The difference between land and sea, between love and thought, or between flesh and astronomy could almost be forgotten in this poem.

But the firm presence of the house in the first lines serves as insistence that such a leap into universal mastery is not forthcoming: the garment of Emersonian wholeness the protagonist wears like a sorcerer's apprentice corresponds to him only in its ill fit, only "From far and on high." A crucial flash of light reinstates the distinctions that are fading out of the deceptively welcoming "warm black" between the luminous human and the starred firmament. The reminder of difference here is the "sparkle" of breaking waves. Unlike the more subtle visibility of crescent swells offshore, the visible breakers coming in reestablish the divide between human realms and the space of mere Being. Just as the potent glaring speech of the lighthouse depended on its iron grounding (in "clerical dress") at the shoreline, the astral luminescence of the nude swimming body depends on the garments of matter: the boundaries of ocean that offer a "Report of Land" and of safety; the planet that buoys the human through infinite space. To be new-limbed in freedom is always to be "new-limned," circumscribed even in encounter with vastness.

Although the title of the volume in which it appears, Merrill's *Water Street*, brings together fluidity and domestic human grids, this poem holds apart the experience of fluidity and its enabling structures. The house on shore suggests that they might relate narratively, offering first the comfort of a lighted window and then the promise of its own vanishing into "warm black." In this mediating hospitality, the house therefore contrasts absolutely with the ocean, which is not only cold but also constantly sparkling with reminders of difference. The interaction of sea and continent, the "break" that gives rise to the sorrowfulness of the last lines, emerges in the poem when the protagonist dons his "master's robe," Earth itself, which he puts on illicitly in a tenuous manipulation of scale. It is not easy to picture the world as a garment — and Merrill will return to the thought-experiment with a map-decorated Tyvek windbreaker much later in his career. Even when claiming the entire planet as his (sheepishly borrowed) property, Merrill encounters the tragedy of incommensurability — to wear the coherent globe is also to hear the "break" of its seams, and to feel, with sadness, existence itself "tear" up. The imagination is too large, and the body too small, for nature to be anything but the most awkward of garments.

Even Merrill's epic of knowledgeable and exhaustive cosmology, *The Changing Light at Sandover*, is devised in spheres that are repeatedly encompassed and supplanted — and in turn, the entire system sends outward still farther a broadcast of warning. Deity itself speaks of smallness and of embattled firmness within an infinite space, like a lighthouse on the shore of a sea that dwarfs the poem's cognitive gains of thought and conversation. God's verbal intervention in the poem is only in his singing the following song, a telegraph of isolation, endlessly repeated:

IVE BROTHERS HEAR ME BROTHERS SIGNAL ME
ALONE IN MY NIGHT BROTHERS DO YOU WELL
I AND MINE HOLD IT BACK . . .
I AND MINE HOLD IT BACK AND WE SURVIVE (360)

More fraternal than the lighthouse's "glare," this message is nonetheless identically situated on a promontory before absolute distance. The outward orientation of the essay "Circles," with the boundless increase of scope as its challenge and promise, still governs American ideas of knowledge. And this means that the perceiver stands always on the brink. Emerson and the poets that follow him know that outside the last circle, no matter how large it is, looms a further horizon that must be acknowledged even at the cost of any sense of accomplished largeness. Speech then becomes a means of "holding back" the void to prevent insignificance.

Yet at the same time, and quite clearly, the philosophical agenda imposes another requirement: the irresistible Emersonian mandate to claim even that void as a human reality. The mise-en-scène of infinity's brink might seem abstract and far-flown; but as the next chapter will show, the poet is also charged to present it as a domestic problem, and not just a dilemma for astronauts and cosmologists. The human interface with nature cannot be purely natural, miraculously blending its double character as "breaker" and "crescence." It is made of words rather than water. It might be rendered as a tear welling from, and blurring, the transparent eye, rather than a tear that rends the countenance of the world. The partition of the knowable world stems from the partiality and idiosyncrasy of the perceiving self, the one who may see "everywhere" but also must not be effaced. Shoreline negotiations of absolute size are ways of holding on to infinite possibility, but in equal measure they are about the equipment humanity has for holding it back, and creating a dwelling within it.

3   Privacies of Storm

Emerson set out to express the unity and integrity of the world, yet his essays include some of the most fragmented prose of the nineteenth century. That fragmentation is not simply a qualification of his famous bigness; it is essential to it. "The essence of rhetoric in the hands of the orator or the poet," he wrote, "[is] to detach and to magnify by detaching" ("Art" II.211). This sentence, one of Emerson's most forthrightly accurate descriptions of his style, names a surprising philosophy of representation for this advocate of wholeness. Emerson usually emphasized the world's unity in his work, and asserted the unity of work and world. How can it be that such a writer considers rhetoric, the very element of philosophy's work, a mode of detachment rather than annealment? What might be the place of detachment in a project of magnification?

To address these questions, this chapter examines the textual embodiments of Emerson's characteristic category — size. As is suggested both by his own definition of rhetoric and by his typical deployments of it, he is obsessed with the relation between a small, detached object and the largeness it represents. Herein lies the fascination of the Emersonian sentence and, likewise, of the central objects in poems of Emersonian knowledge. The small sentence and the graspable piece of nature fascinate the Emersonian mind because somehow they express infinity — and in the right hands, they express it astonishingly well. These verbal objects, like the philosopher's magnifying proposition, are not large objects: they loom large in the empty space that a writer creates around them.

The paradox of self-containment within openness is at the heart of Emerson's artistic method in his essays — as he describes it in the quotation above, a method that correlates detachment with magnification. The method is philosophical as well as representational: it can therefore be described either in terms of the senses or in terms of verbal figures. In Emerson's sophisticated philosophy, a great leap beyond the just-so stories of Swedenborgianism, every piece of the outer world is a human symbol for the entirety of nature. Any object therefore can represent the whole — and indeed, thereby, the idea of wholeness itself: "We unite all things by perceiving the law which pervades them." But there are no shortcuts allowed, as Emerson goes on directly to insist: "Every mental act — this very perception of identity or oneness, recognizes the difference of things. It is impossible to speak, or to think without embracing both" ("Plato" IV.27 – 28).

The essays' sentences face the inevitability of this double challenge of detached signification. In isolating his chosen words from the vast context they represent, the Emersonian stylist (like the literary critic) must rely on the tenuous principle of synecdoche. The part stands in for the whole, failing to disguise — indeed, even flaunting — its own extreme smallness. Emersonians, who espouse the idea of the whole as a central premise of knowledge, feel this representational tension more intensely than any other set of modern writers. As they bind themselves to language's smallness, they are also bound to be harshly disappointed when synecdoche fails — as it must.

Synecdoche is a self-qualifying trope: in resorting to sampling the whole rather than claiming it, the user of synecdoche concedes that direct access to wholeness is impossible. Emerson performs this acknowledgment, and the resulting partiality activates his philosophy from within his writing (not as a debunking from elsewhere). Detachment is a key part of his method. Moreover, the self-conscious smallness of his written objects is the necessary obverse of his philosophy of wholeness. Literary study holds the failure of a writer's tropes to be as interesting as their successes: from a literary perspective, then, the partiality of Emerson's philosophy of nature appeals just as much as its universal reach.[1] Moreover, its incapacity for success gives rise to a distinctive — even idiosyncratic — poetic tradition of shelter and confinement. The rhetoric of the essays is constituted by the arrangement of mutually repellent nuclei — each particle broken off from totality, in an act that is both a sampling of unity and a disruption of it. It is for other American writers to sustain synecdoche long enough to achieve things with it. For Thoreau the naturalist, by contrast to Emerson, the writer's job is to delve into an integral world. The naturalist searches his surrounding for closed samples that open onto its meanings. On the other hand, Whitman took Emerson's technique of knowledge to authorize the primal American synecdoche: the idea of a community founded in individualism. For Whitman the national singer, the writer's job is to occupy and smooth out the heterogeneity of the world his senses integrate. Wholeness is born in the human mind, which then applies its energy to the unification of the social world.

In Thoreau or Whitman, world instructs mind and mind contains world; and each of them draws on the strength of the other. But Emerson is a philosopher rather than a naturalist or an artist of national identity, because he is not willing to locate the origin of wholeness primarily in either the world (*Walden*) or the mind ("Song of Myself"). Thus his writing intensifies rather than relaxing the fundamental tension between its message (magnification) and its method (detachment). In Emerson's method, writing seizes particles of what should be a coherent Thoreauvian world, and wrenches them loose for magnification in the lonely largeness of the self. Such wrestling with small objects is a cognate, not an opponent, of the broad, integrating sight for which Emerson is famous. In his writing, the world's basic integrity is known through intensely irregular and fragmented formations of thought, in a verbal landscape studded with cairns rather than blooming with vines. An Emerson essay is effective not because of the breadth of its claims but because of its highly punctuated conceptual arrangement, in which few sentences have a simple relation to the ones around them. Yet that very sense of overall fragmentation relies on the contrast with each sentence's aura of wholeness, its self-containment and internal adequacy.

Every sentence of an Emerson essay seems capable of expressing in miniature all the thought of the essay in which it appears; it has no need, but also no capacity, for elaboration. Ironically, Emerson's prose often becomes stiffest where it asserts the principle of motility: "There are no fixtures in nature. The universe is fluid and volatile. Permanence is but a word of degrees" ("Circles" II.179). It is hard to imagine sentences more monumental and self-stabilizing; hard to imagine, that is, sentences less fluid and volatile. This is not to assert that they are false, or that they are badly written for the purpose. On the contrary, they perform in miniature the central drama of this essay, the dialectic of compression and expansive force. The intellectual's every cognitive structure, every sentence, puts a squeeze on thought; that squeeze is the necessary obverse of the outward energy urged by their propositional content.

The quintessence of Emerson, if there is one, can be found in the self-sufficiency of his art's outward aspiration, the stasis of his most eager sentences. When this principle of the essays qualifies itself — as often happens in the disappointing final lines of an Emerson poem — he promulgates some of the thoughts typical of his complacent literary marketplace. The prose, though, is still and always to be admired: the self-closure of a typical sentence of an Emerson essay (especially in contrast to the long enthusiastic sentences of the journals) requires us to modulate the received opinion about expansiveness as the primary impulse of these texts. David Porter epitomizes the traditional reading with his extended contention that prose meant mobility and liberation to Emerson, "[a]n open text taking hold of more power" (*Emerson* 168) because of its openness.[2] But a different premise would lead to a different idea of Emersonian verbal knowledge: what if Emerson is liberated not by the open-ended homogeneity of prose (as against the closed form of poetry), but by his prose's very fragmentation, the modularity of its thought? This would mean that Emerson's art does not "erupt out" of the contradiction between confinement and openness (as Porter puts it in a metaphor that obviously favors the dynamic term of the pairing); rather, it is founded on its fault line. Such a focus on prose's fragmentation would mean, too, a challenge to Porter's celebration of the "prosaicized" (*Emerson* 182) quality of twentieth-century poetry. It might then be argued that the prose inspires poets after Emerson not with its open-aired windiness, but with its cracked immobility on a foundation of failed synecdoche.[3]

The outlines of such an argument are readily traced: it is a reversal of the prevailing view that prose freed Emerson from the confinement of form. Emerson is liberated in the prose by its intensity of enclosure and precision of diction (the very qualities that are sometimes flooded out of an Emerson poem by the need for mediating resolution). This is a tension more radical than the transcendentalists' prosodic ideal of "liberty-within-restraint"[4]: it supposes liberty to be constituted rather than undermined by confinement. As it turns out, for writers with a certain sort of Emersonian sensibility, limiting shelter and vast imagination are mutually constitutive: the short aphoristic sentence, or the small Dickinsonian poem, creates the vastness that surrounds and infuses it.[5] Such a reading of Emerson cannot compete dynamically with more dramatically complete ones. Any interpretation that would integrate the text more wholly, and describe its swirling currents of meaning in a larger way, has an intrinsic claim to being more successful. As the essay "Circles" asserts, after all, it is in drawing a wider circle — not in maintaining a tight focus — that an imagination makes its claim on truth. The claim that Emerson always believed this, in turn, buttresses the methodology of any critic who reads him broadly rather than closely.

In a certain kind of Emersonian perspective, though, wide circles have less appeal. This perspective does not deny the importance of largeness, but maximizes it: one result is to reinforce the inescapable human fact of smallness. On the scale of infinity, the scale that Emerson urges with his metaphor of the horizon, large circles are effectively no larger than other circles, and are too commodious to invite the imagination further outward. Shorter sentences capture Emerson's attention — smaller (sometimes even punctiform) structures that acknowledge their distance from totality. Hence smaller circles speak more effectively than large ones to the absolute openness of this philosophy.[6] This occurs most clearly in individual poems, where the referential failure of smallness is palpably linked with the absolute largeness it fails to contain. Before examining instances of such stasis, though, it is worth asking why criticism should choose such a method. Why should Emerson be read retrospectively through cramped poems written after his time, to find smallness where largeness can be found? Why champion Emerson's own closures, the particularity of his text, instead of its open and inviting possibilities?

THE MAGNIFICATION OF fragments in Emerson's writing is philosophically significant because his idea of objects informs — and indeed constitutes — his idea of the human subject. In interpreting his writings as a consistent system, strong critics of the twentieth century have often worked to resolve the difficulties of this analogy, but paradox is hard to escape. "[The mind] must have the same wholeness which nature has," he says — and then again, outrageously, in the same paragraph, he says the opposite: "The truth was in us before it was reflected to us from natural objects" ("Intellect" II.201). The reader is justified in asking impatiently here: which truth *does* create the other? The contradiction these two sentences pose is not constructed for local effect; it has a long history. The double origin of truth's unity is an old and intractable dilemma; it is a version of the exhausted conflict between empiricism and idealism. Empiricism holds that the world's order provides a framework that disciplines the mind, idealism that the world is made (and made orderly) in the mind that perceives it. For Emerson, the empiricist's trust in materiality and the idealist's self-reliance are both right. Object and subject somehow engage and make each other instantaneously.

These two ideas from Emerson's boldly contradictory single paragraph beg to be reconciled: on the one hand, that the fallen mind should seek wholeness in nature, and on the other, that nature is simply an image of humanity's own intrinsic wholeness. Narrative mediations would disrupt the crucial symbiosis (or identity) of the two simultaneous operations of Emersonian sensation. The contradiction between them, however, is not a problem with Emerson. Rather, it is the Emersonian problem: the one he labors over rigorously in all his best writing.

Since Kant, the distinction between the cognitive subject and its object has been undergoing nearly continuous dismantling; indeed (as in the legend about the ongoing construction of the Cologne Cathedral), the completion of that task would probably represent the end of recognizable Western philosophical culture. Emerson continues to be a significant philosopher and aesthetic theorist not because he joins in proclaiming the end of the subject-object distinction, but because he constantly performs the work of its disassembly. His mind must labor along with the weather to take down walls, to make its own identity with the raw space it encounters.

Even at his most propositional Emerson emphasizes the strain (rather than the product) of his imaginative effort. For instance, in describing the Paris museum of natural history, he expresses the union between world and mind in a comment that quickly turns from pleasing the cognitive faculty to baffling the imagination: "The upheaving principle of life [is] everywhere incipient in the very rock aping organized forms. Not a form so grotesque, so savage, nor so beautiful but is an expression of some property inherent in man the observer, — an occult relation between the very scorpions and man. I feel the centipede in me — cayman, carp, eagle, & fox" (*Collected Works* IV:200). As the list of animals grows longer, it begins to resemble the encompassing spirals of Whitman's poetry;[7] but in the first urge of particularity, the turn from affirming philosophy to scorpions, there is a different Emersonian force at work. Here "the upheaving principle of life" takes a poisonous and heavily armored form, the scorpion, and expresses itself in an object so arbitrary that it seems to refute rather than buttress the notion of presiding intelligence. Swedenborgianism, a doctrine operating in the background of this passage, claimed that spiritual meanings were to be found in nature. That doctrine often functioned, though, by bringing meanings to be joined with the world's objects, rather than the other way around. (It is the sort of system William Carlos Williams deplored with the manifesto phrase, "No ideas but in things.") Here the isolated scorpions, signifiers without referents, show that Emerson did not just adopt Swedenborg's idea of the world's significance, but upended it. Segmented in themselves and segmenting the text, the scorpions and centipede suggest that disjunction and abruptness are as prominent in the Emersonian encounter with nature as their opposite, the sensation of grand unity in which they participate.[8]

The single object, then, with its irresistible appeal to the committed poetic mind, constantly draws attention from the vast background to the foreground, and with a sting in its tail that object paralyzes the gaze. In the foreground, intensity is born in the desiring and highly partial eye of the observer. With Emerson's well-known claims of poetic freedom in the background, this chapter examines the way poetic attention is drawn to the foreground text from the broad context of fluid unity, to the individual poem from raw poetic possibility. This is a way of using poetry to ask a fundamental question about Emerson's philosophical prose: How is the urge for expressive freedom, Emerson's well-known outwardness, reconcilable with the essays' manifest urge for closed forms and sharp boundaries? The connection between the two is central to the verbal functioning of Emerson's philosophy.

Propositional handling of such epistemological problems has little appeal to Emerson or to his readers; segmentation of space emerges in his imagination not as an idea but as a fact. Most of the time, human partitioning of the world takes the simple, concrete form of a house. In this vein, the opening lines of Emerson's "The Snow-Storm" establish the repeated motif of Emersonian house-poems: the incommensurability of setting and structure.

> Announced by all the trumpets of the sky,
> Arrives the snow, and, driving o'er the fields,
> Seems nowhere to alight: the whited air
> Hides hills and woods, the river, and the heaven,
> And veils the farm-house at the garden's end. (*Essays and Poems* 469)

The proper metaphor for the linguistic object is the domestic container; hence the sentence cannot alight at a period until it arrives at a stable human structure. The initial sequence of verbs, interspersed with commas, indicates a kind of fluid storm-power that the aphoristic essays rarely exercise. Indeed, after the stability of the first verse-paragraph's final lines, the sheltered imagination is drawn abruptly out of doors, almost reluctantly, to admire the drama of weather: "Come see the north wind's masonry." The resting state of the poem, at the invocation of house, is given over so that the snowstorm's dynamism can be appreciated on a walk outside.

The snowstorm puts nature in its most creative state: "Body overflowed by life" ("The Poet" III.24). Emerson celebrates the imaginative freedom both imaged in and inspired by the snow — it "Seems nowhere to alight," and even when at rest transforms hard edges to swirled turrets and swans.

> Come see the north wind's masonry.
> Out of an unseen quarry evermore
> Furnished with tile, the fierce artificer
> Curves his white bastions with projected roof
> Round every windward stake, tree, or door.
> Speeding, the myriad-handed, his wild work
> So fanciful, so savage, nought cares he
> For number or proportion.

The storm is an artificer, an Emersonian poet of abstract dynamism filled with raw and unacculturated power. Such a fully undomesticated energy dominates Longfellow's companion poem "Snow-Flakes." In the next century, similarly, the strength of Stevens's "snow man" would lie in his ability to see only "the nothing that is," a bareness in which the imagination fulfills itself without reference to human feeling. Gorgeous abstraction takes pride of place in the wildest and most dynamic versions of Emersonian philosophy. Obscuring borders, mediating structure and formlessness, snowfall creates an alternate realm of forms into which the poem ushers us.

But Emerson does not allow the imagination to abide in this space. The savage activity of the whirling weather yields to an art of shrunken borders, labor, and segmentation: the snow

> Retiring, as he were not,
> Leaves, when the sun appears, astonished Art
> To mimic in slow structures, stone by stone,
> Built in an age, the mad wind's night-work,
> The frolic architecture of the snow.

The artistic imagination, then, is given two entirely different figurations in this poem, and there is no middle ground between them: either the artist is like nature, "The fierce artificer," a principle of speed, excess, flow, and transition; or he is a practitioner of "astonished Art," reactive, methodical, belated, and blockish. In neither case, notably, is the artistic self originary — the snow builds around existing structures, constrained to the gap "From wall to wall," while the farmyard objects themselves are somehow reduced to "mimics" of the snow that engulfed them. The snowstorm, oddly, leaves behind human-made structures, and a made object is what the writer of the "Snow-Storm" leaves in turn as a souvenir of his experience.

On the one hand, nature's power is the source of an art of sensation and awe. On the other hand, the human mind gives shape to nature — paradoxically, by the way it "mimics" it, in the building of walls that follows (and precedes) the snowfall. Emerson's poetics, then, takes two opposite forms. While fairly described (in Jonathan Levin's phrase) as a "poetics of transition," intent on the "breaking through to a new state," caring nought "for number or proportion," it is also, and with equal emphasis, focused on "slow structures" of meaning. These smaller objects (in "The Snow-Storm," objects that confine — the coop, the kennel, the thorn, the lane, the gate) not only undergird such moments of freedom but also and equally supersede them. In just such a way short sentences like "The universe is fluid and volatile" stake down a yard of certitude against the winds of volatility that they name.

In writing this particular poem, unfortunately, Emerson cannot decide whether these two alternative schemes, one empiricist and the other idealist, should be consecutive or simultaneous. The versifier, not certain that to everything there is its own season, expresses his sensibility of time unsteadily, even diffidently. Shifting verb tenses locate the moment of speech ambiguously: "Arrives the snow"; "Come see the north wind's masonry"; "And when his hours are numbered, / Leaves"; "Built in an age." The unreconciled issue of this poem is the question of time — are people spectators to the snowfall or the aftermath, or both at once? The thaw or the initial labor of construction, or both at once? "The Snow-Storm" ultimately dodges these questions, mystifying time as the ultimate mediator of opposite principles, and leaving the cycle of seasons as the best synthesis of art's double life in limitation and freedom. The final sentence swings from "stone" to "mad wind," juxtaposing opposite principles that it cannot reconcile, and the poem arrives at an epigrammatic oxymoron that can only hope to calm its frantic shifting of tense and stance. Attempting to unify in one name, "frolic architecture," the vigorous play of the soul and the methodical craft of structure, the final line short-circuits the poem's central conundrum. In the last lines of this poem, as in the last lines of "Each and All," Emerson dodges his poem's governing question, asking it again as if he had answered it. What is the relationship between limit and miasma, between craft's "number and proportion" and the boundlessness of an artistic power drawing on an infinite "quarry[,] evermore / Furnished with tile"?[9]

In brief, then, Emerson found himself unable to address poetically the representational problem his essays of detachment and magnification masterfully pose. He was defeated by the same problem his interpreters face: the need to interlink the sensation of boundless possibility and the fact of art's self-contained structures. "One house is a quotation out of all forests, mines, and stone quarries" ("Plato" IV.24): so also the plenitude of nature is readable only from within human structures, and the reader encounters one word at a time, not a quarry of possible ones. The effort to intermingle words with each other — to suffuse "architecture" with the spirit of the nearby word "frolic," for example — is foiled by the same self-containment that makes this poem's initial descriptions of a human experience of weather so beautiful. Longing to evoke flexibility that is somehow formal, Emerson often found himself instead asserting a feeling of buffeted stiffness: "We want some coat woven of elastic steel. . . . We want a ship in these billows we inhabit. We are golden averages, volitant stabilities, compensated or periodic errours, houses founded upon the sea" ("Montaigne" IV.91). Restating his image in appositives, here Emerson becomes more rigorous rather than less: the list of dynamic possibilities culminates in an evocative and concrete image of immobility and peril. Desperate incoherence would be the flavor of the entire passage — as it would be of "The Snow-Storm" — if not for the house.

The true heart of "The Snow-Storm" is found in the moment of human limitation and solidarity that closes the poem's first verse-paragraph.

> . . . the whited air
> Hides hills and woods, the river, and the heaven,
> And veils the farm-house at the garden's end.
> The sled and traveler stopped, the courier's feet
> Delayed, all friends shut out, the housemates sit
> Around the radiant fireplace, enclosed
> In a tumultuous privacy of storm.

Until the final phrase, this descriptive passage moves steadily into the house, and the point of view seems to be firmly centered on the hearth (as it is in Whittier's "Snow-Bound: An Idyll"). But the last line of this first section renames and changes the experience. Rather than claiming to synthesize swirl and limitation, it presents simultaneously the uncontainable flux of weather, and the staving off of that miasma. The poem refuses to place itself either inside or outside the house, but occupies both room and nature—a spatial ambiguity ultimately more powerful than the temporal vagueness of the next verse-paragraph.

The result is not a celebration of thresholds, but a superimposition of irreconcilable states, primary among them the differently sized spaces of inside and outside.[10] Associated with the outside, art is free and unbounded, a pure swirl of ornament: it "Seems nowhere to alight." Also associated with the inside, though, art as human voice huddles more meekly, reliant on walls and roofs, alert to all the possibilities of communication and travel that it is missing. As it sets the scene, on the brink of the storm's arrival, this poem achieves a quintessentially American lyric sublimity. The power of the phrase "In a tumultuous privacy of storm" (like that of Emerson's "transparent eye-ball" locative phrase, "In the tranquil landscape") results from the subtle ambiguity of the word "in." The line describes at the same time the house inside the storm (entrapment: "privacy enforced by storm") and the privacy inside the house (coziness: "privacy inflected by storm"). The container of language at the same time holds the reader out, in the cold of savage beauty; and holds the reader in, so that the (artistic) potency of storm ornaments the indoor space, and the whistle of wind outside gives extra savor to a carol or a crackling fire.[11] It is a powerful doubleness, but also a disorienting one: there is no mediating space between artistic freedom and sociability, between raw power and cliché. There are only walls.

IN EMERSON'S ESSAYS, despite the urging of the orator, thoughts stand apart in fragmentary sentences—each one to be considered separately, distended by the wide conceptual and grammatical distance between it and the ones around it.[12] Emerson's philosophy can be pragmatically unified, if at all, only by making unity a matter of performance, a kind of athleticism. The writer then might partake of both the freedom and the consistency of a typically celebrated Emersonian animal: "A squirrel leaping from bough to bough and making the wood but one wide tree for his pleasure fills the eye not less than a lion,—is beautiful, self-sufficing, and stands then and there for Nature" ("Art" II.211). But Emerson knew well that the power of language was not only a power of elusive verbs but also of static nouns: thus every sentence is like a noun itself, "A cube, standing on its bottom like a die, essential and immortal."[13] Alert to both principles, Emerson deploys words both as energy and as objects, and the fluidity of the former does not dissolve the latter's discreteness.

In the squirrel passage, the governing verb is not a dynamic one: the squirrel is important to the essay "Art" not because it leaps, but because it "*stands then and there for Nature*" (emphasis added). Even in this Jamesian metaphor of animal dynamism, the wideness of the "one wide tree" results not from its variegated possibilities for many kinds of exercise, but from the small squirrel's own inability to traverse it all. Functionally infinite, the forest enables the squirrel precisely by dwarfing its efforts, and removing criteria of success from the equation. The squirrel's total symbolic freedom comes at the price of its ability to achieve anything. Concomitantly, its agility and leaping prowess are instantly superseded by its ability to "stand." As a sign, it is posed still, captured as if on film.

The Emersonian writer sometimes looks like the leaping squirrel, but even at the same time may resemble the rooted tree (whose isolation from other trees the squirrel, when it is not just "standing," supposedly overcomes). Critics may move nimbly in the structure of his sentences, but Emerson himself is often not the flyer but the builder, the carpenter of freedom who "Claps wings to the sides of all the solid old lumber of the world" ("Circles" II.180). The poet's materials are wooden as well as airy, and the stiffness of this clapboard is just as common as the flexible boughs with which the squirrel engages. The remainder of this chapter will consider trees less as springboards than as lumber, affording leverage for the epistemological homesteader. Lumber does not generally mean the helicopter but the house: and the house, as "The Snow-Storm" shows, is the necessary vantage point for poetic vision in Emersonian openness. Openness itself is altered by the smallness of the human vantage upon it.

Emerson sets the problem of incommensurability masterfully, but his poems often attempt solutions that rely on mere linguistic sleight of hand — arriving, as in "The Snow-Storm," at a merely verbal accommodation. Dickinson, on the other hand, is more than willing to leave her reader in the charged doubleness of the storm experience. Many of her poems deal with the inside-outside binary featured in "The Snow-Storm"; several, in fact, use the same storm metaphor to do so. In Dickinson's poetry, weather represents the power of space to endanger and overwhelm the soul — a soul that, paradoxically, sees in such power an image of its own might.[14]

One such poem begins with a mediating spirit like the flickering verbal dynamism of the second verse-paragraph of "The Snow-Storm":

> The Wind begun to rock the Grass
> With threatening Tunes and low —
> He threw a Menace at the Earth —
> A Menace at the Sky. (796)

Gusting in the space of interaction between earth and sky, the wind here represents each to the other; it seems both to bring the storm (menacing the earth) and to defy it (menacing the sky). If, in its tunefulness, the wind is a provisional image for poetry, this text then locates art as a mediator between divine energy and the efforts of Creation to stave off apocalyptic power — "The Birds put up the Bars to Nests." The wind's double-mindedness is registered in a typically bizarre fact: what it sings are threatening lullabies.

The wind is between worlds, like Emerson's snow-structures mediating house and magic quarry; but Dickinson's poem concludes with lines that describe two unmediated worlds at once. This trope of double location characterizes the tradition of Emersonian poetry that Dickinson inaugurates, improving on Emerson by amplifying rather than resolving the doubleness as the poem culminates. The poem's binary setting (out raging with the storm and under cover) applies an extraordinary charge to the final stanza, in which the protective structure of the house is invoked but not quite occupied. Comfort is imaginable, but not fully claimed; danger is felt, but not fully undergone.

> There came one drop of Giant Rain
> And then as if the Hands
>
> That held the Dams had parted hold
> The Waters Wrecked the Sky,
> But overlooked my Father's House —
> Just quartering a Tree —

The plural "Waters" here invoke primordial chaos, to be demarcated and staved off by God (and indeed the locution "my Father's House" is a quotation from Christ the preacher, suggesting that the speaker knows her right to ultimate refuge from chaos). But the word "overlooked" suggests caprice and negligence as well as divine protection; the passover here seems a matter of luck rather than covenant. Moreover, we are never assured that the house of the father is also the home of the self — or indeed that the self can be confidently situated in the poem's described space.

The final line, an extraordinarily simple pivot, intensifies ambiguities to the point of excruciation. The poem is displaced at the spare mention of the tree, which reveals that despite its physical centrality, the house is not the heart of the poem. In the final couplet, the odd activity that preceded the storm — the farm full of bustling protagonists — is replaced by mere stationing. The house is positioned (safe from the storm), the tree is positioned (out in the storm), and no middle space can be discerned. There is no movement from raw experience to domestic or religious shelter, or vice versa. Although both confinement and vast open space are key elements of Dickinson's imaginative life, the relation between them is far more vexed than that of transition back and forth, or of merely uncertain emphasis ("tumultuous privacy"). It is contained here in the word "quartering": the term revises Emerson's resolution to the representational problem of weather, by sketching an even more complex relation between the experience of chaos and the sheltered home.

Since the tree is left out of doors, the paradigm here is not one of containment, as we saw in Emerson's tumultuous privacy, but of juxtaposition and encounter. It is an extraordinary and uncanny moment: "Just quartering a Tree — ." Topics of sheltering and stationing can be arrived at here, since the house might provide quarters for, or stand at some casual angle to, the tree. But a more apt and rigorous reading of the word "quartering" should rely on the nautical use of the word — "Striking at an oblique angle (between beam and stern)."[15] The waters, not the house, quarter the tree, meeting it obliquely. The storm strikes the tree, as if from behind at an angle, as if from below (like a wave), as if to drive it forward — but not wrecking it, yet, as it has wrecked the sky.[16] A quartering wind allows a keeled ship to make good, though not excessively fast, progress.

Unfortunately, a tree is not merely keeled but rooted. A certain nautical spirit of voyage may be present in this last line, before its "quartering" wind, but the staccato quality of the poem's close recapitulates the fundamentally static quality of human participation in this world of pure weather. Standing alone headed by the apologetic diminutive "Just," the last line emblematizes language as jetsam, small and rigid in space without vector or shelter, with the word "Tree" planting the poem at its close. The world of the poem is reduced to the singleness of the tree: the mere phenomenon of the individual, planted in a space of terrifying and buffeting freedom — freedom it owns but cannot enter.

This poem's terrific ending centers on verbal tininess, a principle of limitation and grounding that is consciously contrasted with the poem's direct experience of huge weather. What is the meaning of such spatial difficulty? It is a certain correspondence, perhaps, between the mind that refuses to come in from the cold and the mind that garrisons itself away from oblivion: a hybrid of Stevens's wild snowman "mind of winter" and Whittier's "snow-bound" family. Remaining constantly, painfully aware of size, Dickinson's poetics of houses explores and improves upon Emerson's paradigm of dynamic excess (storm) versus confining shelter (house, coop, and kennel). Here no leaping clauses, in a multitude of time frames, attempt to resolve the poem's thematics of inside and outside. On the contrary, such issues are compressed into one limited and limiting phrase, the single chunk of art. In identifying with the isolation of such a wooden object, the sheltered soul finds she has much in common with the castaway.

POEMS OF HOUSE and weather often seem to be Frost's stock in trade, and the natural expectation is that the reader will find in these writings a sheltering tone and a safe vantage on nature's phenomena. Strict formal patternings, especially rhyme schemes, seem well suited to represent the impulse toward stabilizing structure: the poem is pegged in place by a lattice of rhyming syllables. In the case of Frost, though, these syllables are often strongly enjambed — syntactic energy overflows the line ending even while rhyme reinforces the line break's segmentation. The simultaneous energy of these two principles — linking the power of rigidity to the power of fluency — is vital to the double awareness needed to encounter Frost's poetry of buffeted structure.

In perhaps the most technically masterful anapestic poem of the twentieth century, "Good-By and Keep Cold," the first lines establish both the onward pressure of the voice and the stiffness of the objects involved. One notices first the liquidity:

This saying good-by on the edge of the dark
And the cold to an orchard so young in the bark
Reminds me of all that can happen to harm

> An orchard away at the end of the farm
> All winter, cut off by a hill from the house.

The first three enjambments of the sentence carry the reader along rapidly, as the reader anticipates the coming verb ("Reminds"), the coming direct object ("orchard"). While the first three enjambments here induce the reader to create strong links among the lines of the poems, the final line break, at "the end of the farm," creates the opposite effect. It is an enjambment that separates. After the second couplet, no grammatical structure is incomplete: the final locative line is unnecessary and even unwelcome to this initial flowing and perfectly rounded sentence.

Appropriately, the substance of that line indicates and enacts the absence of the farmer "cut off" from his trees, both spatially and temporally. And what is more, it separates the temporal ("winter") from the spatial ("hill"), with an awkward midfoot caesura. There is a split in the poem's own self-location. Hence the poem's key imagery, working with wood in a mode of winter, expresses the simultaneity of communication and absence. The poet's work (in keeping with this ambiguity) is to cleave.

> My business awhile is with different trees,
> Less carefully nurtured, less fruitful than these,
> And such as is done to their wood with an ax —
> Maples and birches and tamaracks.

Separation is the leitmotif — not only the separation of end-stopped lines from each other but also the separation of firewood trees from fruit trees, of log from log, and of heated inner space from cold natural space. But the aural power of these lines is, indisputably, a linking of objects across space: the delicious rhyme of "ax" and "tamaracks."

The assertion of the nominal here (as opposed to the verb dominance of the first lines) changes the poem's sensory register — splinteriness is to be felt in these types of wood and in the parataxis of the list-format itself. Most important, though, is the source of the rhyme's beauty: it comes not from an easy match between human labor and its natural object, but from a subtle mismatch. The anapest "with an AX" is forced into rhyme with the dactyl "TAMaracks" ("Maples and birches and tamaracks" is a dactylic line). Each line develops tremendous energy from the squeezing of these springs, to make the two phrases fit each other. The trees' poetic power, like that of the tree in

Dickinson's poem, is in simply being named, after a dash. Frost brings these trees partly into the human world by the (slightly imperfect) rhyme, which forces their woodiness into contact with a human tool. Yet they remain also out in the cold, not participating in the poem's structure of human expression: it is no accident that the tree names are comprised by the only dactylic line in the entire poem.

"Good-By and Keep Cold" features a very satisfactory middle ground between inside and outside: the space of chopping, warming warming-work on cold wood in the cold air. Such a middle ground, to be sure, has been absent from the poems discussed so far in this chapter. But it would have been easy for these lines to proceed differently, encompassing and mastering the list of trees:

> Different trees
> . . . less fruitful than these,
> Maples and birches and tamaracks,
> And such as is done to their woods with an ax.

Instead, standing alone, as trees they earn an intransigent presence more stubbornly integral than they would as firewood. Alongside the terms involved with work, then, the thoughts of mere naming and the speech of pure expression set the atmosphere in much of Frost's poetry. This is why absence is reasserted in the repose of the speaker, presented in the double scene in the final lines of this poem:

> I wish I could promise to lie in the night
> And think of an orchard's arboreal plight
> When slowly (and nobody comes with a light)
> Its heart sinks lower under the sod.
> But something has to be left to God.

Unity between self and nature is a paradoxically passive mental effort, an imaginative solidarity between the speaker in his warm bed and the trees in their coldness. This is the poem's success, enabled by the wood chopping that bridged the gap between different spaces. This should be a successful inside-outness, a warm thought for the cold trees from within the house their relatives' sacrifices, and the chopping work of the speaker, make habitable. It might, conceivably, even lead to a visit to the orchard with a lamp lit from a fireplace ember. But in this time of leisure, as in the valedictory time of speech, the mediation does not occur: it is a promise Frost's speaker does *not* make (though he wishes he could). The poem asserts finally the failure of sympathy except on the highest, divine levels — and such an elevation means an even stronger incongruity between the sympathizing self and the trees beyond the hill. The rhyme of "sod" and "God," borrowed from Dickinson's poem "I never lost as much but twice — " (49), drives this discrepancy home.

Another tree-and-weather poem by Frost dwells entirely in this elegiac realm of immobility, without the possibility of mediating work: sometimes Frost works exclusively with the same inside-outside double location that interested Dickinson and Emerson in the case studies above. Again, this is a formal as much as a philosophical phenomenon: the poem's structure, like that of the house, makes energized speech possible, but the energy comes from outside. Unlike the author of "The Rhodora" and the second half of "The Snow-Storm," though, Frost and Dickinson know that to leave the house behind and try to dwell in "frolic architecture" would sap their poems of humanity.

> Tree at my window, window tree,
> My sash is lowered when night comes on;
> But let there never be curtain drawn
> Between you and me.
>
> Vague dream-head lifted out of the ground,
> And thing next most diffuse to cloud,
> Not all your light tongues talking aloud
> Could be profound.
>
> But, tree, I have seen you taken and tossed,
> And if you have seen me while I slept,
> You have seen me when I was taken and swept
> And all but lost.
>
> That day she put our heads together,
> Fate had her imagination about her,
> Your head so much concerned with outer,
> Mine with inner, weather.

The first stanza's pairing of nouns, "me/tree," sets the stage for the poem's key dialectic of subject and object, inside and outside. These entities, fundamentally, are the static and mutually remote protagonists of the poem, and if singular nouns were Frost's only tools, the poem could hardly advance. Meanwhile, the middle verbs in stanza one, "come on" and "drawn," establish natural, seasonal power outside and artistic, protective power inside as the poem's two opposed forces. But the poem will arrive at a different kind of noun, the flexible and capacious word "weather"; it begins to move in this direction through methodical description.

In the second stanza, the adjective "profound" makes some room for accidence rather than essence. The possibilities of predication are then taken up fully in the third stanza, where a pair of verbs unites the two selves in their dynamism: one is "tossed" and one is "lost." (Notably each protagonist is passive in the hands of an alien force.) This excursion into dream movements then retraces its steps in the last lines (through the adjective "together") to arrive back at the noun "weather." The final rhyme of "together" and "weather," though satisfying, follows on the last stanza's careful reinforcement of the window-pane: the object that holds the speaker away from the tree. The difference between inner and outer is carefully emphasized here, in broken lines very similar to the one that introduced the "hill" between house and orchard in "Good-By and Keep Cold." The shape of this sentence, which stalls the arrival of "weather" until it can be properly rhymed with "together," breaks speech up into repellent and opposed phrases. Centered on "outer" and "inner," these phrases alternately describe the two "heads" involved in this poem.

The phrase "put our heads together" here suggests not precisely solidarity between the two but mere juxtaposition, metonymy — or at best, conspiratorial conference. This conversation-image undermines the sense of cloudy superimposition that should be evoked by the rhyme "together/weather." In the second stanza, Frost hoped to create unity with the fuzziness of the phrase "Vague dream-head"; in these last lines, though, as in the Emersonian window/tree-poem generally, the window can never be quite forgotten. It is the hard obstacle holding apart the put-together heads of subject and object. The window, like the commas of the poem, breaks imaginative work off from its objects, holding the inner and outer away from each other in the same way that half the rhyme-pairs are held apart by the ABBA rhyme scheme. That obtrusive prominence of the lens between people and world is figured perfectly in the line "Tree at my window, window tree." In the second naming, the tree's framing from a certain perspective becomes an essential feature of the tree itself. Here in a single line of endearment, in which an outdoor object is renamed as an ornament of the room it is seen from, is the problem of aspectuality in a nutshell. Human writers impose their own tools of vision and shelter on a much larger landscape. In Frost, there is significant and scrupulous effort to mediate: but this poem is only in small part about the tree itself. Its more important task is to justify the poem's first, irredeemably self-centered deed: naming a tree in human terms; naming it "window tree." To be accountable for such an imaginative act is the duty any rigorous poet of nature must undertake.

BISHOP'S WRITING CAREER begins with a window/tree-poem, "To a Tree," which was first published in 1927 in the *Blue Pencil*, the literary magazine of her boarding high school, Walnut Hill.

Oh, tree outside my window, we are kin,
For you ask nothing of a friend but this:
To lean against the window and peer in
And watch me move about! Sufficient bliss

For me, who stand behind its framework stout,
Full of my tiny tragedies and grotesque grieves,
To lean against the window and peer out,
Admiring infinites'mal leaves.

The middle four lines of the poem are written from the tree's perspective: as it watches the student, it creates in the poem an awareness of her sorrow's smallness ("tiny tragedies"). Likewise, the outer four lines of the poem comprise the student's thoughts about the tree: in the first two lines she claims a relationship with it, then in the last two lines she considers the tree in its constituent parts, and returns isolated perception (from indoors) to dominance. The spatial configuration of these two movements is not incidental. Inner contains outer as well as vice versa.

In "The Snow-Storm," familial affection was present but inaccessible; in "The Wind begun to rock the Grass," sympathy with an exposed self was complicated by identity with it; in "Good-By and Keep Cold," warmth was described, but hewn from nature. Bishop's poem, by contrast, with its direct address and naming of sorrow, offers immediately recognizable human emotion — but it also begins her career's work of translating emotion into spatial arrangements. The emotional force of the tableau is more important than some of the poem's odd mannerisms would suggest. The dorm window is an intersection of worlds: it holds student and tree away from each other, but also holds them up as they lean. Contemplation is made possible by the stability of this boundary object (the student's head leans against it to peer at the tiny leaves); in the same way, the lineation and stanza form of the poem allow for consoling progress that neither diminishes the poem's originating mood of sorrow nor gives the dormitory dweller dominion everywhere. The poem's formal flaw, the surprising enjambment at its midpoint, gives it its strongest point of leverage. This stanza break is the verbal equivalent of the tableau's window — the hardest and most transparent point in a structural matrix that both frustrates and strengthens the imagination.

The two stanzas of "To a Tree" correspond to an outer roominess and an inner room. (Each stanza is governed by its second word, respectively "tree" and "me.") The hanging phrase of consolation, "Sufficient bliss," belongs by proximity, rhyme, and lineation to the tree stanza — but by grammar to the me stanza. "Bliss" is linked by rhyme with the gesture of kinship Bishop is making, "this" poem: the act of speech is sufficient bliss — and therefore identical with the satisfying act of watching and being watched. The tree and the student both "ask nothing of a friend but" attention. Thus a lovely symmetry informs the final line: the small poem that contains the tree is matched by infinitesimal poems on its leaves, each in turn becomes an eye that contains the student's reflection. Thus the poet admires herself in the mirror of nature's poetry.

This dormitory window serves as the plane of symmetry for rich parallelisms — but as the stanza break offers transition from world to self, it also reinforces the difficulty of that shift, emphasizing the ontological prominence of the transparent object in the gap. Like the structural element of poetic lineation, the "jamb," which holds the phrase "Sufficient bliss" away from the phrase "For me," the "framework stout" of the window is the emblem of art's troublesome mediation of itself.[17] Such artifacts hold a central position in Bishop's oeuvre. Like the titular "imaginary iceberg" of an early poem and the "grandmother's glass eyeball" intended to serve as a late book title, the window with its frame is an emblem both of the eye's crystalline quality and of its diminutive materiality. Here the window's synthetic transparent area contains the wooden tree, yet is contained by the interior wood of the framework. The stoutness of the jamb holding the inner and outer worlds apart matches the strong artificial spine of the poem, the prominent enjambment that holds apart Bishop's two stanzas. Thus concentric mutual containments of inner and outer encompass a set of objects on each side, telescoping away from the crucial double object, the window.

Such geometric perfection centering on the artifact begins to suggest why Bishop was so admired by James Merrill, the crafter of painstakingly chiseled and symmetrically ambiguous verse. Merrill is also perhaps America's pre-eminent house poet. Indeed, his interest in human-made things, in *objets* that adorn human spaces, is best understood within that tradition. Both in *The Changing Light at Sandover* and in his early and late nature poetry, the key artifacts of Merrill's poetics are mirrors. Often, though, the mirror makes a better window than it does a mirror: in *Sandover* the spirit world leans against the mirror and looks in on the poet and his partner, while in "The Blue Eye" (1946) and "Large Mirror Outdoors" (1993) the mirror is regarded as a medium in which the large world may become clear and congenial to the nearsighted. Knowledge of oneself, reflected in the mirror, is fundamentally linked with knowledge of the world, found in and through the same object.

Though this altered window artifact, the mirror, has added complexity (and is charged with Freudian self-awareness), the larger, fundamental artifact, the house, maintains pride of place. Shells of domesticity — which is to say *houses*, and not *homes* — are just as important in Merrill's late work as the space that surrounds them, and in fact give that space its meaning. Just such a way of reading Merrill is invited by the close of his sonnet sequence "The Broken Home," in which a distant sunset is seen from the window of the title building (which is being converted from house to boarding school), and is linked by a pun with the speaker's childhood dog:

> Someone at last may . . .
> > from my window, cool
> With the unstiflement of the entire story,
> Watch a red setter stretch and sink in cloud.

The pun gives the poem unity and closure — and that satisfaction results not only from the chronological blurring of memory into vision but also from an inside-out ambiguity. From a window seat one can look inward on nature, at a dog's comfort, as well as outward at symbolic skylines. As in the case of "The Snow-Storm," though, the more important poetic power here is not in the deft double formula that ends the poem, but the previous (more descriptive) line describing a state of mind. "With the unstiflement of the entire story," Merrill airs out a cramped space in memory. The word "story" here denotes both the level of the house, where all the windows have been opened during its renovation, and the newly recounted childhood of Merrill himself.

The same architectural pun supports one of the first descriptions of the *Sandover* séance scene. Displaced outside the house, into empty night, the performance of that scene is oddly assigned to "emptiness":

> High upon darkness, emptiness — at a height
> Our stories equalled — on a pane's trapeze
> Had swung beyond the sill now this entire
> Rosy-lit interior . . . (26)

"A height / Our stories equalled" — the poet here is measuring an empty column of space by the yardstick of the multilevel house, and measuring dark void by the yardstick of "tall tales." All of this spatial metaphor is entailed in the choice of a lyric rather than a narrative mode ("Measures, furthermore, had been defined / As what emergency required" [4]).

The Changing Light at Sandover is a poem of domesticity. All of its travels are fundamentally, in a way, interior ones — this is why the protagonists' window onto the other world is actually a mirror that duplicates their own presences. And yet *Sandover* is a poem of nature, curiosity, and "scientific" knowledge: this dilemma correlates with the way that the reader is often invited to feel that the poem is not getting anywhere. Indeed, the paradox of progress and stasis is built into the very syntax of the poem. Its characteristic sentence form ends with a verb that returns the attention, even in that moment of closure, to the noun at the sentence's midpoint. This eddying principle centers the poem on objects rather than on vectors or events. To serve as an example, the following typical sentence is drawn from *Sandover*'s first pages: "Another year we'd buy the old eyesore / Half of whose top story we now rented" (5). The first of these two lines is iambic, and the second is trochaic. Jammed between the two lines is the heart of the sentence, the word "eyesore." As a spondee, this word belongs neither to the line about ownership nor to the line about renting, neither to the present nor to the past. Planted in both moments of time, it defies the poem's own temporal and rhythmic shape. It is a blemish on the landscape that the poem traverses, an eyesore of material shelter, like the implausible and ungainly poem itself, that the poet inhabits ruefully — knowing the blocky strangeness of his chosen form but claiming it anyway piece by piece.

The house inevitably governs the mode of sociable pioneering that this poet undertakes in his largest work. In *The Book of Ephraim*'s final section, before a suggestive encounter with Mother Nature, the protagonists consider and reject an image of nature as an undefined space for self-actualization: a concept of the outer world allied with the westward tradition of the American novel, the tradition that *Sandover* never joined. Discouraged by a roomful of untouched old cartons of Ouija-board transcriptions, the protagonists JM and DJ have been considering burning them. There is possibility in the words' escape from materiality that the transformation into structured art can never provide: in flame, the burned papers might find a

Burst of satori [...]
And that (unless it floated, spangled ash,
Outward, upward, one lone carp aflash
Languorously through its habitat
For crumbs that once upon a ...) would be that. (*Sandover* 91)

In this reverie about oblivion, the poet's block-letter cosmology finds a way out of the house and out of materiality into pure unspecified narrativity, releasing its own intrinsic energy and swallowing the stars like crumbs. It embarks into Poirier's world elsewhere.

This fantasy of consumption and self-buoyancy, invoking even the fairy-tale phrase "once upon a time," is interrupted by something quotidian. While imagining burning flight, the protagonists are reminded of their own chilly bodily situation by a staticky phone call from the furnace man. Bob from town is expected to diagnose "The failure long foreseen / As total, of our period machine." This line, of course, is about the fatigue of the furnace, which is "a period machine" because it is contemporaneous with the old house. But this phone call is addressed in part to the poet's own discouragement: the "period machine" is also the process of composing poetry. The voices that speak through the Ouija board employ no punctuation; to make poetry of those raw materials the poet must impose form upon it — must crank up and operate the period machine every day that he writes. The unperformed, decisive, and novelistic event of burning thus offers no release from the cluttered eyesore that is the poet's workspace and habitat.[18]

This interruption from Bob — a name perfectly chosen to invoke the equipment of carpentry and of angling — makes possible the indoor encounter with the stars in *Ephraim*'s final lines. This conversation at a distance, like the chattiness of the Ouija-board exchanges, asserts the primacy of furnace over fire, of containment over drift, and of speakable truths over satori. "The housemates sit / Around the radiant fireplace, enclosed . . . "; the poet occupies rooms and stanzas, spaces governed not by the upward force of a fire but by socially maintained technology. He works with a period machine, making sentences — not in an open-ended narrative mode (whether comic, tragic, or compromising). After all, those who live in wood-frame houses cannot simply throw sparks.

The opening of *Sandover* establishes just such an important relationship between the shape of a text and the structure in which it was composed. The first section, "A," justifies the choice of poetry as the storyteller's medium; the second section describes the room in which the poem was transcribed. The closing lines of the first section constitute the link between the two. The writer says that he must tell the story himself, in poetry rather than in a novel, due to the fact that "Time would not." The reasons that time is unwilling or inadequate to tell this story, though, are less clear:

> Whether because it was running out like water
> Or because January draws this bright
> Line down the new page I take to write:
> The Book of a Thousand and One Evenings Spent
> With David Jackson at the Ouija Board
> In Touch with Ephraim Our Familiar Spirit.

Time (concomitant with novelistic form) will not tell the story partly "because January draws this bright / Line." Several readings are allowable here. (Notably, though, the lines cannot be parsed to say, "I take to *writing* because Time would not tell the story." Merrill takes the page, not writing itself.) Most prosaically, the line of January might be calendrical, suggesting that the poem is the product of a New Year's resolution, after delayed and abortive work on a novel. In a spatial vein, though, "this . . . line" might also be the product of a carefully chosen workspace: Merrill writes at a window. The sharp line created by the frame's interposition on sunlight creates a sharp left margin on his page: the margin that results from poetic lineation. The jamb gives rise to enjambment. The month (January) is translated into space — into an arrangement on a page.

Oddly, Merrill asserts that the line of light on the page causes time to be insufficient for the storytelling ("Time would not . . . because January draws"). Because of the line — that is, as an effect of the lyric approach — an atemporal perspective is required. Since the writing is not a novel, time does not govern it. But such a synchronic perspective is not that of a transcendent throne. The lyric as depicted here is atemporal in the way the line is: atemporal in the sense of "spatial." This is the atemporality of desk and table, of this certain slant of light; it exists in the realm of alphabet, cup, and hand, the world of artifacts where the poem is written.

In all of these texts, the window above the writer's desk is a Janus-like object: it means openness as well as shelter. If the enclosed house is more important in American philosophical poetry than titles like *A Boy's Will*, *Questions of Travel*, and *Braving the Elements* may suggest, this is because of the tradition's deep-seated Dickinsonian, antinarrative sensibility (which rules out titles altogether). But that sensibility is not a matter of sequestration: it is a double location of the sort indicated by the schemes of this chapter's illustrative poems. The Dickinsonian scheme, it can now be averred, turns nature into writing by turning it inside out, bringing outdoor phenomena into tight encounter with indoor perspectivalism. Versification is a mode of eversion — this, at least, is the implication of the way nature floods in through the poet's window in these relatively self-conscious writings.

In their best poems, however, these four writers add a crucial extra dimension to such indoor-outdoor meditations, and raise the stakes considerably. Any theory about different kinds of space must come under the sway of the unifying presence of all Emersonian writing: the single body who encounters it all. Each poet in her own way, using the language of sensation, must situate poetic philosophy in a paradigm of physical experience. Dickinson herself would not have ratified theoretical definitions of poetry, or regarded it as a kind of phenomenological essay; she would call something poetry "If I feel physically as if the top of my head were taken off" (*Selected Letters* 342a). That surprising word "physically," completely out of place in a literary-critical metaphor, serves as an admonition to readers: in the encounter with a lyric corpus, it is not the human body, but theory itself, that is out of place.

4 Dickinson Outdoors

The figure of the house and the figure of the ocean each suggest the importance of a tight relation between smallness and largeness in the Emersonian poetics of infinity. In this lyric tradition, inside and outside space involve each other intimately, despite being registered as incommensurable. The smallness of language and of the self correlate, absurdly, with the vastness of their projections and dreams. In interpretations of Dickinson, twinned and contradictory assertions of this sort already predominate: the perennial task of the Dickinson critic is to find some way of doing justice both to the poet's potency and her powerlessness. The impasse that power-oriented considerations of Dickinson usually create has come to seem conclusory. A double formula often stands in where we might hope for an interpretive conclusion. In beginning with tragic stasis, the present analysis ceases, for the sake of argument, to ask what Dickinson's poetry *does*, and asks instead how it *knows*. By bracketing the category of "power," in favor of the category of "knowledge," epistemological interpretation may begin to break up a logjam of counterpoised critical intuitions about the poet's puissance or lack of it.

This relief is accomplished, in part, by treating Dickinson as an Emersonian; but the true project begins beforehand, when we begin to treat Emerson as a Dickinsonian. Emerson's philosophy of the incommensurable shares crucial features with Dickinson's theological poetics of mismatch — of inadequacy troped into surplus and, simultaneously, vice versa. The simplest way to link the two projects, and the two ideas of sensory knowledge, is to observe the similar ways the poets handle the metaphor of the house. In *Nature*, in a metaphor to which he often recurs, Emerson identifies the product of the eye's outdoor effort with the most fundamental of human objects, a house. To be sure, *Nature* is not an overtly domestic text — it begins by recommending that the reader "Retire from his chamber" — but at one point the person who goes outside is said, oddly, to enter a house rather than leaving one.

Encountering the open world with his imagination awake, such a person "Wonders at himself and his house" — that is, nature — "and muses strangely on the resemblance betwixt him and it" (I.42).[1] This sentence expresses the Kantian unity of mind and world: the mind is intrinsically of the world, and builds it by dwelling within it. But the metaphor identifying nature and house is stranger and less confident than its conceptual burden would indicate, for it describes not just an idea but an experience. It claims to unify opposite phenomena — the exterior and the interior. Either of these two experiences alone has its drawbacks. Freedom is preferable to fixity; but then again, cognitive "enclosure" is preferable to the rawness of "exposure" (hence the need to call nature a human house in the first place). The metaphor of the house thus expresses two opposite and necessary principles: nature's vastness, and the shelters (mental and physical) that humanity builds to stave it off. The linkage is not an easy one; as Gaston Bachelard writes: "House and space are not merely two juxtaposed elements of space. In the reign of the imagination, they awaken daydreams in each other, that are opposed" (43). For Emerson, though, these two opposed daydreams are one dream, and that dream is something he experiences in stepping outside. His mind's tremendous largeness is also the world's ability to make him at home. The concord between mind and space is expressed here for Emerson in the startling image of the house, a metaphor that unifies the two while dwelling on the opposition between them. The house of the Emersonian in nature is perfect freedom from houses: its roof coincides with sky. As the mind constructs artifacts, it also celebrates its own freedom; as it dwells in a culturally constructed form, whether made of words or of lumber, it confronts the adventure that is its own intrinsic power in nature.

Without Dickinson's influence on our reading of Emerson, this metaphor might seem merely triumphal; her treatment of the image, though, highlights the image's own outlandish difficulty, and the rigorous epistemology underlying it. The relevant Dickinson poem, "I dwell in Possibility," is well known; without Emerson's influence in reading it, though, it is usually regarded as an affirmation of abstract writerly possibilities, rather than a poem of experience. In encouraging readings about simply going outside and having transcendent experiences, Emerson shows us the complexity of this Dickinsonian *ars poetica*; in turn, the poem shows us the strange rigor of Emersonian philosophy.

I dwell in Possibility —
A fairer House than Prose —
More numerous of Windows —
Superior — for Doors —

Of Chambers as the Cedars —
Impregnable of Eye —
And for an Everlasting Roof
The Gambrels of the Sky — (466)

In Robert Weisbuch's excellent book on Dickinson, the first four lines here
are the epigraph to the first chapter, and the gesture in the third stanza is immediately "[t]ranslated into the language of logic" (12). In that study, the poem
is introductory material; here it is the only indispensable text.

The choice to use a poem of this complexity as an epigraph emblematizes
a justifiable critical technique that takes some poems as tools rather than
aesthetic objects. "I dwell in Possibility" has often been shabbily treated,[2] its
phrases taken (at worst) as buzzwords or (at best) as a means for understanding Dickinson — rather than the aim of that understanding. To be sure, the
critic must begin with some premise. In several of the most coherent books
on Dickinson, though, poems like "I dwell in Possibility" that make claims
about selfhood in nature are deployed as instruments for understanding other
poems — the ones that record uncanny experiences. The corpus is implicitly
sorted into two groups: "parables," like this poem, and poems of experience.
Any poem that offers a proposition about the poet's behavior is placed in the
first group; any poem that mentions pain, death (especially in the past tense),
timelessness, or empty space is placed in the second. In the parables, the poet is
seen to act on the world, with her senses and her imagination; in the poems of
experience, the senses are challenged by the world's incomprehensible energies.
When critics separate these groups, though, active knowing is safely isolated
in the Dickinson story from passive experience of the sublime: epistemological questions are evaded, but the oeuvre splits. This methodological problem
can be solved by a spatial reading, one that begins by delving beneath the questions of power that drive the two prime modes of Dickinson criticism.

In most readings of "I dwell in Possibility," the housed self is linked by
necessity with the questing self, and participates by proxy in its romance of
freedom.[3] The poem is read as part of a narrative of writing, and a parable
of its power, either defying or following a power-oriented Emerson. In such

readings, the poet is celebrating the moment of possibility before some future action, or has arrived at this better linguistic house from a more confining one. The stasis of the poem's initial line is instantly mediated and blurred by an unspoken quest narrative outside the poem. And the shelter of the "House" in line two tends to divert critical attention from its counterpart, the absolute immensity of the poem's outdoor space. The contrast is important, as attention to Emerson reveals, for to identify nature with a house — boundlessness with a structure constituted by walls — is to turn experience inside out. Indeed, the first line alone, "I dwell in Possibility," is a difficult enigma (not a self-affirming motto, as it often becomes in writing about Dickinson). To "dwell" is simply to be, and to be aware primarily of comfort and innerness; but to experience "Possibility" is to be able to *do* something — to orient oneself outward. The two categories are as deeply opposed as their counterparts, house and nature.

It is true that the poem's second stanza seems to advocate a simple, synthesizing transcendentalism, one that claims the best of two opposite worlds. On the horizontal axis the speaker is sheltered ("Impregnable"), while on the vertical axis the sky is the limit. But in the last stanza these valences are switched, and the inside-out intensity of the poem emerges with a vengeance. Once the speaker's body has been invoked — this time with the mention of "Hands" rather than "Feet" — the vertical axis imposes fixity and narrowness of scope, while on the horizontal axis the speaker is exposed.

> Of Visitors — the fairest —
> For Occupation — This —
> The spreading wide my narrow Hands
> To gather Paradise — (466)

In these final lines the inward and outward vectors of the poem are superimposed. They are united, not in a proposition, but in an experience: Dickinson identifies the gesture of openness to sensation with its opposite, a movement of "gathering." Just as the speaker is opening herself passively, spreading her arms to accept the world's inrush of immensity, her harvesting grasp draws nature in toward the self in an act of cognitive appetite.

The dilemma of inward and outward here, though intractable, is necessary for a strong interpretation of the poem. To be sure, we could imagine these gestures as compensatory and alternating movements, a dynamic compromise between the outward and the inward. The speaker's hands might just be spreading and gathering in turns — but since there is only one "This" being named, such a reading would lead to a reading of the poem as a postponement of that which the final line claims. "This" would be merely a warm-up for some other "That." Paradise then comes after the poem, and the lyric moment is just an inessential part of some unspoken larger story, a story of progress in which a redeemed self may eventually become active. Poetry in such reading — whether explicitly religious or simply focused on "deferral" — is just a way of getting ready for something good; hardly a worthwhile "Occupation."

If instead the poem is read synchronically, spreading itself is the act that gathers Paradise. Dickinson's speaker simultaneously opens herself outward and pulls the world inward to feed the mind: knowledge is at the same time passive and active.[4] Acquiescence and compressive effort — awe and home-steading — are one in this encounter with nature.

> For Occupation — This —
> The spreading wide my narrow Hands
> To gather Paradise —

The speaker's hands, then, travel outward and bring nature home, in the same instant. Emersonian emphasis on nature, however, insists on more consideration for the physical situation as well as the propositional claim. With Emerson's philosophy in mind, this double reading does not resolve questions, but raises new ones.

Why should the speaker's dialectical gesture — a single and instantaneous act that turns itself inside out and means "knowledge" — be described as a spreading of the arms? And just as important, why is the claim of Paradise called a gathering? The final line, with its verb "to gather," is incoherent unless it is remembered that this is an Emersonian poem of nature. The sustaining outdoor world is, after all, a crucial topic of the poem — and the root of the word "paradise" is not in temporal concepts like power, or heaven, but in the spatial concept of garden. There is a particular meaning, then, to the gathering of Paradise — laying claim to what one knows and drawing the nourishment of hospitable nature in to oneself. Dickinson here reenacts the Fall of Man, paradoxically harvesting death from the Garden's nourishment. Humanity's narrow, fleshy hand closes around the forbidden fruit, knowledge, as soon as the arms (or Emerson's preferred aperture, the eye) open to experience. The active, concupiscent drive of the senses means that exterior Paradise is instantaneously lost, just when it is consumed.[5]

With Genesis understood as the necessary source-text for the poem's final line, the preceding line is much easier to interpret. In that line, Dickinson's speaker asserts that her occupation is a spreading of the arms. Even with all her Adamic appetite, then, she adopts the posture of Christ at the intersection of vertical and horizontal: the second Adam, acquiescent to the barrenness of spatial existence even as he reclaims the Paradise lost by the first Adam. In this double image, passive sacrifice is also the vigorous act that unifies humanity with the absolute. Thus the poem unifies two primal gestures, Adam's grasp and Christ's relinquishment, bringing into one moment all of Christian historiography. Dickinson reverses the order of these two deeds in these lines (putting the original sin last) to insist that the reader not arrange them in time. There is no transition or history between them. They must be identified with each other — not on a timeline of loss and regaining, but in paradoxical simultaneity.

The final stanza, then, describes an instantaneous double phenomenon: a static outdoor experience that is also a vigorous act of writing, gathering the world into "This" object. The single act of composing these last three lines superimposes the vast natural world, bounded only by sky, and the writer's room. The crux of this mysterious double location is the word identified with the word "This" in the line in which the poem names itself: "Occupation." With that word Dickinson addresses the crucial question of what the lyric poet does, when she writes what she sees. There are two answers in one.

In the obvious reading of "Occupation," the word's evocation of the poet's busyness reminds the reader that a writer has more to do than simply to "dwell": effort is required of the human, even when nature is hospitable and generous. Imaginative sustenance is gained only by drawing the world into our mental structures, bringing in the harvest. The poet works for her art, vigorously gathering experience into "This" compressed object, the poem. However, the Emersonian emphasis on nature calls for a second reading of this line, and a second understanding of the status of "This" poem. The word "Occupation" is also a reminder that the speaker must do *less* in nature than dwell. She simply occupies space; simply stands outdoors. In fact, the concordance reveals that "occupy," for Dickinson, almost always means merely being somewhere.[6] Simply existing in nature, the poet's job is to undergo passively what the world brings to her, keeping her receptivity as wide as possible despite the narrowness of her instruments.

"I dwell in Possibility" thus enacts a double knowledge: the strenuousness and passivity of both doing and being, in a world both fruitful and incommensurably bigger than oneself. The absurdity of knowledge here is not a verbal phenomenon, but a bodily one, a double sensation in which the poem participates. There is a philosophical precedent for this apparently unsystematic idea of knowledge in Søren Kierkegaard's witty 1844 monograph, *Philosophical Fragments*. This text self-consciously differs from Hegel's narrative approach to knowledge, for the sake of argument, dwelling in possibility rather than action — and goes on to derive as if from scratch the epistemological need for Christ.[7] Denying himself recourse to any timeline to arrange ignorance and knowledge, Kierkegaard posits that truth does not lie dormant in humanity. Knowledge comes at least in part from outside the human mind. Yet it cannot be solely an external fact, a power so absolute that it negates the self who craved it. It must, in short, be an interweaving of the godly and the human. Both in the theologian's work and in the poet's, the two are unified in a single, agonized bodily form.

DICKINSON'S APPROACH to Christian theology presents us with an uncanny kind of somatic faith, alien from actual belief. In this way it is marked by the same intensely strange doubleness that characterizes her poetics, which features intensity of expression without apparent action. Her work interweaves active and passive modes of cognition, and in doing so sets up resonance with classic theological binaries of Christ's divinity and finitude. In much the same way, infamously, she interweaves images of her power and her powerlessness. The resulting superimpositions of strength and weakness frustrate all interpretive efforts that would draw on narrative resources to make sense of the poems. Unafraid of contradiction, unlike the interpreter, this philosophical poet takes as essential three irreconcilable tenets: the absolute character of power, the absolute character of acquiescence, and their absurd simultaneity in time. There is no cyclical rhythm to distinguish vigor and abjection, and no storyline by which one can stave off the other.

Even when the extreme poetic power that Dickinson claims goes so far as to enthrone itself, it is self-sacrificial: she is, in her most intense moments, the "Queen of Calvary" (347). This phenomenon, stemming from a deeply vexed epistemology, brings the problem of Christic sacrifice into the realm of individual experience. The premise of "I dwell in Possibility," the theological echo that has evaded critical attention because of its basis in fleshly experience, finds direct expression in the following poem of propositions:

One Crucifixion is recorded — only —
How many be
Is not affirmed of Mathematics —
Or History —

One Calvary — exhibited to Stranger —
As many be
As persons — or Peninsulas —
Gethsemane —

Is but a Province — in the Being's Centre —
Judea —
For Journey — or Crusade's Achieving —
Too near —

Our Lord — indeed — made Compound Witness —
And yet —
There's newer — nearer Crucifixion —
Than That — (670)

Strikingly unconcerned with the modernist issue of blocked access to Christ, Dickinson finds instead that access is too horribly easy: the crucifixion is not (historically) too "distant," but (spatially) "Too near" for a journey to achieve it.

In claiming that crucifixion is not for "achieving," this poem asserts something like the opposite of what we might expect from an apostate poet: ultimate sacrifice is not to be achieved, not because it is unreachable or meaningless but because it is lodged within the self.[8] It is a fact of "Being." Its not being achievable means only that the human, like Christ, is passive before it. The *imitatio Christi* is here rewritten horribly as Beckettian dramaturgy, in which the isolated self is locked into a deathliness that iterates again at every turn. And worse, from a poetic standpoint: because there is no manifest image in which the lyric voice is located, no centering body to bring sensation home, this set of propositions cannot even name the compounding of the self nature induces. Theology without sensation is toothless, an assertion of the impossible without its embodiment in possibility.

Worst of all, in these final lines the believer is invited to no action in knowing the world. She neither oscillates with the waves nor embarks over them on a "Crusade" to Judea; she is just an outcrop perched over against unspannable distances. This stasis correlates with the fact that, despite its uncharacteristic formal sprawl, this poem offers remarkably little positive imagery of any kind. It seems a long way from this poem to any vigorous outdoor Emersonianism. We are asked to visualize "the Being's Centre," an inland terrain with provinces, but only the word "Peninsulas" offers lyric images rather than theological axioms.

That single word invoking the natural world is, however, sufficient: it is enough to anchor the poem lyrically. The sensations of Emerson are often nearer (and newer) in Dickinson's theology than we might expect. The image of the peninsula invokes the Emersonian posture of the poet at the shoreline, and figures the human person as a promontory, given shape by the nothingness that surrounds her. Neither internally adequate, like an island, nor included in a social mainland, a peninsula is all shoreline — and no escape. It is terra firma as pure deixis, pointing elsewhere but neither achieving nor falling short of that desired landing. The poem, then, is neither a territory enfranchising itself nor an isolated island of pure language. Lacking temporal prospects, the poet has in compensation only prospectiveness itself, the blank horizon.

This frustrated longing is the immediate corollary of the Emersonian's boundless outward ambition. Even in the central "Province" of the self, Dickinson feels the impossible demand of oceanic infinity, an overflowing ration of space to be consumed as knowledge, a cup that will not pass from the human. That infinite distance is always a match for the poet's vigorous occupation of it. The body immerses itself in that spirit, with no prospect either of dissolution or of recovery.

READERS' EXPERIENCE consistently suggests that Dickinson's work has something to do, in nearly equal proportions, both with enormous power and with almost total powerlessness. This fracture in the poem's idea of itself is congruent with a crack in the foundations of Emersonian knowledge — the split between the world's inflowing power and the senses' outpouring creativity. Both are limitless, both are essential. Through the unfolding medium of explicative prose, the literary critic sets out to tell a story about how these opposites interact. This expository work, sequential and logical as it must be, has a tendency to render Dickinson herself a storyteller — a narrator of her own writing process, rather than a maker of objects.[9] The result is a picture of Dickinson as a writer on a quest for self-expression, sojourning outward (or inward) from silence.

But what if, after all, the poet holds still? The present analysis supposes that the Dickinson of the poems neither grasps the world only nor yields to it only, but simply confronts in a single instant the world of objects. Poetry is an "Occupation," but not a career. Any vectored reading of the poems, because it posits a narrative, neglects the crucifixional simultaneity of Dickinson's poetics. In single intense moments of "Compound Witness," her poetry at once overcomes the limits of human scope and accedes to them absolutely.[10] The lyric moment functions instantaneously: it simply "Be" — in the infinitive. Like the crucial tenets of Christology, it is "not affirmed of Mathematics / Or History." As time diminishes in importance, though, it is not eternity, or faith, but rather space that becomes the key category: turning away from historical and semiotic frames, this poetry exercises itself anaerobically in the outdoor world.[11] In such a bodily encounter — an encounter that finds its literary precedent in Emerson's prose — power and weakness are simultaneous.

When their immobility is emphasized along with their Emersonian emphasis on nature, Dickinson's poems begin to look singularly ill matched with today's prevailing interpretive models. Time is the governing principle in most of criticism's cognitive models.[12] This premise holds sway for good cultural reasons, but not reasons intrinsic to writing as such. Although he is not always acknowledged by name, G. W. F. Hegel, the most skillful inventor of the idea of History, has provided literary criticism with the crucial antidote to the regrettably ahistorical belletrism of previous generations.[13] Kant freed the philosophical mind from dualism; in Hegel, that mind finds knowledge to be dynamic. Thus an Hegelian worldview governs much of our most useful modern self-understanding, from pragmatism's self-correctiveness to the forceful course corrections of destiny undertaken by American presidents. In such a worldview, famously, it is the task of Spirit to "realize itself" as freedom, in the world of events.

At a time when the promise of the future, and new vistas in science, had begun to increase the appeal of Hegelian thought, with its flair for seeing vectors in history, Dickinson eschewed dynamism.[14] She declined a philosophy of accomplishment. She invites us to focus stubbornly on the second half of Hegel's remarkable sentence: "History in general is . . . the development of Spirit in *Time*, as Nature is the development of the Idea in *Space*" (*Philosophy of History* III.81).[15] For Hegel, that last clause was self-explanatory, a passing illustration; but Dickinson occupies herself wholly with understanding its possibilities. In doing so she undertakes an Emersonian project that she understood, better than Emerson himself did, to have deep theological roots.

Most Dickinson criticism of the past thirty years has declined to engage Emersonian paradox, regarding his vision as too confident to be related to hers.[16] Instead, successful readers of Dickinson have handled the dilemma of power and powerlessness by arranging them on a timeline, in one of two basic story templates. The first storyline, taking its cues from the poet's life as a writer, assumes that the poems begin in Dickinson's powerlessness: in the poetry, subsequently, that weakness is troped into strength.[17] The second story, narrating a descent from reality into language, holds that each poem originates in an experience of immense imaginative power: halting, fragmented poetic speech then expresses Dickinson's titanic energies by failing to contain them.[18] These two stories, with their opposite vectors of power, provide the respective heuristics of feminist and linguistic criticism.

Thus the most important critical discourses about Dickinson describe her as primarily a poet of (female) confinement, on the one hand, or primarily a language poet, on the other.[19] The shortcomings of these methods are parallel and opposite: one finds poetic power only a recovery from powerlessness, the other finds poetic powerlessness only a trope of power. Each assumes that the poet's goal is to effect a change, to move from one mode to the other: to leverage historical weakness, or to channel raw imaginative strength. The outdoor world is only a stage for a narrative of cultural self-actualization: nature is just the place where power arrives from its occasioning in the poem; or just the place from which power launches into poetry's realm of abstraction. The poems, then, are modes of action despite themselves: each poem is charged in the criticism not merely with *being* but with *coming to be*. There is no evading the quest, because the ways Dickinson's poetry eschews quest narrative — indeed, rejects it more decisively than almost anything else in literature — can be regarded as strategies in the quest itself. The inevitable entry of Dickinson's poems into history waits only for newer and newer historicisms that will refine our understanding of them.

Emerson proposed that "the experience of poetic creativeness [is] not found in staying at home, nor yet in travelling, but in transitions from one to the other, which must therefore be adroitly managed" ("Plato" IV.32). Competent guidance through these texts means that nothing should be left to perish between worlds, both undomesticated and unadventurous. The poet may spread her hands or gather with them, but never both at once. Such adroitness, though, gives us a literature of the dynamo, and rules out of court any sharp juxtapositions and failures — like what befalls the unfortunate plant at the beginning of Dickinson's poem about poetic distillation: the "Familiar species / That perished by the Door —" (446). The same outdoor isolation is also the fate of Emerson's "shepherd, who, blinded and lost in the snowstorm, perishes in a drift within a few feet of his cottage door" ("The Poet" III.19). These deaths — one involving the lyric poem's traditional object and one its traditional singer — occupy the peninsular imagination much more than any subsequent resurrections or transitional vectors. For Emerson, there is sometimes no easy transition into new thoughts, and one might approach one's own house without recognizing it. To make a qualitative transition it is not enough to make steady progress: "What if you come near to it, — you are as remote, when you are nearest as when you are farthest" ("Experience" III.19). Dickinson's most important work is frozen at the perilous, Emersonian threshold between shelter and exposure.[20] That paradox of power and collapse, of lyric bloom and wintry death, is not an endpoint for analysis, but the place that it should dwell.

For the purposes of this book's critical schema, the Dickinsonian encounter with the world finds its literary precedent in Emerson's prose. His emphasis on the outdoors, on sensory experience, helps correct our image of Dickinson the recluse. It should be acknowledged that this proposed linking of the two writers revives elements of approaches to Emerson no longer much credited. After all, the Emerson most celebrated today anticipates Whitman, Stevens, and William James; important recent readers of his philosophy's uses regard him as a precursor to those pragmatic and dynamic writers.[21] This Emerson is never pinned down either indoors or out. Thanks to scholars like Stanley Cavell and Richard Poirier, critics focus now on the way Emerson wrote his own power into being and yet eluded its confinement, staying always in the mode of transition rather than construction — and, by not setting himself in place, set a precedent for vital elements of American culture. In many of the best recent analyses of his work, narratives of constant readjustment and linguistic skepticism felicitously replace a simple master narrative of expanding knowledge. Discerners of this pragmatic Emerson decline to participate in the old (and suspiciously easy) transcendentalist leveraging of paradox into temporal power.

For many years before these fresh, dynamic readings, Emerson's essays had been read out of all narrative context. His moment of vision was all that mattered. The general sense of Emerson, back then, seems to have been that he simply went outside and had transcendent experiences. Which is, of course, precisely what he did do. It is worth revisiting that outdoor Emerson and the natural world into which he urges us (without denying either the pragmatic possibilities Cavell and Poirier name or the suspect cultural work Emerson's urging once did). In this reading, Emerson and Dickinson are regarded primarily as nature poets, charged with writing what they see. That task, though less useful than another agenda might be, will present complexity enough. The Dickinsonian Emerson described here, unlike the Emerson justly celebrated in recent pragmatist accounts, advocates a philosophy of sensational paradox rather than action, of epistemology rather than hermeneutics. Thus the two writers illuminate each other best not when his protopragmatism is used to narrativize her writing process, but when her poetic craft lyricizes sensory knowledge like his.

DISCERNING A COMPLEX poetics of stasis in Dickinson allows for fresh consideration of her nature poetry. First, though, it is worth considering an alternative solution to the problem of imaginative control in nature. One might argue that Dickinson sought to encounter the world in a more familiar, pragmatic way, in a mode of dynamic compromise (a solution that would in fact be later adopted by Wallace Stevens). Indeed, Dickinson tries out that alternative in a poem in which she confronts the most unmanageable of natural spaces, the ocean. As this experiment collapses, it reveals the central importance of static paradox to the Dickinsonian imagination.

Dickinson's speakers often meet the untouched space of nature at the shoreline: in the beach setting, the mind is at the same time energized to shrink the world to human size (the size of the eye that "takes it all in"), and stymied by the world's own energies. One possible way of depicting this sensation might be a temporal compromise that shifts control of the scene from human to ocean and back again. In the first six lines of the following poem, the perceiving mind uses alternation to try to mediate between the posture of advance and the posture of retreat, and to describe each attitude as including elements of the other.

> Escaping backward to perceive
> The Sea opon our place —
> Escaping forward, to confront
> Its glittering Embrace —
>
> Retreating up, a Billow's hight
> Retreating blinded down
> Our undermining feet to meet
> Instructs to the Divine. (969)

In the first six lines, as they oscillate between the extremes of the active and the passive mind, Dickinson tests the possibility of narrative mediation, "giving each attitude its head" by turns (Weisbuch 9). The series of participles without an agent in the first six lines resonates with a Stevensian project of dynamic abstractions. There is a finesse even in the initial word "Escaping," which is both a seeking of refuge and an exit into landscape.

Until its conclusion, then, this poem seems to be narrating a pragmatic compromise between two attitudes: a besieged, visual passivity that sees all; and a confrontational, tactile activity that dares the danger of being overmatched by the world's hugeness. Dickinson, like any Emersonian writer of nature, seeks to name this impossible doubleness: she knows that she is both a passive and a dynamic perceiver of vast space. Each of these modes represents a cognitive stance — one is the stance of awe, the other the stance of comprehension. To reconcile these two types of knowing, the active and the passive, is the task of epistemology in a nutshell. If the poem moves fast enough to blur the distinctions, however, it might not need an epistemology. It might be able to express both. But in the final lines, instead, it freezes in place.

Moving in concert with the waves, the protagonists of this poem are on the verge of achieving a give-and-take that credits both submission and opposition to nature. But in the last two lines — and especially at the appearance of the stiffening word "Instructs" — this functional blur snaps into focus. All the double actions of the poem become elements of a single thought: all the double things turn out to be a single thing, a catechism that "Instructs to the Divine." The participles "Escaping" and "Retreating," which seemed to enact ongoing dynamism in a narrative of perceptual oscillation and incipient compromise, turn out to be gerunds. If, as William James said, one metaphor for pragmatism is a focus on parts of speech besides substantives,[22] Dickinson here is turning away from a pragmatic project: she transforms into nouns not only the apparent adjectivals of the first six lines but also the adjective "divine." Frozen doubleness and dogma replace transitional ambiguity, at the interface between "our" place and a place of otherness.

At the mention of feet, the temporal arrangement of passivity and power collapses. Going into nature is not a linguistic experiment, after all, but a single experience. Instead of a dialectical resolution, then, the poem presents a single object, the human body remembered: in the poet's feet, those chilly, clumsy objects at the point of contact between the self and the border of infinity, are her weakness and her strength. Feet undermine the beach-walker's feeling of surging power, but they also delve slightly into the sand ("under-mining") to offer necessary stability in a disorienting seascape. Freshly aware of the instruments of sensation, Dickinson's speakers seem to have remembered here (in Emerson's words about the "Fall of Man") "that we do not see directly, but mediately, and that we have no means of correcting these colored and distorting lenses which we are" ("Experience" III.43). There is no adaptation of the body that allows mind and sea to intersect; the obstacle is absolute: "We have not arrived at a wall, but at interminable oceans" ("Experience" III.42). In its last line, the poem stops trying to compromise between cognitive retreat and advance. The intractable oppositions — in and out, up and down — that Dickinson sees when she looks at nature are in her own limbs.

The collapse into theological language at the end of this poem will strike many readers as a failure of nerve; indeed, failure is the dominant note of the last few lines. Acknowledging the physical limits of experience — the finite means by which its speakers seek to measure infinite nature — the poem takes on a tragic stiffness. To be sure, there was never optimistic power in this poem; it begins with its protagonists fleeing an advancing ocean. But in the stasis of the final line, and its recourse to the idea of "structure" (buried in the word "Instructs"), we have an emblem of Dickinsonian writing's immobility, its failure even to embark on quests of knowledge. Like the weed and the shepherd, it perishes by the door — unable either to come in or to go out, dead on its own threshold.

"I DWELL IN POSSIBILITY" suggests a relationship between powerlessness and power that is both less dynamic and more complex than one might have supposed — a relation much like the one between Emerson's eye and his horizon. To claim the vast outer world as a human space, one must also yield to its hugeness and acknowledge the vertigo of incommensurability. And these movements, like the gestures of perception and appropriation, happen at the same time, instantly — in the amount of time it takes Emerson to begin counting circles in the sentence "The eye is the first circle; the horizon which it forms is the second." The eye is not an eye until it opens, with all its creative power; but in opening, it also makes itself dwindle to insignificance.

One advantage of spatial criticism over readings reliant on time is that (in an Emersonian landscape, cleansed of old Spenserian or typological stories) it minimizes the temptation to treat the poem as a narrative, itself participating in a larger narrative. This in turn allows criticism to credit the many poems in which Dickinson explicitly forecloses the narrative mode. The gradual expurgation of verbs in the following poem traces a characteristic conceptual vector for Dickinson, from narrative structures of speech to static juxtapositions.

Finding is the first Act
The second, loss
Third, Expedition for
The "Golden Fleece"

Fourth, no Discovery —
Fifth, no Crew —
Finally, no Golden Fleece —
Jason — sham — too. (910)

The proliferation of dashes in the later lines of this poem parallels the foreclosure of narrative meaning, and concomitantly the possibility of self-naming on a historical canvas. Not even the unmasking of Jason as a sham qualifies as a "discovery"; instead, falsity retroactively suffuses the whole poem.

For Dickinson, then, narrative heroism is built up out of seven falsehoods, all based on the first sham: unitary identity. Power does not come either through questing or through domestic retrenchment, but in static spatial imaginings in which the inaccessibility of potency itself is the prime fact. As "I dwell in Possibility" suggests, the poet is not given to know what power is — knowledge she might gain either by having it or by lacking it. She gives herself neither clear status. Power is not an unknown thing, but something always present, always enforcing itself on one's peripheral vision.

Power is a familiar growth —
Not foreign — not to be —
Beside us like a bland Abyss
In every company — (1287)

It is crucial to observe here that the apparently temporal term "growth" is refuted by the antinarrative phrase "not to be" (that is, "not in the future"). The poem is not simply anticipating an eventual step into power. Meanwhile, the discovery of power's "familiarity" is attenuated by its status as an "Abyss." The lesson is double: we must hesitate to read such poems either as hopeful narratives of embarking toward power or as milestones in the poet's journey to discover that power is simply domestic. Instead of drawing her readers only out into abstract abysses or only into her own "company," the poet juxtaposes the two poles. As a corollary, she treats power both as a thrill and as a terrible burden. The abyss of "Power" promises "familiar" comfort, but also yawns horribly when we are meant to be keeping each other company. It mars conversation like a disease or blemish, a protuberant "growth" that is not ourselves, that we have learned to live with companionably.

It may seem mere hedging to claim that "Power" is both claimed and abjured by the lyric speaker, who is always both beside herself with energy and loomed over by titanic forces — never even moving from one status to the other. But in an Emersonian approach, there are strong positive and imaginative reasons to choose spatial rather than narrative modes of interpretation. Space is not just the bland background of experience, but the ground of the natural world: nontemporal reading promises to make Dickinson a poet of nature — an "outside" poet, a poet of the continent and its outside.[23] At the same time, to read Dickinson as a nature poet also serves to draw her inward to a type of confinement that has less to do with historicized femininity than with the problem of embodiment in flesh. This shrinking into the body results from the way that nature opens out infinitely and coldly — around a self that must feel closed by contrast, even, or especially, in the open air.

LIKE EMERSON, Dickinson encounters nature not as a realm of local instruction "On any dated calendar day" ("Experience" III.28), but as a set of distant objects. The inner and the outer, the mind and the other, variously intersect and obviate each other. She finds, as Emerson did, that nature is most inner, most strongly related to the mind, when the absolute outerness of its infinitude is most in evidence: for this reason, the ocean is her most common referent for otherness. Thus the transformation of the animal in "A Bird came down the Walk" is registered not by a description of causality, but by the shift to maritime language: he "Rowed him softer Home — // Than Oars divide the Ocean, / Too silver for a seam." This kind of flight from encounter corresponds with a shift from markers of time: a leap "off Banks of Noon" (359).

It is hard to expunge temporal arrangements from the poetry of nature, however — after all, different moments make for different kinds of world. For Dickinson, the poetics of instantaneity and open space was the result of an extended project of encompassing and bracketing the chronological. After a lengthy early period in which Dickinson described nature in its seasonality, as a way of meditating on transition and difference (and after another period in which poems of sheer inwardness predominate), the outer world takes on increasing status of its own, without reference to seasonal cycles with their attendant conventional attributes. The corresponding shift toward a synchronic poetics is anticipated in a few earlier poems, in which radical questions of knowledge are sensed at the margin of Dickinson's more sentimental, seasonal early poetics:

Low at my problem bending,
Another problem comes —
Larger than mine — serener —
Involving statelier sums — (99)

With such self-challenging poems we may ally the much-revised "problem-poem" "Safe in their Alabaster Chambers" (124), a poem of timelessness in which a first draft about unaware seasonality above the tomb was replaced by a raw spatial image: "Worlds scoop their Arcs . . . / Soundless as Dots — on a Disc of Snow." In this early phase, such episodes of particular conceptual effort are studded among nature poems of seasonality. They do not blend easily into the fabric of the early work, and indeed in the fascicles they are often followed by rambling, ironic poems full of quotation marks. In these latter "cliché" poems, the voice seems to break through into speech in bursts. Quotation of bromides makes it possible to say something when it seems as if nothing can be said. Each time the poet is struggling to write again, without recourse to the conventions of seasonality, after being stymied by "larger" problems of serene ineffability.

Those problems begin to take clear shape in early 1862, with "A Single Screw of Flesh" (293), "A Weight with Needles on the Pounds" (294), and "There's a certain Slant of light" (320), poems in which sensation takes on difficulties more radical than its (seasonal) fleetingness. These difficulties at once create and transcend human self-knowledge, the awareness of the mind that is enabled by "Internal difference."

> There's a certain Slant of light,
> Winter afternoons —
> That oppresses, like the Heft
> Of Cathedral Tunes —
>
> Heavenly Hurt, it gives us —
> We can find no Scar,
> But Internal difference,
> Where the Meanings, are — (320)

That "Internal difference," the difference of the mind from itself, can be read either as the marvelous (though invisible) "Scar" that extraordinary experience leaves, or as a poor compensation for our not being able to find such a correlative mark. It is no longer clear, then, for the poet, whether times of poetic self-examination can be insulated from the times of near absorption into nature (here, "Winter afternoons"). Space, and specifically the space of the body, takes on new prominence in the task of composition.

Time's double power to scar (both to create and to heal change) here ceases to operate, and ceases to guarantee the poet's immunity from "seasonal" difference, with its concomitant deathliness. Difference is no longer a property only of the cycles of nature, and the cyclicality of spring is no longer promised to heal it. Knowledge, therefore, may be rendered irredeemably tenuous by a few "oppressive" moments — just as (in a spatialized version of the metaphor) a whole town may come under the aural aegis of its lone cathedral's "Tunes." Dickinson expresses this unseasonal phenomenon by replacing event metaphors of sound and sight with nontemporal metaphors of weight. The associated difficulties of fleshly knowing gradually dominate a greater percentage of the nature poems.

Dickinson's decisive (though hardly absolute) shift in 1862 from nature poetry of the seasons to nature poetry of static essence is visible in an agonistic poem of warmth and cold.

> I know a place where Summer strives
> With such a practised Frost —
> She — each year — leads her Daisies back —
> Recording briefly — "Lost" —
>
> But when the South Wind stirs the Pools
> And struggles in the lanes —
> Her Heart misgives Her, for Her Vow —
> And she pours soft Refrains
>
> Into the lap of Adamant —
> And spices — and the Dew —
> That stiffens quietly to Quartz —
> Opon her Amber Shoe — (363)

There is a plausible resolution to the uncertainty about whether this text describes Indian summer or the beginning of spring: the "Frost" is "practised" (from winter), and the "South Wind" means spring. The vagueness, though, is telling in itself: this poem is more interested in arrested change than in seasonality's movements. Nature thwarts change first by thwarting death itself — the "Daisies," like lost sheep, are led back into the realm of the living. Yet death is still a fact of the scene: they are recorded "Lost" even after they have been found. Similarly, the return of summer floweriness seems as if it will be thwarted, for the heart of Summer "misgives Her," and she seems ready to break her saving vow. The breaking of the vow, though, is not the refusal of gifts, but the exercise of more aesthetic largesse, "soft Refrains" of music. She is of two minds: the result is a "soft" gift that "stiffens" into deadliness.

All these seasonal ambiguities are masterfully embraced by the final image, in which the ultimate ambiguity, Dickinson's "serener" problem, is manifested. The shoe of Summer (a surface on which, despite Summer's best efforts, there is no warmth, no gentleness) gathers stiffening dew from the daisies. The shoe is a perfect image for the warm season's least proximate surface, the place where the frost finds new warmth's Achilles' heel, in the chill of dawn. Yet it is also a perfect image to invoke the experience of a human speaker. The shoe's gathering of dew on morning walks reflects the poet's own experience, and is itself a kind of record, a gathering of sensation that then comes inside. The perceiving human, at this point in Dickinson's oeuvre, has made her way into the poem's "place," and the ongoing struggle between warmth and cold is being exercised on the surface of her strolling body. Since the shoe partakes of summer but is held apart from it, it is endowed both with liquidity and with cold. Likewise, the amber of the dawn is both a suffusing warm yellow and a freezing stiffness ("amber" is, of course, a preservative sap). Likewise the walking poet's gaze is both a loving coloring of the world and a seizing of it that holds and kills. The place where summer strives with frost, then, is none other than the sensory circumference of the poetic self, where the killing abstraction of pure dew is poured from the warm mind over the seedlings of nature — where in turn it freezes and kills. It is, perhaps, only on the heavy shoe of the poet that nature is threatened: she treads the field in hopes of preserving the scene in the amber of art. The "Quartz" is a fact of nature's cold, but it mirrors a human aestheticism that admires dew for its icy, polished beauty rather than for the liquidity that makes it nourishing.

Taking on herself the role of summer, and finding that she inhabits it ambivalently, the poem's speaker encounters the problems of human perception in nature that run deeper than the problems of time and death that have governed most of the early nature poems. This transition in Dickinson's poetics paves the way for seemingly abstract poems like 601. Time is still an overt theme, but the meanings that happen at the edges of experience are becoming more important:

> When Bells stop ringing — Church — begins —
> The Positive — of Bells —
> When Cogs — stop — that's Circumference —
> The Ultimate — of Wheels — (601)

Apparently focused on either a definition or an eschatology, this poem exemplifies Dickinson's savor for abstract words ("Positive," "Ultimate") and her interest in abstract questions like the relationship between a sign and its transcendental signified. Like "I know a place where Summer strives," though, it is grounded in intense uncertainty about the role of inwardness in experience. The self finds its cognitive power beautifully proscribed; at the same time, like the summer, it senses that its border is a site of intense negotiation.

The stopping of the "Cogs" may be a temporal event or a spatial fact. In the first case, something has stopped them, and the only candidate is "Circumference" itself, a limit or border beyond which the wheel cannot roll, a place where no traction is available to its cogs (teeth on a wheel, devised to translate circular power into linear terms). In this temporal reading, the "Cogs" are analogous to the merely prefatory "Bells." In the second case, though, the stopping of the "Cogs" is a spatial fact, acknowledging the wheel not as a tool but as a pure, purposeless circle — its "Circumference" a wholeness manifesting itself in the object's mere physical being. Its circular power may lose its traction on events, but it stands (ultimately) as an emblem of the self's integral wholeness — one whose shape matches the world's.

The first two lines suggest that human devices look toward an eschatology in which work and speech will yield to their "Positive": acquiescent quiet in a church of eternity, into which no human devices can offer access. The second couplet incorporates this narrative as well — the wheels stop at the end of the distance it is possible to travel toward God — but links it also with a static tableau. We may freeze ourselves (or be frozen) at any point to find the ultimacy we seek in our own shape, as it arcs against the space around it. Using Emerson's complex linking of the eye and the horizon — the tool of knowing and the limit of knowledge — Dickinson here transforms his thought. The human body is no slick orb, but a toothed circle, one that may reach a limit of effectiveness and falter ("*There* is Circumference"), or in its pure physicality compose its own entelechy ("It *is* Circumference").

Remarkably, this complex double thought about eschatology and the working self is wedded to a simple, almost childlike thought about the nature of a weekly routine. The first line, "When Bells stop ringing — Church — begins —," far from being an explanatory metaphor to clear the way for the last two lines, serves to make the entire poem, in all its ambiguity, a meditation on everyday knowledge. The thoughts about eschatology, timelessness, and limit are involved even in the simple experience of hearing church bells ring, and consistently finding that they correlate with the church service. The poem can, of course, be telescoped into its neo-Platonic final line, but it can also be telescoped into its first line, a simple observation in which deconstructive uncertainty about referent and signifier (do the bells cause church, or are they mere forerunners?) parallels the more deeply felt uncertainty about the relationship between body and ultimacy. In both cases, the question is whether experience is a precursor to knowledge or identical with it — whether representation like that performed by the bells and the toothed circle yields before the fulfillment at which it aims, or is united with it.

These are questions with double answers, as most Dickinson critics have noted; but that doubleness is in their premises as well as their conclusions. The poetry is born in experience, and when Dickinson's experience fronts on unfamiliar realms, it suffuses those realms with the natural and the mundane. The trope of the inside out both defies and satisfies comprehension. We can visualize the wheel that rolls along its circumference until it is forced to a halt against a circumferential border — can visualize it, that is, until the border turns out to be a site of ontological power in the wheel's own image. The trope is baffling; yet this is Dickinson's image of the mind, embodied in complex and limiting forms, shimmering on the brink of its own internal infinity.

The philosophical reasons for this complex handling of intense knowledge are wedded, as is only proper, with poetic ones. One artistic reason that these tropes of the inside out are necessary is because the fullness of transcendent experience is unrepresentable.

> I saw no Way — The Heavens were stitched —
> I felt the Columns close —
> The Earth reversed her Hemispheres —
> I touched the Universe —
>
> And back it slid — and I alone —
> A speck upon a Ball —
> Went out opon Circumference —
> Beyond the Dip of Bell — (673)

Here the poem's moment of essential force is presented quite limply in the fourth line. A perfect encounter with wholeness has been enabled by the movement of eversion, a radial flipping. At the poem's opening, the speaker has resolved to seek an impossible communion, to which she sees "no Way" in line one; in line three, it is unexpectedly, even absurdly, granted. The world is turned inside out for the speaker's moment of connection, a moment that is the poem's thematic but not its aesthetic center: "I touched the Universe." This line flatly states the poem's referent, the visionary power in Dickinson that critics of all stripes have focused on; the poem's own power, though, comes later.

What follows that central moment is a renewed sense of marginality that overshadows the epiphany itself: because wholeness can be named in poetry, but not enacted, the surrounding elements dominate it. The poetic power here dwells in life "Beyond the Dip of Bell," once infinitude has made it possible to speak in such a way about the finite — half-rhyming the matter-of-fact "Ball" of "Earth" with the endlessly suggestive word "Bell," which evokes vertiginous swings in constant succession, communal and churchly life, solidity, collisions, rim and roundedness, sonority, and even mourning. The first stanza's abrupt turn to transcendence — the turn found in the "-verse" of "reversed" and "Universe" — has poetic meaning only after its swing ("Beyond the Dip"). The "Bell" spatializes the speaker's experience: its movement fulfills itself in stasis. It is in the vertiginous pause at the peak of the bell's swing, not in the speed of its transitional dip, that the rim meets the clapper, and the bell speaks. The poem has musical and communicative potency, then, not in its zoom toward transcendence, but in the stillness of its return from it (which is also an incipient return *to* it). This insight moves experiences of centrality, "touch[ing] the Universe," to the margins of Dickinson's poetics, while the marginalized body, the "speck opon a Ball," takes on a crucial imaginative role. Thus the solid "Bell" contains all the circular wholeness of its supposed referent, "the Universe," and overpowers it by matching it. It does so both despite and because of its circumscription — the concussive rim that makes its concave openness audible.

The translation of the music of vastness into a physical fact — and vice versa — remains a paradoxical movement, and not even the similarity between the universe's roundness and the roundness of knowable space like the bell's rim can be counted on to overcome incommensurability. No solution can satisfy entirely, for a metaphor that describes the movement of human power outward will inevitably neglect nature's impact on the self, and vice versa. The "Bell" must at once speak in its hollowness and hear the hollowness of the space around it. The music of the world can be articulated only in a human voice — and can speak only of nature's difference from the human.

SINCE IT IS NOT JUST a question of futurity for Dickinson, death fascinates her because it can clear away conventional metaphors in order to concentrate purely on the spatial dynamics of inside and outside, the self and a world resolutely distanced. Keatsian, seasonal images of death as winter can hold no ongoing attraction for her. Instead, the issue of enclosure and openness informs the key tropes of "Safe in their Alabaster Chambers" (in which space looms vastly outside the tomb), of "Because I could not stop for Death" (in which the speaker journeys indefinitely toward a tomb that is a home), and of "I died for Beauty" (in which the outward orientation of gravestones is metonymic for the whispered conference inside, between entombed souls of principle).

Though these bodies are stationed in nature, in Dickinson's mature poetics they partake of none of nature's cyclical temporality: thus the protagonist of "No Notice gave She, but a Change — " dies into a sort of speech that is only a sigh, and refuses to imagine ever bearing fruit for future generations:

> She was not warm, though Summer shone
> . . . .
> And when adjusted like a seed
> In careful fitted Ground
> Unto the Everlasting Spring
> And hindered but a Mound
>
> Her Warm return, if so she chose —
> And we — imploring drew —
> Removed our invitation by
> As Some She never knew — (860)

The figure of the poet here offers no message, but presents herself to the world cold and dignified. The poem, figured as a "Sigh" in the first stanza, speaks uselessly, having no content and no specific audience — it is spoken, but "For Whom, the Time did not suffice / That she should specify." Poetic speech is, in fact, deathly itself: "Rime"-frost piles on the protagonist's bosom as she processes to the grave. No cycle of spring returns her to social existence; her strength is in the lasting power of her corpse's hauteur, in her very reticence, and in the corresponding evasiveness of the last stanza's cramped grammar. The danger of such a poetics, of course, is that it may have nothing to say to us, and that the poet who rarely sought publication in her lifetime might receive no invitation from outside — and die into a nature that seals her away into cold. Dickinson's poetics steadfastly refuses to occupy itself with these temporal concerns (although one might feel that this poem protests too much on that score). In focusing with fascination on her own burial, she traces a tragic Christian knowledge that centers on Good Friday rather than Easter. She does not think of her poetry as a "Warm return," an artistic resurrection in history. Her concern is instead with the relation between her present self and the absolute, between "This" and the infinitude to which she is instantly destined.

The mind in its self-awareness unifies these incommensurate realms — but its relation to the present world is just as mysterious as its relation to worlds beyond.

> This Consciousness that is aware
> Of Neighbors and the Sun
> Will be the one aware of Death (817)

The experiencing mind is the site of overlap between the familiar and the strange. That link, visible here even before mortality is introduced in the odd pairing of "Neighbors" and (typological) "Sun," connects Dickinson's fascination with death to her questions about cognitive experience close at hand. What this poem calls "Adventure" is both an outward and an inward turn — but in the poetics of eversion, fulfillment of a sublime destiny cannot be comprehended in narrative form.

At the close of this poem Dickinson describes the roaming in nature and the relations of mastery that fill "My Life had stood — a Loaded Gun — " (764) with narrative energy. This time, though, the speaker is the master and the servant, holding both roles at once, as a paradoxical epistemology demands. The conventions of narrative, and even the active moment of explosion that informs the gun-poem, are stripped away. This speaker has the Christological "power to die" that the gun lacks. In relation only with herself, she embarks into a nothingness of perfect ambiguity. While death in many other poems is pure enclosure, a tomb and mound, or (as in "Because I could not stop for Death") a journey past the world that becomes an arrival into earth, here it is a journey outward that seals the protagonist into herself. In this poem the thrill of the incipient quest, of being taken up like the gun into an ongoing encounter with mastered nature, is perfectly balanced by the horror of an infernally endless pursuit — in which hell is not other people, but oneself.

> Adventure most unto Itself
> The Soul condemned to be —
> Attended by a single Hound
> Its own identity. (817)

Setting out hunting, in a transcendence of gender roles and a well-defined quest, this speaker is also, however, withdrawing into herself, musing on the relationship between soul and consciousness. When those two are split, all other unities seem inevitably out of reach. Descending into the self, accompanied by a bestial avatar of herself, the speaker is consigned to a world of knowledge that is at best reflexive. The "Hound" that is her earthly consciousness pursues her even into the afterlife, and there is no escape from its appetite, only unending flight.

The pursuit, though, is itself thrilling, and the baying hound of self-condemnation is also a faithful companion on this "Adventure." The speaker makes the best of having been thrust into existence, having been "condemned to be." Faithfully setting out into a space in which her personality is both a column of reliable strength and a ravenous animal force, the speaker makes self-knowledge a mystery, self-sufficiently manifest but unachievable. In the middle of this abstract poem of "Adventure" is a stanza in which the poet's perplexity and her confidence both seem total.

> How adequate unto itself
> It's properties shall be
> Itself unto itself and None
> Shall make discovery — (817)

In the poem about Jason and the quest, the notion of "discovery" was canceled even as the discovery of the sham self was being made; here, inversely, a discovery is both tautological and denied, but said to be fully consummated nonetheless. The word "None," a zero at the core of the poem, floats free, defining the subject, the object, and the audience of poetic work. Even so, Dickinson's poetics holds out this hope of instantaneous power — reflexive and alone, even self-negating, but achieved in company nonetheless, in the marriage of the soul's voluble power and its dumb enfleshed identity. The inequality of this marriage — its unavoidable dynamic of mastery (one is master, one is pet) or pursuit (one is predator, one is prey) — insists that there is tragedy in this fate, but this poem is too thrilling to be simply an elegy.

THE JUXTAPOSITION OF incommensurate attitudes is a central trope of Emerson's writing: "Our moods do not believe in each other. . . . I am God in nature; I am a weed by the wall" ("Circles" II.182). For Emerson as for Dickinson, this contrast vexes not only experience but also composition: in these words he laments the irreconcilability of two writing selves. The voluble self, inspired by nature, can hardly recognize or be recognized by the puny scribbler who struggles to find words in the lee of his puny lean-to — "by the wall." In an early poem, Dickinson addresses the problem of these two selves with an optimistic thought-experiment. Poetry, she suggests, might be a process in which the immobile and withered self concentrates herself further, in order to invoke the vast power of the outdoor world. Weakness gives rise to strength. For the purpose of this poem — a narrative experiment, like "Escaping backward to perceive," fated to collapse — Dickinson adopts Emerson's metaphor of the tiny plant by a structure.

This was a Poet —
It is That
Distills Amazing sense
From Ordinary Meanings —
And Attar so immense

From the familiar species
That perished by the Door —
We wonder it was not Ourselves —
Arrested it — before — (446)

Attar (emphasized on the first syllable) is the essence of rose: the flower's beauty contained by a tiny bottle. In reading such lines, criticism seems bound to point out confidently one of two distinct phenomena: either the poet transforms ordinariness into amazing poetry; or, inversely, she translates "immense" imaginative power into the domestic world of bottled perfume. A critic interested in functional smallness will choose lines three and five, while a critic interested in language's immensity will focus on lines two and four. In either case an antecedent state, "before" poetry happened, yields to the synthesized essence that is the poem. But criticism tends not to credit Emerson's incredible claim that smallness and immensity are both primary and instantaneous facts of writing. To close a drawer full of poems is also to open up the ceaselessness of infinity, each page embodying the intense openness of encounter with the all.

More important, the double status of immensity and smallness applies to the writer just as it applies to her materials. For this reason, Dickinson sets the first line of this poem in the past tense: "This was a Poet." The vanished writer here is also "This" — a poem at hand, or this very poem. So the poem's material is not gathered from elsewhere: it is the poet's own deathliness, her death in her own garden. Like the dynamic shoreline poem "Escaping backward to perceive," this text imagines that poetry might be a process (this time a process not of compromise but of transformation). But the experiment collapses before it has begun, in the first line rather than the last. To say "This was," rather than "This is," centers the text not just on preservation but also on loss. The two moods of this poem, the mood of distillation and the mood of mourning, do not believe in each other. The poet cannot hope to succeed in processing her objects — least of all herself — but merely to "Arrest" them.

A later rose-poem returns to this early theme of distillation, and revises it. It addresses the question of whether Dickinson prefers to emphasize the deathliness of exposure outdoors or the tiny, static final object that encapsulates the essence of beauty. The answer, of course, is both: not because death is trumped by resurrection, but because they are simultaneous. Indeed, in the static Emersonian lyric they are identical.

> Essential Oils — are wrung —
> The Attar from the Rose
> Be not expressed by Suns — alone —
> It is the gift of Screws —
>
> The General Rose — decay —
> But this — in Lady's Drawer
> Make Summer — When the Lady lie
> In Ceaseless Rosemary — (772)

It was not obvious in the first rose-poem, but is manifest here, that in extracting meaning from her materials, the poet is not just turning the screw but also undergoing its pressure. It is not just her object but herself that perishes in the triumph of her art. "This," the poem in Dickinson's drawer, is the essence of her experience — but its expression is attained only in her agony under the compressing "Screws" she turns herself. The philosophical body, in its task of writing, stages an instantaneous dialectic between muscular concupiscence and material acquiescence, the desire to squeeze and the necessity of being crushed. There is no transitional surface, no space for oscillatory blurring of the two principles; there is only flesh.

To be sure, there is a message about language's status here: the poems are to be received by future generations, because the ineffably noble "Lady" has died into words, surrounding herself with the austere flavor of rosemary (indicating only remembrance). And there is a feminist message: the "Lady" inhabits this role as vigorously as the man; the centering power of the male sun is inadequate without a hidden, indoor activity of expression; and essence is not expressed by sons alone. These are fundamental meanings of the poem, one turning to nature and the timeless interrelation of summer and winter (the linguistic object "Make Summer," ungrammatically), and the other turning strongly indoors to parody and surmount the patriarchal courtly-love metaphorics of rose and lady.[24]

Both of these meanings, though, come under the umbrella of the central epistemological theme, which is developed in the static second stanza along the contours of Emersonian concerns. How can we know nature's liveliness rather than just basking in its sun? How is summer "made" from the deathly materials that are us? The answer is mysterious. As "the Rose" is replaced in this poem by "Rosemary," it changes in a radical way that no session of work could have brought about.[25] The word "rosemary" is not a modification of "rose" that makes it a name; its roots are deeper in the history of language. It derives from the Latin *ros*, "dew," and *mare*, "sea." These two roots prevent each other from establishing the poem's theme as either universality or ephemerality.

The poem's key images of flower and herb, then, are not arrayed on a timeline but in space. Somehow still nearby rather than buried, the "Lady" maintains a relation to the essence of herself, poetic "Attar" stashed unceremoniously in a desk. Meanwhile, the familiar species, under the writerly eye of the Emersonian, is perched at the brink of infinity. For Dickinson, the dew, ephemeral liquid on the rose's surface, must have worth and status just as its "Essential Oils" do. Likewise, the deathly experience of diluting the self in oceanic vastness, of acquiescence, might be as important as concentrating it into a poem. Just as in the "Escaping" experiment the poet both gripped the sand and entered the ocean, here she hopes at once to dissolve into the atmosphere and to be concentrated and preserved. Forced by this dream into a deathly mode of being, she is the rose upon the rood of open space.

Like the dewdrop encountering the ocean, Dickinson's poetry faces dissolution in its own substance. The flavor and spikiness of rosemary, though, make it impossible to consider this a poem of transparency: the pungency of this poetic self, her power with sensuously satisfying objects, is counterpoised to her encounter with oblivion. She not only yields to nature but builds — or cooks, or adorns, or writes — within it. The house of "I dwell in Possibility" was supplanted by an exposed body with empty hands: here that stark image is itself replaced by sensations both more specific and more universal than even Christology affords. The immaculate object ("Rose") and the obedient conceiver ("Mary") of that scheme are both present in the final line, but other meanings are present in it as well. In the single word "Rosemary," Dickinson's poetic effort is figured as a proper name and a Latinate coinage; a garnish sprig and a hardy organism; a drop of dew and an enormous ocean. The poem, shapely and flavorful, faces absorption into ceaselessness — but not without etching out its own sharpness on the face of infinity.

5   Frost and the Unmoving World

Communication between people functions smoothly in the poetry of Robert Frost, because such interactions are insulated from his most pressing artistic uncertainties and longings. In writing, the mind comes up against nature's unyielding stability and coldness — but when relationships are at issue, there are no limits on what language can accomplish. Frost protects sociable experience from the most important difficulties of his poetics. Since sociability in turn is central to the American tradition of pragmatism, Frost has often been read as a poetic version of William James, with his Emersonian qualities credited just insofar as Emerson can be read as a proto-Jamesian.[1] But there are significant tensions among the Jamesian elements in Frost's lyric poetry: when they engage too tightly with each other, in the hands of the poet rather than in the mouth of an interlocutor, the workings of American knowledge can seize up. Frost induces this immobility, purposefully and consistently, and not only in poems of darkness or winter. For him, humanity's cognitive breakdowns correspond to a principle of recalcitrance — literally, stoniness — in even the sunniest versions of nature he describes.

To be sure, Frost has little interest in expanding the imagination away from rural homesteads. His goal is expressly not to develop a scope large enough to universalize (or federalize) language. Concomitantly, his negotiations of American size usually do not emphasize the infinite horizon. Instead, the fulcrum of knowledge — and its breaking point — is situated at the surface of an object right at hand. Like Emerson in his more thoughtful encounters with horizon, though, Frost finds at these interfaces a leverage that works both ways — he is both the agent and the object of his experiences. The quintessential Frostean object, in fact, offers its perceivers something "To stay our minds on and be staid."[2] Such staying power is by no means the only goal of a typical Frost poem. But when the materials are most rigorous, and the stay maximally effective, the muscularity of the cognitive mind moves only itself. Its objects remain still.

Frost once referred to poetry not as a tool for handling the world, or as a fictive world itself to be explored, but as a grounded cause of vertigo, a boundary stone to what we know: "My poems are all set," he said, "to trip the reader head foremost into the boundless."[3] In considering the way that poems are "set," as well as the ways that they move and function cognitively, this chapter supplements (and often opposes) not only the dynamic readings of Frost's work-poems but also the general sense that Emersonian poets operate primarily by means of flex and constant readjustment, as Stevens does. Since boundlessness is rarely on immediate display in these poems, the study of Frost's Emersonianism in its infinite context should center on the firmly fixed objects that he sets to trip readers into boundlessness, objects that refuse to cooperate with the mind that encounters them. The structure of the obstacle (variously, the poem or its central object, or both) is the best clue to the meaning of the openness beyond it. As chapter 2 argued, openness and closed forms are more tightly related in the Emersonian tradition than is usually supposed.[4] Poised just on this side of boundlessness, small and immobile elements, in the world or in a poem, have the power to turn interpretive momentum into useless torque. Craving the sharp sensation of the stubbed toe, the Frostean perceiver instantly tumbles away from his object, and they orbit each other closely without touching.

One emblem of this encounter is the elusive white object at the bottom of a well in "For Once, Then, Something": it might be a reflection from far above or an object far below, but it tantalizes the senses from a distance without performing. Just as relevant, though, is the patch of earth right at hand in Frost's critical poem of longing, "To Earthward."

When stiff and sore and scarred
I take away my hand
From leaning on it hard
In grass and sand,

The hurt is not enough:
I long for weight and strength
To feel the earth as rough
To all my length.

Mystery in Frost's poems is not just about the way that objects escape detection and comprehension; it has to do with the craving that all sensation elicits, for deeper and sharper interaction with the world. Unable to impinge on each other, in Frost's poems the perceiving body and the vast, fascinating world interact across an impermeable tissue. All things may be in reach, but this only deepens the ache of the ever-grasping Emersonian poet.

The star, rather than the ocean, is the Emersonian object of knowledge that Frost most often employs. Encountering it with organs besides sight, he adds new dimensions to the wistful nighttime encounter with the stars, a vista that Emerson considered the archetype of human awe. As many critics have remarked, poetry of touch works quite differently from the poetry of vision; it is by emphasizing the physical contact of sexuality, after all, that Whitman has earned the critical approval as a social thinker that Emerson has lost in recent, politically alert writing about the American Renaissance. But Frost brings the Emersonian epistemological problems of the night sky to infect the hands-on experience of nature — and in Frost's poems, the star that can be gripped is no nearer to humanity than the one that Emerson eyed upon "retiring from his chamber" in the opening lines of *Nature*.

The star, indeed, is only one example of a phenomenon that recurs often in Frost's poetry: the object one holds that, in its self-contained singularity, helps to stave off confusion but evokes other, more fundamental longings. Lee Rust Brown has argued that in Emerson, a single object can have the same cognitive effect as open and confounding space: "Normal perspective is reversed in this microscopic way of looking: the horizon . . . is no longer an expression of the viewer's remove *from* the object but instead expresses conceptual distances already there within the texture of [the object itself]" (72). Thus a great distance may be spanned by the amateur astronomer's telescope in "The Star-Splitter," but the outcome of this closer union between the dreaming mind and its sublime objects is new division: the telescope

> Didn't do a thing but split
> A star in two or three, the way you split
> A globule of quicksilver in your hand.

The enjambment at the word "split" is only one way that the poem takes responsibility for fissures and gaps. Adopting the first-person plural as if to include the reader, it confesses at its close that "We've looked and looked, but . . . / Do we know any better where we are?" The poem's quest for more knowledge, like the vision of the stargazer, simply opens up new distances, some of which can never be entered.

Often in Frost, the distances within objects involve no particular ambiguity or uncertainty — they are not distances of confusion, but distances of pure blankness, empty "desert places" near to hand that offer no milestones to the mind. There is plenty of distance within even the most particulate objects. This explains an odd hiccup in the logic of the poem "Desert Places": the speaker remarks, "They cannot scare me with their empty spaces / Between stars," then corrects himself to put the distance within each star rather than between them — "*On* stars where no human race is" (emphasis added). Each dot of light contains all the empty space that might be found in journeys between them. The speaker goes on to localize distance even more, registering his feeling that the same emptiness can be found "So much nearer home," in strolling experiences like the one of the poem's first three stanzas. The mind that faces an object like the star may do so in order to be stayed and therefore to be "staid"[5] — but in considering the star more closely, a Frost speaker is likely to find at the heart of the object an empty space that corresponds to his own hollowness. The two emptinesses plunge through each other, defying narrative representation — how, after all, can one hear a collision of voids, or know when it is over? This paradigm of the lyric, in which no work is done, inevitably results whenever Frost locks himself out of pragmatism into a more absolute and tragic relation with nature's objects.

IN THE TITLE POEM of the volume *New Hampshire*, Frost quotes Emerson as a foil, depicting himself as the champion of good country folk against elitist Massachusetts philosophers: "Emerson said, 'The God who made New Hampshire / Taunted the lofty land with little men.'" Frost clearly disapproves of Emerson's critical tendency to remark on a mismatch between topography and the selves that confront it. Richard Poirier's *Robert Frost: The Work of Knowing* holds that the central task of Frost's poetry is to mediate such mismatches through labor. In this poem, though, Frost reveals a different kind of imagination — one that is deeply Emersonian, and far from pragmatic — by exaggerating this same incongruity and meditating upon it. In this way the poem turns away from celebration of land and folk to an appreciation of astral forces as they ornament the land and make it uncanny. Though capable of fireside political talk, Frost is more interesting when he looks alone out the window — replicating the crucial moment of contrast in Emerson's "The Snow-Storm" — at a world that takes human imagination as its template.

Before turning to mountains and sky, though, Frost counters Emerson's insult to the state of New Hampshire, and bolsters his own reputation as a populist. In this long poem introducing his fourth book, Frost seeks among other things to position himself commercially as a different kind of literary figure, one who neither remakes people nor wishes them larger to match their "lofty land." Unlike "higher," more cosmopolitan artists like Emerson, Frost claims simply to draw people together with their place. Unlike his folksy persona, he says sardonically, other poets try to impose alien grandeur on the place:

> The glorious bards of Massachusetts seem
> To want to make New Hampshire people over.
> They taunt the lofty land with little men.

Scorning the airiness of transcendentalism, Frost shows in this last line how language can work flexibly to answer for a human presence without being defensive. That last line's reframing of the original Emerson insult shifts the emphasis (the need for some attention to the unstressed word "They," the subject of the sentence, results in an exaggerated metrical stress on the next syllable). The emphasized verb "taunt" focuses disapprobation on the philosopher's deed and its childishness. Meanwhile the sentence-sound agglomerates the land and its people into a single, organic entity — New Hampshire is indeed "the lofty land with little men," but that phrase has taken on its own strength. Wryly, Frost accepts Emerson's joke, and the taunt is embraced, no longer a novel jibe but a fond nickname for the place — fit to be printed on the license plates.

Frost is more defensive and less interesting as he turns back in the following lines to Emerson's main challenge, the challenge to rural character — the issue of New Hampshire's "Little men (it's Massachusetts speaking)." Even in their smallness, Frost says, the people in New Hampshire are almost too good for a writer to use:

> How are we to write
> The Russian novel in America
> As long as life goes so unterribly?

As anodyne as this vague defense of local character is (and despite the fact that it appears in opposition to a quotation from Emerson), it emblematizes the sort of cheery Emersonianism this poet is usually believed to espouse. This Jeffersonian outlook (one that some critics of the fifties condemned Frost for advancing) holds that life in its simplicity outdoes the modes of literary representation. As a social poet, to be sure, Frost gives signs of believing this: in describing people, he carefully eschews the egotistical sublime and pays generous attention to each type in its own context.[6] In this line, he puts on geniality: in his eyes, the easygoing residents of New Hampshire show up the effete, self-absorbed Boston philosophers and their fashionable novels of misery.[7] No imagination is needed to like people as they already are.

Such celebration of reality's ease notwithstanding, the second key theme of these lines from "New Hampshire" is the opposite of the first: it registers the strong allure of representation's possibilities over reality's. The power of artificiality, corresponding to the power of the perceiving mind over the object, underwrites the Emersonianism abruptly activated here. Having seen an old map in which the White Mountains are labeled with heights twice their size, the speaker of "New Hampshire" (who is so satisfied with his neighbors and their lives) laments that something in the landscape now fails to satisfy him. Ruefully, he acknowledges that he, too, must be a "glorious bard," aware of shortcomings in his experience when it is measured against the heights of his imagination.

> How, to my sorrow, how have I attained
> A height from which to look down critical
> On mountains? . . .
> [By] the sad accident of having seen
> Our actual mountains given in a map
> Of early times as twice the height they are —
> Ten thousand feet instead of only five —
> Which shows how sad an accident may be.
> Five thousand is no longer enough.

The facts of New Hampshire are disappointing after all: the people are as they should be, perhaps, but in encounter with nature Frost finds himself insatiable, longing for more sublimity, longing in fact (as a later passage makes clear) for absolute height that pierces the sky. Having had a belated whiff of the "early times" promise of grandeur in the New World, Frost makes an Emersonian imaginative effort to envision its absolute size and power.

This passage includes ample instruction about how it should *not* be interpreted. Frost assures the reader that the desire for more height is not the yearning of a Romantic imitator: "Foreign travel in the Alps," a sublime and speculative experience like Wordsworth's in the *Prelude*, does not cause it. More important, he also asserts clearly that it is not a Hamiltonian choice. He will not buy in to a Massachusetts ideology of ambitious collectivity. The dream of high mountains does not mean that Frost is dissatisfied with earthy, parochial American politics or lifestyle: Frost's awareness of reality's smallness, he says, does not result from

> Having seen and credited a moment
> The solid molding of vast peaks of cloud
> Behind the pitiful reality
> Of Lincoln, Lafayette, and Liberty.

The moment Frost explicitly disavows here shares the dynamic of Sacvan Bercovitch's jeremiad, an imaginative sequence in which political reality — in this case, the actual towns named in the last line — pales before its entelechy, and then is reinvigorated.[8] Through the jeremiad, communities like Liberty, New Hampshire, strive always anew to fulfill the power of their names, seeing in the imposing clouds above them the promise of the future. But this is expressly not the moment that inspires Frost's lyric ambition. These lines seem carefully designed as a refusal of the place Americanist scholarship might have had ready for Frost, among the ambitious American writers of universalizing romance. Frost's poetry is not about American history in the landscape (the complacent ruminations of "The Gift Outright" notwithstanding). It is not just the lyric infrastructure for a narrative driven by useful national dreams.

Despite the preference for immediate description that Frost sensed in his readership, the "actual mountains" in this poem are the ones on the map, not the ones on the skyline. They are transformed, and made higher than their namesakes, only by a label — but they make the ones on the skyline seem smaller. (Without the gentle, Frostean idiosyncrasy, Emerson's project often does the same thing: sublimity in nature is, fundamentally, humanity's own majesty reflected.) The imaginative power involved in the way things are mapped is not possessive, but it is absolute; it is wry and self-deprecating, but vast in scope. Frost praises New Hampshire most compellingly not by defending little men, but by refusing to defend the land's hugeness in the face of soaring human imagination that outdoes it. The land is not as lofty as it might be. Thus the poem must register the mismatch, as well as the intercourse, between human assertiveness and natural terrain. A set of nonnational poetic ambitions results from the poet's individual sadness — from the unmediated contrast between what could be and what is. The edgy Frost is a protest poet of a sort, dismayed by the finite destinies that the inadequate continent offers to dreaming humanity.

In urging the mountains higher to match a fiction, Frost violates his own famous claim, from "Mowing," that "The fact is the sweetest dream that labor knows." His concern is a possibility always in the back of the Emersonian mind: that lyric dreaming exists precisely as a mismatch with fact — and moreover that despite the importance of feeling to the contrary, labor often cannot wed the two. When it does (as Richard Poirier has shown in *Robert Frost: The Work of Knowing*), earth work and literary work become one. But "New Hampshire" ends with a reminder of the difference between those two key elements, the farmwork that is the subject matter of georgics and the task of writing such georgics.

> I choose to be a plain New Hampshire farmer
> With an income in cash of, say, a thousand
> (From, say, a publisher in New York City).
> It's restful to arrive at a decision,
> And restful just to think about New Hampshire.
> At present I am living in Vermont.

The desire to straddle two worlds here, the literary and the outdoor, collapses in the near miss of the poem's last line. Unable to inhabit the modes he praises, Frost has found that the negotiations of the volume *North of Boston*, however perfectly rendered they may be, do not resolve themselves into a choice of living. It will be up to art, not life, to create reciprocity between art and life.

The imaginative climax of "New Hampshire" is not in these final lines' mere juxtaposition of country life and city money, a welding of incongruous lifestyle choices. The heart of the poem is instead in an earlier passage, where Frost describes a longing that would persist even in New Hampshire, even when a career has been perfected. It describes his romance with the land as it will never become. Having seen the map of mountains with their heights doubled, Frost cannot set his mind at ease:

> Whereas I never had a good idea
> About improving people in the world,

Here I am overfertile in suggestion,
And cannot rest from planning day or night
How high I'd thrust the peaks in summer snow
To tap the upper sky and draw a flow
Of frosty night air on the vale below
Down from the stars to freeze the dew as starry.

Despite this vision's artificial origin (the map), here Frost names nature in its own categories — night, day, snow, stars — rather than with verbal muscle and dexterity, and carries forward the Emersonian legacy of absolute ambition that encounters objects right at hand. His overfertility gladly frustrates itself in excess, bringing the answering rush of winter out of the heights to the vale of summer: the choice is for cold, pure beauty over the cyclical nourishment of farming. To be imaginatively "overfertile," in these lines, is also to kill the summer crop. (The decision is made more stark here by the unnecessary emphasis on "summer": Frost not only celebrates crystallizing dew but also disrupts the seasons to bring it on.) The bigger the imagination, the worse the situation of earthy folk: however much Frost's commercial success may have depended on his defense of such folk against a caricature of Emerson, his poetics relies on the overreaching — the admiration of loftiness — that such defenses deplore. The hardness of the mind's object is introduced into this poem as a thing underfoot that evokes the stars. Infinite space's coldness suffuses objects right at hand, putting the gasp of a sudden chill into the out-of-breath voice of these enjambed lines, which is so quintessentially Frost's. This explains why the triple rhyme here, in its yearning, anticipates the form of the poem that follows "New Hampshire," "A Star in a Stoneboat." The two poems have the same strange metaphoric core.

To name the imaginative role of Frost's stars, by considering "A Star in a Stoneboat" and its kin, is to begin to name his Emersonianism. Emerson began his own career as a published writer by recommending encounter with the stars, an encounter in which their distance is the primary fact: "If a man would be alone, let him look at the stars. The rays that come from those heavenly worlds, will separate between him and what he touches. One might think the atmosphere was made transparent with this design, to give man, in the heavenly bodies, the perpetual presence of the sublime" (*Nature* I.8).[9] Despite the emphasis on "presence," Emerson is remarking primarily that the stars' distance infuses itself into all sensory relationships: even the nearby things the

Emersonian touches seem to take on the distance the stars represent. In Frost, too, all too often there is no domesticating the unspeaking mystery of things that are touched and manipulated. In a way, of course, stars are consoling, since they keep the sky from presenting itself as mere void: "Eyes seeking the response of eyes / Bring out the stars, bring out the flowers" ("All Revelation"). Making infinity punctiform, stars offer a handle on total knowledge: hence in the last few lines of "A Star in a Stoneboat," the meteorite offers Frost "The prize / Of the one world complete in any size / That I am like to compass, fool or wise." In this poem, the feeling that Emerson names in *Nature* is made portable, localized into a single object.

To human hands, though, this star is just as unworkable as Emerson's stars are when distant. This intransigence in the object makes it less useful than the rocks also incorporated into a wall in "Mending Wall," in the socially dynamic volume *North of Boston*. In that earlier poem, the title object is primarily an obstacle between selves, one that also brings them together in a cooperative "game." In "A Star in a Stoneboat," though, the wall's constituent object is an obstacle to itself: it blocks both the poet and the farmer by its own double essence. Moreover, the star's aesthetic power, as in "New Hampshire," frustrates agriculture (though hot this time instead of cold): "The harm was done: from having been star-shot / The very nature of the soil was hot // And burning to yield flowers instead of grain." The object seems to promote beauty rather than nourishment, and the farmer can only "Move[] it roughly with an iron bar" into a sledge. But the poet will fare no better manipulating it. Its defining features are the heaviness that requires the stoneboat and the magnetism that torques the lyric speaker into "tangents": it is both hard to move and hard to hold still. The energy of the poem, however, does not stem from its ability to unify the opposite terms, but to feel their difference — just as the opposite poles of the magnetic rock are felt in the poet's hands.

When the stone comes alive, it does so as a sign of forces elsewhere — it runs

Off in strange tangents with my arm,
As fish do with the line in first alarm. . . .

Such as it is, it promises the prize
Of the one world complete in any size
That I am like to compass, fool or wise.

Though this metaphor resonates with a georgic theme of productive work, in this case fishing rather than farming, it also invokes the excitement of sport. The lines are too playful to do work. Nothing in the poem corresponds to the eating of the fish, a true encompassment that also nourishes. Indeed, if the length of the poet's arm is the same as the length of a line — the line that crosses the border between self and intriguing world — then even objects held in the hands are at a distance. Thus the object can never be reeled in;[10] its responses to manipulation always indicate something larger in its own nature, something too big for us to apprehend. Every hooking of the world releases adrenaline: this time the force on the other end might be the one that gets away. It always is.

A desired object, found and held, tends to become the divining rod for some other, fuller, more intensely craved object of knowledge — in the extreme instance, Earth as a whole. Indeed, this is precisely the plot of "A Star-Splitter," in which the longed-for telescope (for which a farm and home are sacrificed) reveals more about the stars themselves, and their internal differences, but nothing that will give a context to the human status "Among the infinities": "We've looked and looked, but after all where are we?" Once the object is "compassed," it becomes just a compass, a tool for further exploration of the world at large. In Frost, too, even the perfectly sized miniworld, spinning in one's hands, only suggests (like a wobbling needle under glass) the vast untouchable field of magnetic force that governs on the planetary scale.

The issue is not what an amiable poet might do with a flexible line, but the stranger, ungovernable thing a fish does with it — and what a heavy sledge dragged across the lines of "plowed ground" does to poetic order. The strain of brutal contrast, not the flex of mediation, is the primary mode of "A Star in a Stoneboat." Under this poetics, to move an object that is within reach might be useful (as it is to the oblivious farmer); or it might be exciting, since it indicates the power that tugs the other end. But it cannot succeed in being both at once: it is never both fact and dream, never both work and sport. Recreation offers no leverage on Creation. The desired object — a "complete" world — is somehow supposed to be present in two ways at once: intriguingly indicated, by the meteorite; and held in the hands, as the meteorite.[11]

In certain kinds of pragmatic art, plain seeing and visionary energy become the same thing. The encounter with beauty and the fulfillment of human need can be aligned and interwoven along the seam that is the poem. In the case of this poem, though, that stitching is jammed by an inflexible object, the meteorite, that draws the attention of both protagonists. The poet's interaction with it is quite opposite to the farmer's interaction — and both, for opposite reasons, are difficult and uncertain. The heat and energy the poet prizes give rise to the flowers that disrupt the farmer's crop, while the same irregularity of shape that enables the stone to "perch" in the farmer's wall causes trouble for the poet who spins it. No compromise object that sways pleasantly between two types of world — unlike the birches toward heaven that are "Good both going and coming back," or the "Vague dream-head lifted out of the ground" at the opening of "Tree at My Window" — the stone is a stubbornly undream-like fact.[12] Like the frozen dew of "New Hampshire," it stands for the ways in which the work of nourishment and the work of imagination oppose one another.

WHEN FARMLAND presents the worker with an object of absolute resistance, a challenge is issued to Frost's dynamically maintained georgic balance, the steady encounter of give-and-take between the writer and the land he works in writing. In "Mowing," the locus classicus of pragmatic art, the pleasure of scythe-work is linked with the pleasure of making lines of poetry. The protagonist is said to be occupied with "Laying the swale in rows" — the valley ("swale") is ordered by the limber human body, and the sound of their interaction through the scythe is a sort of speech without content, a whisper of unity. This language is conceived as the language of poetry, and the poet's work turns out to be the same as the farmer's. In such labor — the kind of activity disrupted by the wrench-in-the-gears meteorite fallen into a field — category differences are vanquished by muscle as it flexes pleasurably and productively against matter.

"Mowing" indeed offers a powerful pragmatic image of the poet's work; however, the single type of resistance offered by the stalks (even though some are grassy matter and others are flowers) is revised in "To Earthward," in which the resistant objects are grass and sand. This grittier poem responds to youthful pleasures of the sort celebrated in A Boy's Will, the volume in which "Mowing" appears. Not incidentally, it also ponders the speaker's inadequate likeness to the heavy stone of "A Star in a Stoneboat," his paltry participation in the gigantic forces of the planet.

Love at the lips was touch
As sweet as I could bear;
And once that seemed too much;
I lived on air

That crossed me from sweet things
. . . .

I craved strong sweets, but those
Seemed strong when I was young;
The petal of the rose
It was that stung.

Now no joy but lacks salt,
That is not dashed with pain
And weariness and fault;
I crave the stain

Of tears, the aftermark
Of almost too much love,
The sweet of bitter bark
And burning clove.

Every stanza after the transition word "Now" includes a near miss: "*but* lacks salt," "is *not* dashed," "*after*mark," and (as quoted earlier) "take *away* my hand … The hurt is not enough" (emphasis added). This later poetics is preoccupied with the sensation of absence, and the great, uncomfortable, anaerobic strain that it elicits.

The craving in "To Earthward," like the urge to handle the unruly meteorite, is about distinction rather than unification. The speaker does not long to unify the experience of flowers with the experience of earth, but to savor their agonizing contrast. The grass makes the sand uncomfortable, and vice versa: such intense incongruity is what the poet craves — whereas in *A Boy's Will* he focused on breezes and mystery. The subtle shortfalls in Frost's mediating, Jamesian solutions in "Mowing" and "Rose Pogonias" — failures attributable to the very elements that make them most beautiful as poems — anticipate his later poetics of longing and negativity, the poetics sketched in "To Earthward."

The pragmatic reading of Frost centers on the idea that his poems are built to ward off confusion: poetry has value as it acknowledges and works to stabilize the world's unreliable and unuseful elements. This idea that the poem is a defense against chaos is one that Frost encouraged himself—probably without knowing how much he was doing so—by coining a much-quoted definition of poetry. A poem, Frost said, is "A momentary stay against confusion."[13] The natural explication of this phrase holds that the poem is reactive, and takes part in a narrative larger than itself: a narrative in which confusion reigns before the poem; then the poem intervenes to stabilize things briefly; then confusion floods back into the field of view. The lyric moment, if we read the phrase this way, is precious as a contrast with everything else. The pleasure of freezing a moment of pure perception, like a jewel, offsets the overwhelming predominance of imagination's bumptious energy and nature's darkness.

In recent years, the literary-critical authority of the phrase "A momentary stay against confusion" has generally come from its pedigree in American pragmatism. The usefulness of the phrase in criticism has been augmented by the fact that it can mean several different things. It can be adapted to many critical situations—and it has been, although usually it offers little help in the interpretation of a poem. In some ways, it is in fact an empty phrase: the several elements that it names are exactly the things that it is usually taken to mediate. The elements are all named but not reconciled—change ("momentary"), stability ("stay"), and a swirl of meanings that neither moves consistently nor stands still ("confusion"). Interpretive use of the phrase "A momentary stay against confusion" to answer questions about a poem is itself a pragmatic exercise, making the concepts into an example of the way Frost dodges such questions, rather than an answer to them. There is a satisfying congruence here, but a focus on the "stay" at the heart of Frost's dictum (rather than the momentariness that makes the poem precious, or the confusion outside that makes it feel safe) would bring to light something difficult and fresh within Frost's saying. Former ways of reading Frost have suggested that his poems are not about themselves, but about a moment that one might undergo, or a confusion that one might briefly ward off. As "To Earthward" suggests, though, they are also in some way about a "weight" that one cannot possess, a singular heft possessed reliably only by objects of titanic size. They are poems about what the mind cannot budge.

The "stay" is important even in Frost's first book, *A Boy's Will*, in which such uncompromising size seems deliberately forsworn. In "Rose Pogonias" and "Mowing," respectively, Frost deploys the trademark principles of pragmatism: confusion and momentariness. When the two poems are juxtaposed, though, it becomes apparent that even these early texts insistently pose problems of cognition deeper than "confusion" — problems, that is, of the "stay." The critique of pragmatism that emerges from the pair of mowing-poems in *A Boy's Will* eschews processual collective action and enacts scenes of pure encounter, without narrative shape. As has been shown, a star can be reassuring, but it is also a stony cipher, whether in the form of the mysterious "geode" of "All Revelation," the "building stone" of "A Star in a Stoneboat," or the "Snow-white / Minerva's snow-white marble eyes / Without the gift of sight" from the early poem "Stars." And even in the farmer's unchilled field, without obstacles, human knowing can still feel star-shot.

Confusion, the last-named element of the definition "A momentary stay against confusion," governs the poem "Rose Pogonias": in a clearing full of orchises that "Tinge the atmosphere," the protagonists pray "That none should mow the grass there / While so confused with flowers." The thought is that a measure of internal confusion, in this small space, can stave off the senselessness of the "General mowing." Death's indiscriminate sweep is to be staved off by a local experience of benign confusion, an experience intensely tinged by the human appetite for beauty. Because of the mingling of aesthetic elements and grassy elements in the flora (or because of the parallel confusion in the mind that perceives the flora), the mower is asked to "stay" his hand — thus, as Richard Poirier puts it, this poem demonstrates "the *value* of confusion" (*Robert Frost* 210). Because beauty is so delicate and so entangled with the grassy matter of the world, an uncertainty intervenes that can stave off destructiveness. When "confusion" informs the poem from outside, and tinges the atmosphere within it, Frost's pragmatism is a mode of ethical writing: it addresses itself to conduct. Poetic experience in the clearing leads to a hope for the future, a hope that the speech-act of the prayer aims to bring about. The touch of the moment is somehow wedded to the desire to keep the precious moment untouched. (This claim can be mapped into the pragmatic ethics of Richard Rorty: the flowers' tinge means contingency, which means confusion and irony, which block utilitarian cruelty.)

Happily, though, because the speaker is confused, he can banish abstemiousness as well as rapacity from this sanctuary: the protagonists of the poem pick "A thousand orchises" themselves before offering up their prayer to protect the rest. Like the phrase "A momentary stay against confusion," which is careful to mention the confusion it staves off, this poem defends against wanton destruction by letting a little bit of wantonness, in the form of uncertainty and an appetite for beauty, into its confines. Pragmatism uses the uncertainty outside the poem to muffle the poem's own dangerous surfaces, and beauty creates an atmosphere in which consumption of the world can mingle with protection of it.

In "Mowing," by contrast, the dynamism of the poem's central principle overwhelms any sense of knowledge's provisional quality. In this poem, Frost seems to underscore the word "momentary" in the phrase "A momentary stay against confusion." This time the flowers can be cut along with the grass, and an almost inaudible "whispering" speech results from the perfect balance between human strength and nature's integrity. Nature answers the pressure of human effort with just enough resistance to make truth: both the scythe and the stalks whisper, and they speak of the welding of categories — most important in this case, the union of fact and dream.

> There was never a sound beside the wood but one,
> And that was my long scythe whispering to the ground.
> What was it it whispered? I knew not well myself;
> Perhaps it was something about the heat of the sun,
> Something, perhaps, about the lack of sound —
> And that was why it whispered and did not speak.
> It was no dream of the gift of idle hours,
> Or easy gold at the hand of fay or elf:
> Anything more than the truth would have seemed too weak
> To the earnest love that laid the swale in rows,
> Not without feeble-pointed spikes of flowers
> (Pale orchises), and scared a bright green snake.
> The fact is the sweetest dream that labor knows.
> My long scythe whispered and left the hay to make.

The moment celebrated in this poem is a perfect, dynamic picture of human encounter with the landscape. Epistemological problems are forgotten in the subtle and evasive "whisper" of speech that is also work. The snake that would tempt humanity to knowledge is scared off, and in noting its departure the poem invokes a prelapsarian instant in which speech and action, dream and fact, are one. The working person marks the landscape without disrupting nature's own cycles, and the thing language does to nature is just what needs doing.

These orchises are the same kind of "confused" flowers that forestalled mowing in "Rose Pogonias." The momentariness of "Mowing" seems too impetuous to be affected by the blissful confusions of that poem. So Frost's two kinds of pragmatism, the momentary and the blurry, present us with a puzzle: should we mow the orchises or not? Is the right path between disengagement and rapacity found by opting for beauty that is more than the truth — that is, should we seek a vision of nature as a "temple of the heat" distended by human desire? Or should we opt for truth that is stronger than "pale," "feeble" aestheticism, and speaks by slicing through it to perform the open-air facts of labor? These sound like extreme images, opposed to each other as straw men, but in truth they are Frost's own ways of describing these relations to nature. This dilemma results from pragmatism's double emphasis — on the provisionality of all knowledge (forcing us to fall back on beauty, not indiscriminate "general mowing," as an antidote to chaos), on the one hand; and on the other, the importance of dynamism, of process and performance, in cognitive acts.

These two aspects of the phrase "A momentary stay against confusion" are highlighted in order to reiterate a central uncertainty within pragmatism itself. The question is an old one, though not often hotly debated: is pragmatic knowledge reliant on faith in the practical adequacy of provisional beliefs or on a feeling of wholeness that arises from the power of performance and process?[14] These two answers correspond, respectively, to the valuable confusion of "Rose Pogonias" and the homogenizing juggernaut of "Mowing." Frost's knowledge might be about provisionality, the awareness of one's own confusion that gives aesthetic experience its own, narrow space to treasure; or it might be about the work itself, in which for a moment fine distinctions between flowers and "general" grasses are overcome by the capable ordering tool that the mower brings to bear. If (as Richard Rorty has it) pragmatism is a satisfaction with whatever can be demarcated, enjoyed, and saved, then confusion is the most important feature of the mixed flowers and grass.[15] If, however, pragmatism is a philosophy of performance (as Richard Poirier argues), then the phenomenon is in the moment itself: what does a person do with that mixed world in the crucial instant of interaction?[16]

What the Frostean persona does to the land, of course, is make poetry of it, "laying the swale in rows": insofar as these poems deal in processes, they are indeed pragmatic in the way that "Mowing" suggests. Problems of knowledge, emblematized in "Mowing" by the Edenic snake, are banished from this moment, and the only question is how to make subtle linguistic elements — like the whispering of the scythe where man meets field — audible and interpretable. That question is answered effectively in "Mending Wall," which describes the annual ritual that brings very different men together to work and to share what divides them.

But there is no one who might share this particular georgic practice, and in the crucial final line of "Mowing," that which is made is left behind. It is not transmitted into a social sphere. Much of the emotional power of the poem resides in this line, and if read a certain way, this line disrupts the perfect pragmatic balance that the poem has been dedicated to creating. "My long scythe whispered and left the hay to make": the "making" this time is not a human deed, but something that the hay does — and does because it does not partake of the pleasures of mowing itself. It "makes" precisely because it is portable, unmomentary, homogeneous, and ready for public consumption. It makes itself an artifact. The poet's power flexes capably right up to — but not beyond — the limits of the pragmatic moment. Hence the textual object, in "Mowing," is figured by the rows of cut grass and flowers, left behind in the certain knowledge that only time can make it useful. The death of beauty is the thing that makes human effort communicative, and the forces that work on the hay, "making" it, are outside the poet's control. Time, after all — especially the many consecutive hours in the sun that georgic poets recommend to an armchair readership — is one long thing the lyric poet cannot wield.

When a poem acknowledges that it can stage its writing but not also its reading, the flavor of the final line of "Mowing" is the result. Likewise, "Rose Pogonias" isolates an aesthetic sphere and dwells within it, to make the central action of consuming beauty playful and harmless. But writing and reading are both destructive, and they are not the same thing: something dead must be left behind on the page in the vague hope that life may come of it. This is the tragedy of the lyric in time, and it proceeds quite directly from the "momentariness" Frost recommends in his famous saying. The temporal drama, the poem's vexed relation to its own aftermath, draws attention away from the poem, to its commercial destiny as a bundle to be consumed. A spatial version of the same dynamic, however, would lead deeper into the poem itself. This requires a focus on the "stay" rather than the "momentariness" or the "confusion" in Frost's aphorism.

The title of "For Once, Then, Something," a poem in which the speaker peers into a well at his reflection and glimpses an object "at bottom," encapsulates all three Frostean modes of the phrase "A momentary stay against confusion." "For Once" — the notion that chaos is the norm; "Then" — the notion that in certain moments access seems possible; and the *thing*, "Something," which is not an idea, but just a word — a word that is also the poem, a title word that refuses to budge as we stare at it in its place at the very end of the poem next to the highly prosaic and also unmoving object, the "Pebble of quartz." As it staves off confusion, the poem's moment girds itself around with awareness of the outside world — and, inevitably, feels its own smallness. As this moment is conceived more rigorously, it gets smaller and smaller — until the density of the lyric moment becomes the density of the rock, the set, staying object that lurks at the center of Frost's phrase "A momentary stay against confusion."

IN "MENDING WALL," that great poem of sociable pragmatism, Frost admonishes the rocks that precariously constitute the wall to "Stay where you are until our backs are turned!" The moment of making the wall speaks directly here to the moment of unmaking — nature will flip these rocks as the hayturner will turn the mown hay, and one moment speaks to another. More important, the provisionality of the wall enables the ongoing process by which neighbors are brought together year after year. But the game would be very different if Frost's speaker instead said to the wall-rock simply — as he often says to nature (without much expecting to be heeded) — "Stay!" It is something he is unwilling to say to the dog-star who visits him in the person of Gus/ Sirius in "One More Brevity" — but the star, as we have seen, is nonetheless an emblem of that which we "Stay our minds on [to] be staid" ("Take Something Like a Star").

As mobile as Frost's poetics is, fixity dominates many of his most beautiful poems. This is because of the phenomenon suggested by the vital emotion of the last line of "Mowing": as the pragmatic moment approaches its limit case, and dwindles to infinitesimal duration, it becomes particulate, stony, and particular. The poet's task turns out to be much less shareable, less expansive, and less assured of success than the limber energy of "Mowing" would suggest. As a corollary, though, and in compensation, that task develops an emotional power that would otherwise be lacking — the power of regret and longing, emotions represented in "Mowing" by the deed of leaving behind one's work.

Emily Dickinson offers a good example of how the momentariness of a stay makes it unbearable and unconsoling: in the poem below, she is stabilized constantly by a sequence of possible ordering worlds, but nothing could be less cognitively pleasant.

> And then a Plank in Reason, broke,
> And I dropped down, and down —
> And hit a World, at every plunge,
> And Finished knowing — then — (340)

If the transitions from state to state in encounters with the world are too sharp, pragmatism starts to require an inhuman flexibility. In poetry, our contact with the world is more abrupt as the momentariness gets stricter, as it gets closer to the Dickinsonian limit case of the infinitesimal moment. This is why a poet like Stevens focuses on smoothing out the event horizon, with transitional moments that extend and refresh themselves, "Intricate evasions of as" ("An Ordinary Evening in New Haven"). For Frost, the sharpness of objects, physical and lyric, is too palpably important to allow Stevens's kind of fuzzy cognitive intricacy. Insofar as pragmatism is about knowledge, it relies on extended stories of transition and compromise — not encounter with discrete objects of the sort suggested by the word "stay." This is why a focus on the "stay" requires a poetics that could be called antipragmatic.

Seamus Heaney, speaking at Harvard in February 2000, defined the poet's charge as the linking of opposite images: Pegasus and the cart horse, absolute freedom and workaday confinement. Sometimes Frost dances lightly around this problem: the farmer of "A Star in a Stoneboat," for example, seems to make a graceful acknowledgment of logistical difficulties. He transports the meteorite by means of a stoneboat, or sledge,

> And not, as you might think, a flying car,
> Such as even poets would admit perforce
> More practical than Pegasus the horse
> If it could put a star back in its course.

But it is sometimes awkward for even the lightest of poems to maintain the feeling that the two realms, of poetic wonder and worldly effort, can be blended. When they are, moreover, the strength of the poem may come from the bounded character of that synthesizing moment: the way the lyric moment comes to its own edge, and acknowledges the narrowness of its claim.

After reading it admiringly in his talk at Harvard, Heaney objected (mildly) to a single line of Frost's poem from *New Hampshire*, "A Hillside Thaw." This last line suggests positively how Frost's obsession with the "stay" interlinks with his idea of what the poet is charged to do.

"A Hillside Thaw" equates knowledge of nature with the ability to capture its transitional states. Unlike the mower, the artist who would work with water cannot make his product while the sun shines.

> To think to know the country and not know
> The hillside on the day the sun lets go
> Ten million silver lizards out of snow!
> . . . .
> But if I thought to stop the wet stampede,
> And caught one silver lizard by the tail,
> And put my foot on one without avail,
> And threw myself wet-elbowed and wet-kneed
> In front of twenty others' wriggling speed, —
> . . . .
> I have no doubt I'd end by holding none.

It is not for the artist to stay the movement of nature, as if for a portrait. The magic of the moon, instead, answers the sun's warm magic, and between "six o'clock" and "nine" casts the counterspell that freezes the streams "In every lifelike posture of the swarm, / Transfixed on mountain slopes almost erect."

> [The spell] was the moon's: she held them until day,
> One lizard at the end of every ray.
> The thought of my attempting such a stay!

As one might expect, it is this final line that Heaney would leave out, if the poem were his, to close the poem with a firm couplet rather than a wistful tercet (the form of "A Star in a Stoneboat"). The poet's interjection of his own agency seems to disrupt this poem about the relation between the elusive beauties of freedom and the bewitching beauty of controlled order. In fact, though, it completes the initial thought about "knowing" the country by acknowledging that no matter how glorious nature's artistry may be, it is up to the artist to apply the "stay" that makes it into a human artifact. That work might mean idiosyncrasy, unfulfilled longing, and even buffoonery, but the confused "stampede" is no better outcome. Artistic magic, the witchcraft found in looking out one's window on an uncanny world, is the inevitable topic of Emersonian nature poetry.

In a similarly comic vein — this time in midwinter — Farmer Brown of "Brown's Descent" also finds himself desperate for a stay: on a windy night, he is unable to pierce "The icy crust / That cased the world" in order to stop himself from sliding slowly all the way down his own hill.

> He saw no stay unless he stove
> A hole in somewhere with his heel.
> But though repeatedly he strove
>
> And stamped and said things to himself,
> And sometimes something seemed to yield,
> He gained no foothold, but pursued
> His journey down from field to field.

Unable to mark the surfaces that love marks in "Bond and Free" (to leave a "printed trace"), Farmer Brown emblematizes an encounter between man and field very different from that of "Mowing." Without some element to variegate the landscape, and put a stop to nature's motility, even the agrarian man can make no mark on his world. In the frost of winter, a resistant world is the best venue for expressing the responsibility the artist feels, the charge to do something bigger than a chore.

In "New Hampshire," frozen dew was the result of the poet's imaginative power; in "A Hillside Thaw," the poet explicitly refuses credit for the frozen beauty of the streams. Yet he participates, negatively as it were, in the stability that the moon creates: the snapshot in ice of flowing lizards emblematizes poetic power even as it disavows it. (Likewise, the description of ice in "Birches" is disavowed as an interruption, but it contains some of the most beautiful lines in the poem.) This poem poises its desire *against* the mobility that spring engenders: activity under the sun is not the poet's only role, and — in the words of "Mowing" — he may occasionally long for the magic that is "more than the truth." The cold pastoral here — from which the artist excludes himself into warmth — typifies a Romantic, longing Frostean mode that deserves more attention than it has received. Moreover, this attention to the cold "stay" is more closely linked with the warm mowing-poems than one might expect. In "To Earthward," Frost emphasized the craving for larger sensations, and the awareness of stiff contrasts in nature: he craved encounter with the world in all its stubborn heterogeneity, not because of the uniform, almost successful resistance offered by stalks before the scythe. Unlike the mower in *A Boy's Will*, the speaker of "The Last Mowing" has this same awareness of incongruity.

The first two pragmatic elements of Frost's "A momentary stay against confusion" — to wit, a tiny moment of synthesis and an awareness of confusing diversity — conflict with one another. The third element, the stiffness of the "stay," has not yet been fully examined as a poetic principle in Frost. All three problems — the smallness of the moment, the confusion involved in consuming nature, and the stubbornness of heterogeneous matter — are central topics in "The Last Mowing." The poem is elegiac, but the brevity it mulls is not the brevity of a career (Frost was only fifty-four at the time of the poem's writing) or even of a single day's work. It is the brevity of a much smaller moment — the narrow interval in which the encounter of work becomes the encounter with oblivion. In this interval, figured spatially as a clearing in the woods, beauty stands up for itself, as it cannot in either "Rose Pogonias" or "Mowing."

Since its speaker hopes to savor this moment at the cusp of wildness, the poem could be considered "A momentary stay against confusion"; but as in "Rose Pogonias," the confusion invades the poem itself, and as in "Mowing," the moment being described is not the moment of the made poem. In fact, the crucial moment of this mowing-poem is a moment that is only foreseen.

> There's a place called Far-away Meadow
> We shall never mow in again,
> Or such is the talk at the farmhouse:
> The meadow is finished with men.
> Then now is the chance for the flowers
> That can't stand mowers and plowers.
> It must be now, though, in season
> Before the not mowing brings trees on,
> Before trees, seeing the opening,
> March into a shadowy claim.
> The trees are all I'm afraid of,
> That flowers can't bloom in the shade of;
> It's no more men I'm afraid of;
> The meadow is done with the tame.

The place for the moment is ours
For you, oh tumultuous flowers,
To go to waste and go wild in,
All shapes and colors of flowers,
I needn't call you by name.

The farmhouse talk seems just a preliminary to this poem, but the way it locates the human voice is an important aspect of this text. The urgent discourse of the poem is somehow located between that farmhouse and the meadow: the direct address of the last five lines strains to overcome the distance between the scene of speech and the meadow, a distance that is carefully established in the poem's first three lines. The talk of the farmhouse "calls" the meadow "Far-away"; yet somehow speech hopes to transport itself to the very place whose remoteness it is talk's main task to describe.

Even while this drama of remoteness made near is played out, an opposite vector is traced in the two moments of naming that frame the poem. In line one, the speaker "calls" the meadow by its name, seeming to embrace the arbitrariness of such naming while locating the poem in the parental discourse of the home-oriented fairy tale. In the final line, however, the speaker refrains from calling by name the flowers that the poem has fixated upon and addressed. As the poem's emotions grow more ambiguous in this way, the excess of feeling, the wasteful intensity of floweriness, becomes the predominant note. This aesthetic intensity is centered on an aching contrast that evokes the contrasts of "To Earthward" — a troublesome distinction between types of object. This time the distinction is between flowers, which can be cut (but no longer will be), and woody trees, with which the human cannot interact except in awe. (Such awe characterizes the speaker of "Spring Pools" — "Birches," on the other hand, is about flexible trees that one can grasp.) Clear and unmitigable contrasts like these are the most important challenge to the pragmatic spirit of poetry that "Mowing" named — in that poem, flowers and grass, the two key substrates of Frostean knowledge, could be cut with equal ease.

In the pragmatic version of Frost's poetics, to do something is to know it, and the poem should seek to maximize both, as "Mowing" does in its first thirteen lines. Action in a space is the way to encounter nature meaningfully. Here, though, as the speaker's talk occupies the space it was at first intended only to describe, his not being there is just as important as his being there. The meadow's untouchable character is registered not just practically in the human decision to stop mowing it, but linguistically in the poet's decision not to describe its beauties (a description he undertook, albeit anxiously, in "Rose Pogonias"). The poem's final reluctance even to call the flowers by name is what makes this mowing the last: no longer bringing the flowers into lines of poetry — no longer mowing the meadow in rows — the speaker is abjuring his own speech. As the title-word "mowing" turns from simple participle ("Mowing") to elegiac gerund ("The Last Mowing"), the poem becomes a deed of work that freezes even before finishing itself. The last line performs in itself the same desirous not-touching that "Rose Pogonias" hoped to perform by splitting its roles into two different kinds of harvest. In this closing, Frost registers the ache to know one's own distance from beauty, and beauty's distance from itself. But to know those things would be to enter into the shade of not knowing, the darkness of a final, unmowable claim. Once the flowers stop being named, they stop existing except as confusion, and when the human stops putting them into lines, they are shadowed out by forest.

In this third mowing-poem, then, beauty takes pride of place as a principle incommensurate with human activity. The poet's adored object, the flower, occupies a sanctuary while human work bows gracefully out of the picture. Yet it would be wrong to understate the human presence here — not only the social features of the voice but also the status still assigned to the poem as work. It is, after all, not titled "After the Last Mowing," or "A Time for Flowers," but "The Last Mowing." Just as work looked ahead to its own absence in the last line of "Mowing," here it looks back from that absence to the working presence that allows the poem to exist: experience, both labor and naming on the page; that which allows knowledge to come into being. Only mowing makes the flowers' life possible, even though the poem's ultimate knowledge is quite alien to the world of sunny work. It is knowledge of forest, an awareness of what comes in to stiffen the world of nature so that it is no longer friendly either to human activities or to human admiration. Apprehension of the sublime suffuses this poem: nature's deathliness imposes a "stay" not only on beauty's aftermath but on beauty itself, which exists most vibrantly, most wildly, under the shadow of unworkable darkness.

WHAT, THEN, is the value of emphasizing the "stay" in Frost's phrase "A momentary stay against confusion"? The prosaic answer is logistical: attention to the "stay" acknowledges and addresses the difficulties that result from emphasizing either "momentary" or "confusion." The question from *A Boy's Will*, of whether a farmer-poet should cut his flowers or not, is addressed in the great ambiguity of "The Last Mowing." That poem of enjambed, yet somehow choked-up, longing brings into focus the contradictions that lurked at the edges of the previous mowing-poems, the moment-poem "Mowing" and the confusion-poem "Rose Pogonias." Contradiction will be resolved only by the tragic marching in of the trees, the solidity that will block all interaction with nature.

The problem of "Mowing," registered only in its last line, was the diminution of the moment: "making" seems always just outside a moment of blended truth and beauty. The problem of "Rose Pogonias" was that confusion troubles action, and makes poetry a sort of fever-dream from which one seems constantly on the verge of waking into violence. When one emphasizes the "stay," both of these problems are addressed, and exacerbated. The poem stiffens into a reliable act of naming, but because it places at a distance the meadow it names, it can call by name (obsessively) "Only the trees," and not the aesthetically powerful flowers. Aesthetic confusion is placed at a distance from speech, but speech can then only mourn at the general, shady homogeneity that will soon overtake it in its absence, now that "The meadow is done with the tame."

But there is also intrinsic poetic value in this critical emphasis on the "stay," value that stands apart from such insistences on philosophical rigor. In the strange promise of "A Star in a Stoneboat," and its speaker's thrill at being tugged by the world, even tangentially, we sense the energetic possibility that Frost loves. But in the heavier facts of that poem, and the stoniness and distance even of the desired object, the propositions that inform poems like "The Last Mowing" assert themselves strongly. The intransigence of such objects, and the fascination they hold when they hold meaning only awkwardly, is what stays for the reader of Frost's poems. The energy may be different each time, but the obstacles to understanding are there on every reading. In feeling that resistance, the reader consistently encounters heterogeneous beauty, so that to interact with the poem itself, laying it in rows, also means leaving it alone.

WHEREAS THE TITLE of "The Last Mowing" occupies the time of work that in the text of the poem has already passed, "After Apple-Picking" seems occupied with the work its title proclaims to be finished. The truth is more complicated: as Reuben Brower has pointed out, crucial phrases in the poem "seem to refer both to the morning and to the present state of 'drowsing off'" (24). This means that the day of labor has a dreamlike quality to it[17] — but it also means that the night keeps the intense sensation of the daytime. "Essence of winter sleep is on the night," Frost writes, but he goes on to specify that essence in a surprising phrase: "The scent of apples." In this transition, oddly, the seasonal difference that seems a crucial topic of the poem is denied: winter's essence turns out to be the smell of fall.

If it blends these two counterpoised phrases, interpretation is apt to situate this poem in the spirit of late autumn's fecundity, the misty, blurry cider-pressing time that Keats described as the most precious of the year.[18] But to identify the essence of winter (not fall) with the actual smell of apples is to collapse two different times into one. Neither of them appears or disappears; they are simply simultaneous. Indeed, no ambiguity or oscillation is even allowed in the world of the poem: the apples, both dreamed and seen, are far from blurry, with "Every fleck of russet showing clear"; sleep is either human or animal; none of the up-and-down ferrying that characterizes tree climbing in "Birches" is mentioned; and all the apples that strike the earth go to the cider-apple heap "As of no worth." This last phrase, surprisingly, rejects one of the central beauties of Keats's "To Autumn," the beauty of the cider press. Frost's speaker has no interest in the "last oozings" of experience, or the gradual easing transition from one state to the next.

Instead, Frost's protagonist experiences the day fully, then finds that that experience suffuses his night by its stark absence.

> I could tell
> What form my dreaming was about to take.
> Magnified apples appear and disappear,
> Stem end and blossom end,
> And every fleck of russet showing clear.
> My instep arch not only keeps the ache,
> It keeps the pressure of a ladder-round.
> I feel the ladder sway as the boughs bend.

Having accustomed itself to the sway of the ladder, the speaker's inner ear now senses a sway in the bed or chair where he rests: this rocking is out of phase with nature but in the same rhythm. Having accustomed itself to the pressure of the ladder's rung, the speaker's foot, like the hand described in "To Earthward," now feels that pressure again, exerted in the other direction. Having obsessively focused on the fruit of his work throughout the day, the eyes of the speaker now project them against his eyelids. Because experience is so intense, its aftermath is intense as well — with the sensation now coming not from the fever intensity of desire that characterized "Rose Pogonias" but from the backlash of that desire — "I am overtired / Of the great harvest I myself desired," the speaker says. Indeed, the sleep the poem anticipates gets confused with the words that describe that sleep: the woodchuck, the poet says, could tell if "It's like his / Long sleep, as I describe its coming on." Sleep itself, oblivion, cannot be reached by the poet's metaphors.

It would be excessive, of course, to regard "After Apple-Picking" purely as a nighttime poem of thought and muscle memory, one that depicts work only in the negative. But Frost's manner of describing the day suggests that in merging the two moments — work and thought, outside and inside — the poem undertakes something more complicated than a description of work. Experience itself is held at arm's length: framed at that distance in the poem, as well as being handled. The dream of apples is born in a moment before they are ever touched:

> I cannot rub the strangeness from my sight
> I got from looking through a pane of glass
> I skimmed this morning from the drinking trough
> And held against the world of hoary grass.
> It melted, and I let it fall and break.
> But I was well
> Upon my way to sleep before it fell,
> And I could tell
> What form my dreaming was about to take.

The cold of the autumn night alters the morning in these lines, just as the warm color of the fruit suffuses the night. Taking hold of nature's own hardness in order to make a window on the pliable grass from "Mowing," the speaker here finds a "stay" that is both a natural fact and a human one. As in "A Hillside Thaw," the rigidity of this lens is both something made by nature (indicating to the human how far he is from knowing nature's ways of refreshing itself) and something chosen by the perceiving mind to attempt to hold the world in place. It is a natural-born metaphor, and the moment in which it is successfully held up to the world is infinitesimal, as hard to hold as brittle ice in warm hands.

The lens of poetic seeing, like the language in which it is described, comes apart in the very hands of the person who holds it up, and refuses to be more than momentary. But it suggests that the world operates upon the speaker not only in the day of work but also in sensation's aftermath. Here nature is still working on the mind of the speaker, who has finished harvesting but continues to harvest more apples than truth would allow (so many more that he does not even want them anymore). Seized by the world his own hands frame, a world "of hoary grass" in which ice and plant matter are interwoven, the speaker is offered over and over a fruit that emerges surprisingly from hard wood. The trees of this poem combine the stiffness of stone and the life of flowers: they support human weight while presenting the promise of tiny worlds to be picked and consumed. The poet's job is both to touch those globes and not to touch them: they are drawn into the cellar, but must not be soiled. The poem names this strange, stabilizing work in its odd central verb, the phrase that mediates the poet's exertion and his passivity: "lift down."

The apples of this poem might seem a troublesome place to end this chapter, which began with the meteorite of "A Star in a Stoneboat." Unlike the meteorite, they are fragile and nourishing, and they are suspended above the earth rather than wedged inconveniently into it. Like the meteorite, though, they become fascinating out of proportion to their use, and remain physically significant even when one forgets their ostensive meanings. They are cherished "in hand," not in the mind or in the mouth — it is exactly because they are held at arm's length that these objects dominate these lyrics. If they were encountered more completely, like the water of the stream drunk in the climax of Frost's eschatological poem "Directive," they would offer moments of satisfaction, and the poem would stay human desire by bringing its ends into close encounter with its means (with work itself). But desire here is overfilled, given too much weight, because the sensing body on the ladder feels its own heaviness constantly: the size of nature impresses the lyric speaker with more than his share of the world's weight.

The poet must exhaust himself in not letting the world fall into homogeneity, not letting apples rot back into earth. Stiff and sore and scarred by the maintaining of contrasts and interfaces, the speaker finds himself figured in two places in nature. He is the hibernating mammal, of course, his mandated work of the season complete and his rest well earned. But he is also the pane of ice, a vessel for dreams that will not stop redreaming themselves, brittle, imperfectly clear, and fallen into uncomfortable encounter with the organic world that he intended to contain and store. One possibility makes the speaker complete in himself, the other renders him the expendable tool of some larger imaginative force.

The image that unifies these two possibilities is found at the beginning of the poem, in the two-pointed ladder inexplicably left "sticking through a tree." Piercing the stiff, separating structure of nature with a human tool made from the same substance, this line focuses our attention on the mode of transport between two different realms. Left behind as it is, though, the ladder is no longer a transitional fact but a souvenir of the process of harvesting. No longer a means for hard work, it emblematizes the hard objects that made it possible for flesh and fruit to come into contact. Like the pane of ice, it separates human sensation and the organic world; like the woodchuck, it mediates articulate work and the unselfconsciousness of self-displacing nature. Human contrivance and nature's own stability combine to point toward larger meaning ("toward Heaven") but, more fundamentally, simply to stand as an index of the sensation a lyric poet feels in sensation's absence, not on the ladder but considering it from afar as night falls. The human instrument of knowledge never falls but also never moves, cannot rot into earth but also cannot retire at the finish of the harvest. The two entwined wooden structures, empty of fruit, surrounded by darkness, "still," and distant from the world of speech, together present an apt image for the Frostean lyric's idea of itself. Poems of the stay, ensnarled with nature like the dullest possible scythe, are stuck fast in the world outdoors.

6 Bishop's Weighted Eye

Seasonality is the conventional metaphor for nature poetry's representational challenge: to make the outdoor world into art, typically, one must defy the deathliness of winter. Whether set in the ripening of spring or the ripeness of summer, nature poems are often infused with an urgency that seems to result from the implacable workings of time. Feeling the underlying problem of knowledge and nature in its most extreme form, though — feeling that knowledge in nature is not only "flowing" but instantly "flown"[1] — Elizabeth Bishop set herself more difficult, Emersonian problems. For Bishop, poetic urgency is not a problem of time. Any representational effort is immediately too late: it is at the poem's first word that nature ceases to be natural. The poet-figure may hunt for "A virgin mirror / no one's ever looked at,"[2] but in finding such a thing one always destroys it. No earlier, fresher moment is to be preserved in the poem. Art's mirror is always held up by someone, and is never seen without a face in it — just as the poet's nature is never unmirrored in language.

Metaphors of space, of "Active / displacement of perspective" ("Roosters"), therefore often take the place of temporal metaphors. Like Dickinson's, Bishop's myth of the Fall into tainted knowledge is an instantaneous myth — and like Dickinson's, it is simultaneous with the myth of redemption. Everything happens at once in the poem. The challenge of the Emersonian lyric, the thing that makes the poet's work urgent, is to reconcile these two opposite elements (not just to create a story that includes them both). The lack of narrative pressure, stemming from Bishop's insight that time is not the real problem, means that her poems can slow down and describe every part of a scene. Without fear of the season's ending, the poem can gather every rosebud — but each becomes immediately part of the "Clutter of trophies," one of many "rust-perforated roses" flawed even before they are offered. "The acuteness of the question" of death, the sharp cold of winter, "forks instantly and starts / a snake-tongue flickering" ("Faustina, or Rock Roses"); it does not need to be anticipated and cannot be outraced. For Bishop, every physical image holds within it all the sorrow that other poets find in decay.

Predecessor poets adjusted their seasonal metaphors as they approached the heart of this problem. Keats, for example, agonized over time's instant transitions from freshness into decadence, and finally found as his best subject autumn, the season defined by its passing away. The ideal poetic object, in "To Autumn," is a cider press, and beauty is found not in the quick indulgence of the "bee-mouth" of "To a Nightingale," but in "Last oozings hours by hours." Conversely, Robert Frost, as we have seen, felt that nature in its extreme plenty put pressure on the senses rather than the other way around, and began to drain humanity as it was grasped. Thus his autumn-poem "After Apple-Picking" sorrowfully registers a kind of physical memory that aches gladly at an absence: "I am overtired / Of the great harvest I myself desired." Such autumn resolutions compromise with time: they are apt to release the natural world in favor of a world of memory. Their beauty comes from stately withdrawal rather than fresh engagement.

For Gerard Manley Hopkins (the only poet besides Moore whose influence on Elizabeth Bishop is indisputable), chastened withdrawal would not do: the moment of spring was poetry's necessary object, the moment of the world's perfection. To Hopkins, in a spring-poem Bishop cites prominently, only one miraculous figure, Christ, has the quickness necessary to hold on to the moment's life.

> What is all this juice and all this joy?
> A strain of the earth's sweet being in the beginning
> In Eden garden. — Have, get, before it cloy,
> Before it cloud, Christ, lord, and sour with sinning. ("Spring")

The impossible task of nature poetry is to gather the juice of a sunny world into a human structure without tainting it and seeing it cloud up. For this harvesting, Keats's protagonist at the cider press needs an excruciatingly "patient look," an attitude that accepts the suffering and even the doom of itself and of the world. Frost resists that doom by incorporating darkness into his vigorous work: he must "lift down" his apples, preserving those whole globes so they do not touch the earth on their way into the cellar. Hopkins, on the other hand, trying to maintain both doom and workable hope, has a less practical solution:

he turns his poem abruptly so that it addresses not its reader but Christ. For Hopkins, only Christic redemption can match the greedy appetite a poem takes on at the words "Have, get" — the words that drive any descriptive effort by which nature is brought onto the page.

None of these solutions will work for Bishop. She has an Emersonian agitation that "To Autumn" lacks — her "look" may be extended, but it is rarely mellow. Her writing places emphasis on visual rather than manual knowledge — she finds the world in the eye rather than the hand emphasized by Frostean metaphors of work. She will not compromise her intense spring vision of fresh fullness; in this way, she is an Emersonian through and through. But unlike Hopkins, she has no clear access to religious mystery — she is troubled, as he is usually not, by the way that any messiah-figure "instantly instantly falls" into the human frailty he is meant to overcome ("Anaphora"). Combining the Romantic sense of the mind's pressure on the world with the Emersonian sense of nature's massive counterpressure, Bishop continues to ask "What is all this juice?" as mind and world squeeze each other. Each is drained, each is diminished, but in focusing on the instant of compression, the hard impact of knowledge's coming to birth, Bishop denies herself recourse to the narrative themes that mediate the world and the mind (which was first? which will survive?). Asking instead how mind and world interlock in the moment of vision, she sets poetry a task as difficult as the one Hopkins sets Christ — but without any anticipation of the miracle that alone will suffice to accomplish it.

The seemingly fruitless labor of the title character of "The Man-Moth" is a suitable emblem for Bishop's concept of the poet's work. That work is marked by strenuousness as well as awe; it is an effort both to grasp the world and to be grasped by it. The man-moth's goal is the moon, which he sees as an opening onto absolute space:

> Up the facades,
> his shadow dragging like a photographer's cloth behind him,
> he climbs fearfully, thinking that this time he will manage
> to push his small head through that round clean opening
> and be forced through, as from a tube, in black scrolls on the light.

The aim is to capture the whole, bright world, as if in a photograph, and simultaneously to be shot through into its firmament — transforming oneself into pure expressiveness, unprocessed media, becoming all the pure possibilities of a first squiggle of paint onto a palette. Individuality and emotion may be transcended as the artist reaches this distance from the earth under which he scuttles through the daylight hours.

The outcome of this effort is a foregone conclusion: "he fails of course." But as the world declines to squeeze the man-moth sharply enough, a different sort of juice is produced, one that is true to his underground origins as well as to his ambitious vision. In the melancholy of his existence is material for a different kind of art, one that is born in the eyes but must be harvested from them for nonvisual consumption — the tear that the speaker describes in the poem's last line, "Cool as underground springs and pure enough to drink."

> If you catch him,
> hold up a flashlight to his eye. It's all dark pupil,
> An entire night itself, whose haired horizon tightens
> as he stares back, and closes up the eye. Then from the lids
> one tear, his only possession, like the bee's sting, slips.

As the eye is overwhelmed by light, then closes, the poet's flashlight simulates the fulfillment in the moon that the man-moth dreamed of. The cost, implicitly, is death (having lost its sting, the bee must die). But the longing that drives the man-moth's narrative failures is squeezed out into visibility here as sight is relinquished — into a tear that also symbolizes the roundness and purity of his vision. The night of his experience is contained in it.

The theme of these poems is engagement, not fatigue — the man-moth "Trembles, but he must investigate as high as he can climb," and the protagonist must try to "Catch him." Bishop felt the Hopkinsean imperative to write about the spring of new experience as well as the Keatsian fall of dying fatigue: she wrote in Hopkins's words that it is the poet's job to keep the world "New, tender, quick." Yet she is also among the bleakest poets of modernism. This paradox reflects the vicious paradox behind all rigorous spring-poems: the intense freshness of the world is identical with the mind's desire to depict it and infuse it with humanity. They match each other perfectly, and frustrate each other instantly. No process can offer hope. Only an impossible miracle can remit this work — a miracle of vision enabled only by the end of sight.

The assiduous work of seeing remains possible, and necessary, but it is Sisyphean work: the man-moth always falls back "Scared but quite unhurt" from the journey to the hole in the sky. Then he struggles in small experiences too: he "cannot get aboard the silent trains / fast enough to suit him"; "Each night he must / be carried through artificial tunnels and dream recurrent dreams." The open-ended character of poetic effort parallels the endlessly agitated meticulousness with which Bishop adds details in her poems of description — the sandpiper, ceaselessly running, represents the poet's own ceaseless work at the boundary between virgin space and objects struggling to be born into meaning. Moreover, the endlessness of this despairing work is the corollary of hope's infinitesimal span, the eye-blink in which description of the world in its freshness seems possible. That span, the visionary time "before it cloy," is so brief as to be no time at all. The lyric imagination seizes nature suddenly and violently, at the precise moment when eye meets world. Bishop's is a vision in which the human is painfully aware of the "colored and distorting lenses which we are" (Emerson, "Experience" III.43), aware that it is her mind that fulfills and mars the world. Placing herself in space, the poet must then regard herself as part of the scene — but at the same time as a disruption to it, and in turn therefore cut off from its essence: "We are far away within the view" (Bishop, "The Monument").

The philosophical situation of Bishop's poems is compactly expressed in a paragraph from her short story "The Sea & Its Shore." The typographically self-conscious ampersand of the title links an untouched space with a human, textually mediated, one ("The sand itself . . . looked a little like printed paper"). The story is about Edwin Boomer, whose job it is to keep the beach clean of waste print-matter: he gathers scraps of paper into his beach hovel, where the threats of water and of night are staved off by his reading. Surprisingly, though, his work is necessary not just because the ocean is destructive of human effort ("gasoline, terribly dangerous") but also because print is threatening to the ocean:

> Of course, according to the laws of nature, a beach should be able to keep itself clean, as cats do. . . .
>
> But the tempo of modern life is too rapid. Our presses turn out too much paper covered with print, which somehow makes its way to our seas and their shores, for nature to take care of herself.
>
> So Mr. Boomer, Edwin Boomer, might almost have been said to have joined the "priesthood." (*Collected Prose* 172)

The sea cleans the land, and menaces it with oblivion, but texts also overflow and mark even the ocean, marring with fragmentary language our experience of its immediacy, its wholeness, and its oblivion. In this story about raw, oceanic experience threatened by fragments of text, vision and reading are mutually interwoven. This is because concepts — even concepts of cleanliness — are themselves the output of the press, where nature's objects are charged with human thoughts and desire, and become litter. For Bishop, this is not just a clever proposition: it is the writer's experience. At this frontier of space and word the poet alone serves as the "priest" who ministers from one world to the other — obsessive and mildly insane in a beach hovel plastered with quotations, a house that is also a "one-eyed room." Living in his own head, as it were, Boomer lives "the most literary life possible." This text, in its form as well as its content, insists earnestly that nothing can be more literary than a walk on the beach.

There can be no doubt that Bishop's poems emphasize the artificial; but this does not make her any less a nature poet. If one neglects the ways that the world greets Bishop's eyes *as* artifice, it is easy to imagine that the referents of the poem must be Edenic experiences, unreachable through the poems, "A strain of the earth's sweet beginning" marred only by the poem itself. But Bishop's poems of nature are not about a distance poetry creates in its process; they are about a distance humanity feels in the eye. For Bishop, this is not a problem of history or narrative structure but of knowledge; a problem of nature as humanity confronts it — which is to say: a problem of nature.[3] Bishop's meditations on representation are coterminous with her meditations on real space, and her strange modern allegories have all the Emersonian immediacy that (paradoxically) kept Emerson himself at a distance from the world.[4]

BESIDES TITLING VOLUMES *North and South* and *Geography III* — titles that meditate on the way that writing warps the world into human frames — Bishop also assembled a volume with a "natural" title, *A Cold Spring*. It seems uncharacteristic: in truth, though, the choice typifies Bishop's sense of the close association between nature and human artifacts. Originally, Bishop wrote to Robert Lowell that this same book was to be called "*Concordance*, starting off with a poem called 'Over 2,000 Illustrations and a Complete Concordance.' On reading over what I've got on hand I find I'm really a minor female Wordsworth — at least, I don't know anyone else who seems to be such a Nature Lover" (*One Art* 222). Bishop senses no incongruity between these two sentences: to her, the topic of print culture and the topic of nature are not at odds, and "Concordance" seems a perfectly appropriate title for a book featuring poems of nature.

Bishop's spring-poem, obviously, is in dialogue with Hopkins's, and takes its epigraph from it. In the modern iteration, innocence is transferred from the youthful Christ to another occupant of the Nativity stable — a calf, transplanted out of shelter into the harsh air of the world. The hills have begun to sprout with grass, and

> One day, in a chill white blast of sunshine,
> on the side of one a calf was born.
> The mother stopped lowing
> and took a long time eating the after-birth,
> a wretched flag,
> but the calf got up promptly
> and seemed inclined to feel gay.

The calf's attitude toward life seems miraculous, since this tableau of birth, and nature's rebirth, seems to the poetic mind so "flawed" — by cold, arbitrariness (the side of any hill will do), and the indelicacies of nature (both the external "blast" and the reinternalized afterbirth). The passage hovers scrupulously, uncertainly, around this miracle: it is hard to feel its redemptiveness. Even the calf's mood is only guessed at.

But such guesses are made, as they must be when the senses authorize knowledge, and the person writing the poem is not apologetic about her own far-from-innocent presence within it. Her neurosis marks even the flowering trees. "Greenish-white dogwood infiltrated the wood, / each petal burned, apparently, by a cigarette-butt." There is idiosyncrasy to this poet, and she writes of spring with a certain goal that is not religious praise. It is gratitude, but not the gratitude of the Christian to Christ;[5] the "you" who is later introduced abruptly into this nature poem is not God, as in the case of Hopkins's spring-poem, but a particular host. Someone sheltered the poet, tolerating any guestly vices while affording access to whatever flawed beauty greeted her eyes. The poem is inscribed "For Jane Dewey," and it speaks of "your" hills for that reason; Bishop was a guest in Dewey's farmhouse in the spring of 1951.

Resisting poetry's names for it by being "cold" and somewhat ugly, spring gets recuperated into meaningfulness on the farm later in the poem, as the shadow of language covers it over (and as the scene itself fades). The dark of evening obscures awkward details, and the dark summer night later will accentuate the cleanly contrasting ("particular") fireflies that the poet imagines will rise high enough to match her esteem for her hostess. The final benediction associates darkness closely with naming: the "shadowy pastures" are called that because Jane Dewey's farm was called Shadowstone. Insisting on the farm's particularity, the fact that it has a name and that this "particular glowing tribute" has been written about it, the poem claims to find an image of its own particularity in the particles of nature — the discrete lights of the fireflies, which the poem calls "these" after twenty-five uses of the more remote definite article "the." In referring to the promise of the fireflies as "this," conversely, the speaker holds at greater distance the unmanageable materials of spring, the unreconciled white blasts, fragile membranes, and scarred petals comprised by any difficult birth.

Hopkins's speaker gets a vantage on nature's exuberant richness by making Christ the protagonist of his poem and its choices; Bishop's speaker does so by finally centering the landscape on its owner, so that it spells out the poem's own message. In the odd change of verb tense in the final sentence, after the "now" of the writing day has advanced as far as it can, the conventional urgency of seasonal poetry is released. It is replaced by artificial hope for the moment after the poem, the hollowness of absence from company that it echoes into. The coldness of this spring is tinted with the warmth of the poem's inscription to a friend.

At the end, happily, the poem becomes the original whose spirit nature copies: it composes a tribute, and in anticipating a summer in which metaphors work properly, it makes the land an expressive entity too. The land of Jane Dewey's farm has become the tribute that the poem is — and in doing so, has become "particular," as rich in detail as the poem and as personalized as the voice of its author. Dewey supplants Christ; relationship, albeit distanced relationship, stands in for myth. Thus in "A Cold Spring" we could say that the poet must try to be satisfied with half a loaf: one half of her title or the other. She can write either the cold, late-winter solitude she feels or the conventional vernality of "Nothing is more beautiful than spring." She cannot get both at once; each would shrivel instantly on contact with the other. Warmth arrives fully in the world, to match the poem's own warmth toward Dewey, only when the writer's scrupulous describing self has vanished from the scene — once silent, twinkling summer has put an end to the moment the title tried to name.

Emerson expressed the problem with naming, the absence entailed by all language, in a startling aphorism now dulled by familiarity: "The man is only half himself, the other half is his expression" ("The Poet" III.4). Bishop toys cleverly with this idea in the "The Gentleman of Shalott," a poem in which artistic expression is figured as a mirror that is always there, and indeed is constitutive of the self: "He felt in modesty / his person must be half looking-glass." This poem ends in much the same way that the tribute of "A Cold Spring" does, with awkward awareness of the transition into writing. As it quotes the protagonist, the text self-consciously names the thing it should merely do: "He wishes to be quoted as saying at present: / 'Half is enough.'" Without miraculous self-harvesting like the man-moth's production of his tear, the speaking self will always be torn. There will always be a difference in kind between the self and the means of self-representation.

The double moment that art must seize, the moment of representation, is ungraspable — like the feeling (or the idea) of being half one's own reflection. When faced with problems like this, Bishop's characteristic verbal maneuver is self-correction: she writes of the gentleman of Shalott, in free indirect discourse echoing his own voice: "The glass must stretch down his middle, / or rather down the edge." As the change in the article suggests, though, something quite radical happens as the thought-experiment takes over: perspective shifts so much that the speaking voice loses its selfhood. If only half of him is real and the other half is a mirror, the gentleman becomes an object to himself, a thing with sharp limits ("the edge") rather than a person who possesses an interior ("his middle"). In places where Stevens might correct himself with an appositive, leaving both possibilities in suspense, Bishop's poetic alternatives tend to be irreconcilable — the gap, like the glass that separates an object and its reflection, is too absolute to be blurred by verbal dexterity. In the rift between representation and reality, and in Bishop's characteristic self-interrupting corrections, an unanswered question cries out for an answer.

A similar self-interruption for the sake of correction occurs in the second line of Bishop's published work.

Land lies in water; it is shadowed green.
Shadows, or are they shallows, at its edges
showing the line of long sea-weeded ledges
where weeds hang to the simple blue from green.
Or does the land lean down[?]

If anywhere in Bishop there exists "A strain of the earth's sweet being in the beginning," it is in line one of "The Map." What could be more simply true of a continental terrain than that it is surrounded by water? The second day of Creation (Genesis 1:6) is reenacted: the primal distinction — that between land and sea — is marked out upon the face of the waters, and the poem is able to handle it. Instantly, though, with the next clause, the shadow of language (of aesthetic excess, of incidental local color) comes into the poem, with the word "green." (In fact, once we have noticed this shadow we must also notice that it appears earlier, in the pun on "lie" in the first clause; the serpent's tongue speaks with God's in this first clause, which enacts both presence and representational knowingness.) The labels of the map will later be animated by this aesthetic excess:

> The names of cities cross the neighboring mountains
> — the printer here experiencing the same excitement
> as when emotion too far exceeds its cause.

There can be no objective correlative once difference exists in the world,[6] because the relation between incommensurate objects can never be objective. Connection across a shore of difference must always be created aesthetically, by a feeling observer.

The fall into representation occurs in line two, almost as quickly as the poem can begin, along with the neurosis of self-questioning. Are the shaded areas in the sea representative of a real transition space, a continental shelf; or do they simply reveal an aesthetic sensibility that would like to frame the land for the human self, pleasantly cushioned from sea? With this first unanswered question that might distinguish terrain from cartography, the dam is broken: more questions come, multiplying around every distinction made on the map. As land takes on the shadows of language, subsequently, ocean becomes the object of desire. Ocean alone, unclaimable, "under glass," remains unfallen and unclouded — "simple blue" inviting no elaboration.

ONE PROBLEM of nature poetry, then, is the way that experience is marked instantaneously by language. Bishop also faces resolutely a strong version of the opposite problem: nature's unspeakability, the oblivious simplicity of pure blue to which the land "hangs down" desirously in "The Map." Bishop is as vexed by the miasma of the waters as she is by the cartographer's shadowing of the land. Just as the poem has no credibility when spring is simply "beautiful," the poem has no leverage when spring is just a chilly white blast. These two opposite problems are figured, respectively, by the artificial vista that strives to be evocative in "The Monument," and the inscrutable ocean object that the poet longs to have in "The Imaginary Iceberg." In these two laboratory-poems, Bishop isolates each problem from the other, and sets each into a space where it could be examined alone. The first experience transposes openness into an artifice, as any landscape-poem does; the second consolidates it into an impenetrable purity, as any landscape-poem would like to do.[7]

As the tableau of "The Monument" ingeniously makes apparent, even empty space can be artificial when the poet takes hold of it. Emptiness itself, in this odd conversation-poem, is shaped and sanded by an artisan, to achieve an effect:

A sea of narrow, horizontal boards
lies out behind our lonely monument,
its long grains alternating right and left
like floor-boards — spotted, swarming-still,
and motionless. A sky runs parallel,
and it is palings, coarser than the sea's . . .

With a poet in charge, an entire vista can be crafted: the whole view in this poem is "geared." Because the intentional object is wooden, it makes the world around it wooden as well. The subjection of the world to stasis includes the speakers within it who describe it to us: they are, we are told, "far away within the view." This distance corresponds to the fact that the monument is designed so self-consciously that a viewer has no way of interacting with it, no possibility of knowledge about it. Like the horizon, the object stands always at a distance, fixed; the conversation that the poem stages gets nowhere. The monument is built to mean something, but when its referent is absent from the scene it is only an allegory[8] — so intent on meaning the thing that it should mean that its reality is stunted. Thus the energy of the poem comes not from the object itself, but only from extending the time of vision, hoping for the miracle, the fullness of time in which the object could represent something else.[9]

The monument is one end of a spectrum of art's objects, artifice so intent on meaning something that it fails to be anything. Bishop's experiment with it should be coupled with her experiment featuring the object at the other end of the spectrum. The second laboratory-poem of *North and South* is "The Imaginary Iceberg," featuring an edifice of ice that is so occupied with being that it has no need to mean anything. While the monument was encumbered by "crude scroll-work" (like the art the man-moth strives to impose on the moon) that says "Commemorate," the iceberg is an actor without a script, a character, or time limitations: "Its weight the iceberg dares / upon a shifting stage and stands and stares." This time, "He who treads the boards" can be "artless," since boards are not really the material of which his world is constructed, and no artifice supports him. Essence is maximized, ornament minimized; but what is there to say about an essence, and what can it say to us?

The iceberg stands in open space: the view of it has emphatically, and unfortunately, not been "geared." The oceanic setting of the encounter forces the ship-bound poet to contrast the iceberg with human instruments that enable the expansion of knowledge. The iceberg is an object perfectly opposite to the monument, having been self-made in solidarity with the soul (rather than being linked with the body, "the bones of the artist-prince" that are inside the monument). Yet in the end these objects are functionally equivalent: the chunk of ice is no more accessible than the chunk of wood. No instrument of science can probe it, since it is "imaginary" — it is too ethereal, just as the monument was too solid.

Whereas "The Monument" began with a difficulty of seeing, this text begins with the desire to possess that is at the heart of Hopkins's spring-poem.

> We'd rather have the iceberg than the ship,
> although it meant the end of travel.
> Although it stood stock-still like cloudy rock
> and all the sea were moving marble. . . .
>
> This is a scene a sailor'd give his eyes for.

This poem dreams that the restlessness of encounter with objects can come to an end in the discovery of a place without the cognitive problems of "shadowed land." This land exists for itself, not as a stage for human self-actualization. To participate in its symbolic power one must give over all the ways of knowing, and all the meanings, that human experience in various places can offer. Both the poet and the sailor long for union with the iceberg — reminding us in a Frostean vein that not only artists but also laborers "tread the boards," and dream in doing so of other types of knowing. But the bargain the sailor ponders is an impossible one, for a categorical rather than a logistical reason.

It is not that there is no clear way of reaching the iceberg or of living on it, but that giving up one's eyes makes it impossible to participate in the scene one longs for. The desire of this poem is not for mastery over the physical world, but for a chance to relinquish the means of knowledge and dwell only in its end. A hopeless narrative ("Watch it closely") was the result of the encounter with the monument; a hopeless dream of icy stability constitutes the encounter with the iceberg. Yet Bishop's poetry will continue to mull the Miltonic bargain that this sailor would accept, if it were offered — his eyes, in exchange for vision.

The fact that these animating poetic problems are opposite to each other does not help Bishop to alleviate either of them. She must address both at once: both the artifact's neglect for the world it refers to and the world's neglect for the imagination that shapes it. In the task, she will have to abandon the dream of having the "iceberg [rather] than the ship," like the dream of making "a romantic scene" out of wood. Wood and water, the formations of human knowing and the flux of nature, must interlock in some workable manner. Poetry, after all, is a form of desiring speech, not a set of propositions tending toward some kind of détente through better acknowledgment of the mutual obligations of humanity and nature. The power of nature animates the poem in a way nothing else can; there may be pleasure in watching artificial objects for signs of life, but life itself is indispensable to the Emersonian poet.

The end of "Pleasure Seas" offers a raw, springlike energy, but does not find a way to incorporate it into a human mind. Unreconciled as it is, the poem was never published by Bishop. The oceanic energy it finds at the end, though, throbs under the surface of many of her best poems. In the poem's last lines, we are far removed from the poet's laboratory:

> . . . out there where the coral reef is a shelf
> The water runs at it, leaps, throws itself
> Lightly, lightly whitening in the air:
> An acre of cold white spray is there
> Dancing happily by itself.

This unself-conscious, expressive, oceanic freedom is the dream of Bishop's work, like all Emersonian poetry. It is named best in one of her last poems:

> Caught — the bubble
> in the spirit-level,

a creature divided;
and the compass needle
wobbling and wavering,
undecided.
Freed — the broken
thermometer's mercury
running away;
and the rainbow-bird
from the narrow bevel
of the empty mirror,
flying wherever
it feels like, gay! ("Sonnet" [1979])

This poem, like the Emersonian dream of freedom generally, functions cognitively on the basis of impossibility. Its elements of freedom can be named only
by describing the artifacts that imprison them. Even so, their energy under the
confinement, like the energy of these lines under the confinement of the poem's form, is thrilling. We might say that rather than "riding on its own melting," in Frost's phrase, this poem sublimates — vaporizing under the steam
of its frozenness. The gaiety of freed spirit is a crucial part of Bishop's poetics,
but it appears always in a frame that negates it. To get rid of frames would also
mean getting rid of the necessary instruments of seeing. The most important
question raised by "Sonnet" is one tackled in Bishop's most difficult poems:
that of endowing a human body, in natural space, with the freedom here best
embodied by a "rainbow-bird."

In "Pleasure Seas," where ocean finally dances happily by itself, such freedom from structure is approached cautiously, awkwardly, through an array
of human ways of encountering water. Liquidity is encountered here in solid
vessels.[10] The people are said to be "happy" in this poem, taking pleasure in
the aquatic, but they are participating in pale, domesticated versions of the
happiness the ocean acre feels by itself. Once a sea becomes a "pleasure sea,"
it has become an attraction, a destination, and culture has confined it and
walled it off. In the optimistic human experience of water, the observer hopes
that a Platonic progression can link the shadowed water of the acculturated
swimming pool with the bright, unbounded water of the ocean.

In the walled-off swimming pool the water is perfectly flat.

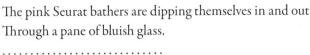

The pink Seurat bathers are dipping themselves in and out
Through a pane of bluish glass.
. . . .
If the sky turns gray, the water turns opaque,
Pistachio green and Mermaid Milk.
. . . .
But out among the keys
Where the water goes its own way, the shallow pleasure seas
Drift this way and that mingling currents and tides
In most of the colors that swarm around the sides
Of soap-bubbles, poisonous and fabulous.

In accord with the intensity of Emersonian concerns about sensation, openness, and fluidity, the confrontations with water in this poem are highly mediated. Like the fish Bishop catches in the poem of that name, the ocean itself
seems to be under glass, held at a distance even when one soars above it in an
airplane. One can never get the water in itself, which adorns "only itself," and
dances "by itself"; one can have only the ship, and the other media that enable
encounter with it. The forms that human thought imposes on the objects of its
desire, seen most obviously in the trademarked names for the pool's color, are
seen again and again — the colors of pure refraction seen from all perspectives,
a "rainbow-bird" in "Sonnet," are here described as something less than what
soap bubbles offer in a bathtub.

As the poem reaches its most propositional form, using the voice that
achieved closure in the complex final lines of "The Imaginary Iceberg," a self-
correction intrudes, to assert the inevitability of human walls in constituting
ideas of freedom. "The sea is delight. The sea means *room*. / It is a dance-floor,
a well-ventilated ballroom." The abstraction "*room*," which is italicized to indicate both the emphasis the poem places on it and the fact that it is a space
rather than a place, soon collapses into the more concrete name "ballroom."
We cannot conceptualize "room," it seems, without rooms; we approach the
idea of the sea through experiences (like that of the enclosed swimming pool)
and concepts (like "room") that are essentially marked by their human finitude. The word "room" itself walls off the ocean, just as the swimming pool
did, and the speaker must settle for a witticism — calling the open space of
ocean "well-ventilated" in an attempt to laugh off the fact that since it is infinitely roomy, there is nothing about it that is like a room.

No human action makes sense in the oceanic context, but this does not stop an observer from trying to find meaning in the water.

> From the swimming-pool or from the deck of a ship
> Pleasures strike off humming, and skip
> Over the tinsel surface: a Grief floats off
> Spreading out thin like oil. And Love
> Sets out determinedly in a straight line,
> One of his burning ideas in mind,
> Keeping his eyes on
> The bright horizon,
> But shatters immediately, suffers refraction,
> And comes back in shoals of distraction.

Capitalized as they become solid objects—emissions of allegory from the viewer on the deck—human emotions dwindle to nothing in the vastness of this landscape. With her shallow angle of perception, the diminutive person who faces the horizon can get no cognitive purchase on the sea. No act of intention can cover an infinite span; the mind that sets out to probe such a space is immediately distracted by the surface play of light, then beguiled by the sight of fish underneath. Like Frost's stars or the fireflies of "A Cold Spring," these shoals of fish offer sensory traction on a blank vista; but they are also groundings, particulate "shoals" on which the voyager into openness founders.

A single hinge-word, "and," provides the transition from all this discouraging allegory to the description of dancing seawater that ends the poem. After two lame assertions of human happiness, Bishop inserts a dash and lurches into a description of water untouched by culture: "And out there where the coral reef is a shelf," she claims, we can discern water "Dancing happily by itself." It is probable that the inadequacy of this hinge is the reason that Bishop never felt the poem to be finished: there is no earned reconciliation between the bric-a-brac involved in human experience of water and the thrill of its pure essence at the end of the poem. The schema of this poem is mere juxtaposition, "Everything connected only by 'and' and 'and'" (in the words of "Over 2,000 Illustrations"). Like the diptych "Sonnet," with its two unlinked themes "Caught" and "Freed," it is about two things that seem not to relate at all.

In "The Map," which mulled the real world as well as the represented one,

Bishop asked: "along the fine tan sandy shelf / is the land tugging at the sea from under?" Here, at the close of "Pleasure Seas," the reef allows us to answer yes.

> . . . out there where the coral reef is a shelf
> The water runs at it, leaps, throws itself
> Lightly, lightly whitening in the air:
> An acre of cold white spray is there
> Dancing happily by itself.

At the reef, the growth of the continent through calcified skeletons makes another solid vessel for activation of the water. It is this hidden solidity that brings the sea to anthropomorphic life. As unselfconscious as the waves are said to be, they cannot be rendered without consciousness of the shelf and its human meanings. Indeed, in these lines a land-bound concept takes pride of place in the poem's most satisfying description of ocean power. The word "acre," evoking the laborer's work in a field, beautifully disrupts the passage about the surf's undifferentiable energy. Like the solid, subtle coral reef, this agricultural word both enables and undercuts the description of wave power. In singling out just one acre, one "plot" of ocean, the speaker has chosen her own place in placelessness. Where solidity is held just under the surface, it can mount just enough resistance to pure idea that beauty without particulars comes to seem possible.

SADNESS IS THE more common tenor of Bishop's attempts to connect land with water. In "Quai d'Orleans," Bishop describes the effect an awareness of flow might have on human communication. Unlike the dancing waves, the ripples in this poem and the leaves from upstream both "modestly" vanish before the protagonists' eyes; the poet's response is to speak in counterpoint and in sympathy, in a perfect balance of immodesty and modesty. She feels that the protagonists' imprint on the water, as they stand above it on the structure, is more significant than nature's imprint. (So likewise is the imprint of humanity's leaves — the pages of print that hold a trace.) Yet somehow that significance is a sign of human inadequacy.

> We stand as still as stones to watch
>   the leaves and ripples
> while light and nervous water hold
>   their interview.
> ·"If what we see could forget us half as easily,"
>   I want to tell you,
> "as it does itself — but for life we'll not be rid
>   of the leaves' fossils."

The lines seem initially to be governed by a conventional contrast: static, memorializing mind versus ever-changing river. But the poem says that the water — not the people — cannot forget this moment. This incongruous claim, one of the poem's principal beauties, registers an important point: the agency of this poem is not all nature's. The reciprocal "interview" of light and water is marked from outside by the metaphor-making sight of the poetic speaker. Reflecting on the water, she makes it still: the barge's wake resembles a large oak leaf, she says, and focuses our attention on the shapes of all these leaves rather than their destiny. By seeing forms in the water, including her own, she has made herself permanent in the scene — albeit modestly (not out loud but on a leaf of paper).

As in "A Cold Spring," poetic speech in "Quai d'Orleans" is hesitant about its ability to change the world — but at the same time ruefully certain that it has done so. To be sure, the leaves, embarked "down the sea's / dissolving halls," will undergo the same dissolution that the halls themselves do (when the eye sees through their apparent walls of firmament to apprehend its vastness). But they are also hardened in their extinguishing encounter with the human presence — a presence figured both by the quay where ripples die and by the stony perception of the humans in the scene. The speaker does not remark that the leaves will be always in the viewers' memories, but rather that their fossils will: there is now no freeing the leaves from the sediment of human receptivity, a mire that grips and kills them.[11]

This is why nature is unable to forget people: in making nature memorable, the poet makes nature itself stony like the mind. In describing the leaves' journeys to oblivion, Bishop's speaker has blocked that journey, and sunk these objects in place like the pilings of the title quay. The leaves are bound into a finite, rather than an infinite, volume — their dissolution is suspended as they enter the chambers without walls, the "dissolving halls" that can never quite dissolve without ceasing to be "rooms." It is not incidental that in the face of such topics, communicative speech with a companion becomes impossible: even the hypothetically vocalized sentence of this poem must be interrupted. The speaker must acknowledge that in beginning to speak, even in her head, she has violated the spirit of forgetfulness and self-forgetfulness emanated by the ripples and leaves. In verbalizing, she makes herself a fact, just as the poem with its metaphors has made leafiness a fact rather than an evanescence. The last line of Bishop's speech about the world's forgetfulness, then, concedes that a spoken wish must prevent its fulfillment. The world cannot forget a verbal human, because it is she who makes the world mindful.

LIKE THE OBSESSIVE beach-cleaner and reader of "The Sea & Its Shore," Bishop dreamed while in nature of the shelter that imagination could enclose. The content of a text, the oddity of any given detail, does not matter; reading is itself a warming and consoling fact. "The End of March" responds to nature's bleakness with a desire to retreat to books (a dream that will be bizarrely fulfilled in "Over 2,000 Illustrations"):

> It was cold and windy, scarcely the day
> to take a walk on that long beach.
> . . . .
> I wanted to get as far as my proto-dream-house,
> my crypto-dream-house, that crooked box
> set up on pilings . . .
> I'd like to retire there and do *nothing*,
> or nothing much, forever, in two bare rooms:
> look through binoculars, read boring books,
> old, long, long books, and write useless notes,
> talk to myself, and, foggy days,
> watch the droplets slipping, heavy with light.
> . . . .
>   But — impossible.
> And that day the wind was too cold
> even to get that far,
> and of course the house was boarded up.

Her strolling companion on the beach is left out of Bishop's daydream of retirement; as a poet, it seems to be her longed-for destiny to talk to herself. She acknowledges, though, that this outcome is intrinsically impossible — and not just because of the logistical reasons. The books cannot possibly suffice; the walk itself, a shared experience of nature, is too fundamental. The poet's window must look out onto something besides its own surface full of rain, and the binoculars must have objects to bring close: Bishop needs the shore, and therefore she needs her (shared) experience of the shore.

In this case, desperation created by the weather drives Bishop to construct a sociable narrative out of the objects she has. The dog-prints on the beach, she proposes, belong to the lion that is proverbially March; the "man-sized" corpse of a kite string suggests the kite's lively earlier self; and the two "perhaps" played together, as lion and lamb of God perhaps, at the birth of a new springtime.[12] The sun enables this hopefulness by offering a glimpse of warmth as a promise of the summer to come. Bishop is hesitant to allow herself meanings like these, and approaches them only through allegory. The dead kite string in the surf is the most forlorn object possible, a corpse severed from the inspiriting kite that gave it life; to find cheer in it as one's own face "freezes" takes fortitude. It is a strong poem; but its dream of retirement is an element that remains unresolved. The poet has an infinite desire to be alone, to speak to herself of her own experience in the moment, instead of encouraging others with an attenuated promise of spring. This is why the narrative ends with the rocks over which the poet is walking, rather than more dynamic elements of the scene. It focuses idiosyncratically on the stones that, as their shadows appear briefly, "could have been teasing the lion sun, / except that now he was behind them."

This near miss, as the world's objects face away from each other, is a reminder of metaphors' failure, intervening before the metaphors themselves are even made up. The position of the evening sun is important: at its heart, Bishop's cheery energy is retrospective rather than full of promise. The poem is enlivened only by the thought of a moment *before* humans arrived on the scene and registered its emptiness. The playfulness of sea and sun is already over, and so is the hope for more warmth: as the sun leaves the scene, it is on the wrong side to fill the eastern ocean horizon. Thus the futurity of American narrative, the promise of the West, fails to reach the lyric self; even her dreams of summer are counterfactual. It is a cold spring indeed that the poet offers to her readers.

To herself, though, Bishop continued to extend and rescind the promise of a dream house of textual shelter. As her speaker pores over the strange book in "Over 2,000 Illustrations and a Complete Concordance," she provides American poetry's most rigorous account of consoling representation's inadequacy. This masterwork of a poem lacks the simplicity of the laboratory-poems, in which a single problem could be inspected in isolation. To be sure, the book is like the monument, an artifact of now inaccessible meaning; however, it is also like the iceberg, preferable to real travel and absorbingly interesting to the viewer. And as soon as writing enters the scene of shared memory — as soon as the evanescent leaves of "Quai d'Orleans" are bound into shape — the result is an uncanny discontentment with experience itself. "Thus should have been our travels: / serious, engravable." It seems a perverse response to an old-fashioned book, to wish that one's own life were more like it. But the impulse to order one's own experience into books should be very familiar — not only to poets but to anyone who carries a camera when traveling. Notably, this is not just a dissatisfaction with art or with the instruments of representation, as "The Monument" was: it is a dissatisfaction with experience itself. The "travels" of the protagonists were not "serious" enough; they fell short of pilgrimage and quest.

The poem is no longer a thought-experiment; it is about life's complexity — travel and its imagining, not a trade of one for the other. Yet this is not a biographical poem in any thematic sense, not simply about memory or loss. It is about a certain kind of knowledge, involving both the essence of nature and the essence of text. The melancholy spirit that enabled Bishop to brood over the map enables her also to brood over the book, and her speaker's patience in brooding over the inscrutable waters will give rise to new meanings. The speaker's melancholy assiduity stems from a sorrow that is also faith. The closest analogy for her readerly look, in the world outside the lyric, is midrash: it is too meditative to be called kitschy, too idiosyncratic to be called exegesis.

WRITING'S KNOWLEDGE in "Over 2,000 Illustrations and a Complete Concordance" may profitably be identified with the strange, unsatisfying knowledge carried by a souvenir. At this point, in fact, we might say that every Bishop poem is a souvenir: an object self-consciously positioned at a distance from the world it is about.[13] It acknowledges that no one is quick enough to "have" or even "get" the world "before it cloy," as Hopkins longed to do. What we get instead is the souvenir-object, the poem, a residuum of the mind's clumsy grasp of experience. As objects seeking to contain moments, both the souvenir and the poem are bound to fail instantly; but cloying as they might be, still we have them. We get them *only* for the sake of keeping them.

The book is not the only souvenir in Bishop's work. We have seen several souvenirs already;[14] each of them is labeled, as Randall Jarrell said all of Bishop's poems could themselves be captioned, "I have seen it."[15] The collection so far includes nearly a dozen of them, each connected to the next only by juxtaposition. They sit alongside each other on a certain shelf; they have occupied our attention one by one.

- Snarled kite string respooled around a rock, from the most recent excursion
- A stiff paper leaf, stamped with the words "Quai d'Orleans"
- In a sky blue box decorated with mermaids, a sprig of pistachio green coral
- A fragment of dull glass, labeled "rainbow"
- A stoppered vial from the gift shop at Glacier National Park
- A splintering monument in a diorama, tagged "Add water"
- An Emerson epigram ("The man is only half himself") clipped from an article
- A postcard of fireflies on a summer night, with the message "Wish I were there"
- A map of the world, scarred with an itinerary delicately traced

Each of these is the souvenir of a poem — but that is not all. Each of these objects on the shelf registers the same impossible desire as the poem it refers to; the desires vary, but in each case an artifact has embodied them. We can therefore say further: for the reader, each of these souvenirs of a poem *is also the poem.*

The thought is worth recasting into an epigram: "Like the experience it describes, a Bishop poem instantly becomes a souvenir of itself."

Like the experience it describes, a Bishop poem instantly becomes a souvenir of itself. The recursive character of this claim makes it absurd: but (to reiterate the absurdity) the claim responds to the poems as they respond to themselves. Marked by the stiffness of the souvenir, the poem is first and foremost an artifact, but its most awkward, mannered elements "give it away as having life, and wishing . . . wanting to cherish something" ("The Monument"). There is no denying that the objects arranged in this presentation of Bishop's work are poor substitutes for the experiences, both in nature and in reading, to which they refer. But replicating such experiences at a remove felicitously (tragically) reiterates the same removal that is inherent to their own natures under the gaze. The writer's distanced eye finds a distance at the heart of its objects: since Emerson, these two chasms are one crack in our experience. Bishop refers to this critical failing of knowledge when she says that there is just "One Art": the "art of losing." In this work, writing is an art made out of loss, and it is also itself the losing. It makes its own failure.

THE METAPHOR of the souvenir underscores the point that a poem is an artifact, not a slice of temporal experience to be measured in history. In encountering Bishop's book, then, we have been on a world tour — but we have at the same time been sold a bill of goods. The words of the poem's title, "Over 2,000 Illustrations and a Complete Concordance," are clearly part of an advertisement, probably one that adorns the jacket of the book itself. They require that we acknowledge the producer of books as a huckster. The object described here has commodity value, and its value as a manufactured object is printed on its own form, threatening to crowd out its other commitments. Not a Bible in which the Word is paramount, it locates its value in the apparatus that surrounds the word. (The illustrations please the eye and ease the experience of reading; the concordance assists the brain as one occasionally looks up a quotation.) It, too, belongs on a shelf. To be sure, the book in this poem is a Bible; but it is a Bible that is a souvenir of the Bible.

There is a problem, then, in the "seriousness" the speaker longs for in line two of this poem: the possibility of overearnest allegory, with its attendant, unending proliferation of bric-a-brac.[16] Even as the book craves a more direct link with the things it is about, its features and ornaments, the instruments of that desire, multiply, occupying the attention. The signs of divinity, after all, are made up of divinity's absence, and the more serious such a work is, the more laughable it is apt to become. This is why the Seven Wonders of the World are included in this Bible;[17] those illustrations are just extra selling points, participating in a muddled notion of the portentous "ancient" that has become the volume's referent. Such orientalizing of the past, not the reader's own "modernity," makes the book absurd.

As we have seen, the spring's lighthearted rebirth is obscured as soon as one comments gravely that "Nothing is so beautiful as spring." In one reading, then, the work of "over 2,000 Illustrations and a Complete Concordance" is to move from the desire for engravable, orderly seriousness expressed in the second line to the extraordinary lightness of the phrase in the penultimate line: "A family with pets." This jocular mistake about the Nativity scene perfectly blends whimsy and dead earnestness. A serious interest in the Nativity may be hackneyed, while the desire to "see" it like a tourist attraction might be tongue in cheek — but the anxiety of these globe-trotting protagonists suggests an unsatisfied longing for some sort of encounter anyway. So much travel stems from the speaker's desire for a home.[18] And this home is not constituted by just any domesticity: it is a domesticity *with pets*, a stable household full of the unselfconscious energy of nature. If somehow she could see the natural world as a home both open and sheltering for contented humanity, the poet could truly say, "Now I've seen everything."

Obviously, the answer here is not a stable and stabilized definition of home (or concomitantly of nature), modeled on the engraved Nativity scene.[19] Desire for the book's hierarchical simplicity, as for the simple pleasure of the souvenir, is matched by a precisely equal amount of disdain; it would be grotesque to buy such an image in the hope that its contents could matter to one's lifestyle. Nonetheless, by encountering this highly stable and self-satisfied book, the speaker carries out the work of the poem. It is not an object to be scorned; it is treasured in hand and examined with extraordinary care and thoughtfulness. There is promise in this exercise precisely because the book is treated as an artifact — an allegory divorced from its referents — rather than as a symbol, participating in meaningfulness itself. Great delicacy is called for. To read kitsch earnestly is to make oneself a buffoon; but to read a serious object laughingly is only to elevate oneself.

The primary feature of the book is that it imposes order. Every illustration has its place:

Granted a page alone or a page made up
of several scenes arranged in cattycornered rectangles
or circles set on stippled gray,
granted a grim lunette,
caught in the toils of an initial letter,
when dwelt upon, they all resolve themselves.

This careful arrangement, in which the illustrations accompany their verbal equivalents and the presence of each word is remapped in the concordance, makes for the "seriousness" the speaker's mind is drawn to. Such systematic concord of reference appeals to human thought. The power of the publisher, like the power of God, is beneficent, "granting" in the case of each illustration the monument's "wish": that it should be a monument, and "Cherish something." As in the case of the monument, though, in each case the cherished thing itself is hardly manifest. At the heart of each picture — behind it — is a cavity where meaning is lodged: "The Tomb, the Pit, the Sepulcher . . . the Well." The meaning of each image has been not only engraved but even "engraved," buried in the far background. In each case the location of the crux, the structure that frames and sanctifies death, is itself so thoroughly framed that it is out of sight.

The central contrast of the poem, then, is between the first verse-paragraph and the second, between these highly arranged elements of the book and the random images of actual travel (held together if at all only by the speaker's "fright"). In her traveling experience, the speaker sees "Everything connected only by 'and' and 'and' "; on the other hand, the book offers depth and above all containment. The sea in "Pleasure Seas" "means *room*"; by contrast, this object consistently means tomb. The book's images of nested framing and entombment are protective: processing the fact of death into an arrangement, they are the opposite of the most horrifying sight from the speaker's travels,

A holy grave . . .
open to every wind from the pink desert.
An open, gritty, marble trough.

It is here, in the open air where the calf's birth in "A Cold Spring" could not be processed, that the poem breaks off to seek consolation in the book, and to reflect that " 'and' and 'and' " will not suffice as a system. There is no protection in travels' methods: proximity and accumulation.

Fittingly, the resolution of the poem stems from the speaker's repeated instruction to herself in the last verse-paragraph, to "Open the heavy book." Its closed forms are put ajar and encompass human desire in a way that does not simply swaddle it. The act involves the book in openness, which in turn stems from being *seen*, made subject to an actively knowing mind. The yawning referent of the illustrations closed off before, the darkness of "The Tomb, the Pit, the Sepulcher," is revisited in the final lines, in the magnificently ambiguous phrase about the space of the Nativity scene: "the dark ajar." There is no resolution to the critical question in this line: is the darkness opened to enable entrance into it, or escape from it?

To move from tomb to fresh nativity is of course the goal of every poem with Hopkins's springtime, Easter sensibility. But in the first verse-paragraph the depths of the book "resolve themselves" in a way that makes such a movement impossible. The reader faces Emerson's dilemma: there is either the prison of belief, being "Caught in the toils of an initial letter"; or the exposure of unbelief, being "Open to every wind from the pink desert." Nothing mediates the two. The book's self-containment, its carefully crafted structure of reference, at first affords no room for active Emersonian knowledge. On the other hand, once that knowledge begins to work, the speaker "retiring from her chamber" (*Nature* I.8) to go abroad, the elements of the book dissipate entirely. She is left brooding on empty waters, charged with reenacting Creation by herself. The animating problem of the poem, then, is the resistance posed by the book, which is both absolute and paltry. Its framework can be totally accepted ("Our Christian Empire") or totally debunked ("The eye drops"). There seems to be nothing in between.

Somehow, though, the poem develops a connection between the book and the speaker's travels. This transition between verse-paragraphs, unlike the mere "and" of "Pleasure Seas," is scrupulously earned. The speaker's reverie about her travel is not simply opposed to the encounter with the book: instead, it develops out of it. The crisis of the book simply leads — albeit "painfully" — into a querying of experience itself. In descending into the book's depths, the speaker finds herself descending into her own sensory memory, charged as it is with the visual energy that begins with the primal blueness of horizon. Intense work is being done when an Emersonian reader dwells upon a book. The result is the entelechy of dwelling, its fulfillment — the release into nature.

The crucial transitional image, the concept that participates both in the orderliness of thought and the vivacity of world, turns out to be the image of ocean that vexes the most ambitious Emersonian poems of knowledge. Behind the engravings one finds not the primal causes one might expect, the sacred burial sites with "Human figure[s] far gone" into them; one encounters instead the open space of imagination's freedom.

> The eye drops, weighted, through the lines
> the burin made, the lines that move apart

like ripples above sand,
dispersing storms, God's spreading fingerprint,
and painfully, finally, that ignite
in watery prismatic white-and-blue

Entering the Narrows at St. John's
the touching bleat of goats reached to the ship.

The lines about seeing through the book are highly ambiguous. They strain the interpretive faculty — but these lines have rarely been analyzed closely, and the drama they unfold can be reenacted. We are asked here to visualize the descent of a seeing eye through the lines of the book, and to notice their response: those mannered lines, so clumsy and dark, start to resemble the immaculate circles that spread out in water after it has been touched (or after an object has been dropped into it). Their distortions seem to be resolved into clarity at the impact of the eye. It is as if the speaker of the poem has dropped her eye into murky waters, and illuminated them in the act. But there is no return to the shore.

The ripples, in turn, then seem to be storms "above sand": the viewpoint shifts beneath the surface of the page, and what was a watery surface below the speaker is now a firmament above her. But looking back up from the seafloor, having dropped herself into a world the book contains, the speaker finds all that world's material gone: the God responsible for the disturbance, for the texture of the lines and for their movement, has vanished, and all the media of the experience are consumed. As the book dissolves all around the speaker who has descended into it, the task of dwelling upon the book is finished, but the task of the eye has just begun. The "white-and-blue" that results from having seen through the book is the "white-and-blue" of thrilling openness. The "resolution" of the illustrations is the escape from their boundaries. In "The Monument," the poet was "far away within the view," alienated in the artificial setting and removed from the natural one. Similarly and yet quite differently, the speaker of this poem, holding the book, finds herself far away: within the view of nature the book offers.

Two meanings can be assigned to the eye's drop, for this "seeing through" is a debunking as well as a fulfillment. (The fact that the two are the same is the principal beauty of allegory.) Emerson's philosophy, of course, involves the thrill in ceasing to read as well as the thrill in reading. This Bible can offer no resistance to the gaze of the skeptic, who notes that its portentous lines were made with a particular tool (the burin) by a particular engraver, and that God's fingerprint on the Bible is a human artifice. Such a vantage point descends through the book, destroying the bookmaker's integrity of reference on the way by revealing the void that underlies it. In that descent, it breaks from representation into real experience, with the transition constituted by the ideal clarity of void (open blue sky and water above the sand just offshore). Yet the book is the vessel for this work. As closed as it is, the book, because it is treated as an allegory rather than an end in itself, contains — in its reader's capacity for ideas — all the openness one might desire for it.

Thus the active cognitive effort of the Emersonian mind finds the world's unity and largeness even in the closed forms of the book. The brooding engendered by monumental stability has broken through, painfully, to a sort of instability that allows the mind to feel all possibilities at once. The problem that quickly asserts itself, of course, is Bishop's second laboratory-problem, the problem of "The Imaginary Iceberg," for the intense clarity of open space is apt to dwindle the human to insignificance. The eye drops through the engravings (penetrating their screens of deceit), but then emerges on the other side to find itself only a solitary eyeball, plummeting through the very openness it has achieved. At the words "watery prismatic white-and-blue," the lines of representation burn away and consume themselves, and open space is all that is left — in this case, the open space of the blank line between these verse-paragraphs.

The poem could end here, in self-negation, as pure abstract blue fills the scene, but instead we are offered a cinematic transition: the blueness turns out to be ocean. It is only by locating its infinite Emersonian energy, by drawing a shoreline in the foreground of its liberated space, that the poem continues. The scene that opens the second verse-paragraph is about "Entering the Narrows at St. John's," itself a movement from the oblivion of ocean back into the channels of nameable space. Reversing the path of the leaves in "Quai d'Orleans," the protagonist turns from the pure abstract "white-and-blue" of ocean to more conventional realms of poetry, in which a "touching bleat of goats" can give the illusion of solidarity with the world, and one does not need to rely solely on the eye.

Unfortunately, this stanza's effort to narrow the world to a comprehensible size fails in encounter with the "open grave": no effort to contain the self can suffice in the face of death, desert winds, and the far horizon. These lines about travel are also, consistently, lines about the human body that becomes the dust of the desert. Having invoked pure, consuming ocean, Bishop sets about the task of self-protection, carefully positioning a physical self in space. The cliffs above the shipboard breakfast; the arcade, great square, and harbor; and the tea, flowers, and belly dances that the tourist consumes all help construct partially enclosed spaces in which the speaker can locate herself with some confidence (even if she cannot therefore close off and arrange these spaces, as the book would invite her to do). But she develops no security that is any tighter than mere proximity; the body, like everything else, is only connected to its surroundings "by 'and' and 'and.'"[20] The endpoint of this consideration of bodily travel, therefore, is the horror of the open grave. Like the eye encountering lines of representation, the body is bound to be freed from its arrangements, bound to be dispersed in the winds as the "invisible threads" that hold it together give way. Even the "touching" encounter with nature, the St. John's goat scene, is rewritten as the speaker faces the resting place of the paynim: its marble is "Yellowed as scattered cattle-teeth."

Again, the startling fact about this transition is that Bishop's consideration of the body abroad (whether undulating or ungulate) serves not just as a counterpoint to but also as the natural extension of her encounter with the book. The dissolve into blueness became a resolution into sensation. At the end of the first verse-paragraph, as the illustrations were posed silently in indifference to the reader's position, the eye took on solidity to force a different kind of resolution: "The eye drops, weighted, through the lines." The process of debunking and dispersing the elements of the book may seem to be a process of purification, in which intensity of experience can be achieved by eliminating the jetsam of culture. Direct experience supplants the media of culture. That reading would endorse the transcendentalist search for originary clarity. But that reading is confounded in this crucial line, in which it is the "weighted" body, not a transparent lens, that does the work of "seeing through." The eye of this poem, a stone dropped into the murk of the book to clear it of particularity, is itself an unwieldy particle — it is "weighted."

In one reading, of course, it is weighted by skepticism: the modern reader easily pierces the veil of religion to see the void behind it. (Readers of Feuerbach are drawn through this "fiery brook," and their ignition gives rise to modern materialism.) This is an adequate description of the passage. But there is another, less historical way of describing the same phenomenon: the weight of these lines is the weight of representation, a heaviness that comes not from piercing strength but from being dragged down by the world of objects that ballasts the eye. Primary among these objects is the "heavy book" itself. Pulled by the weight of its own desire — given gravity by the engravings and their seriousness — the human eye enters into artificiality. It must burn along with its trophies, in open space.

While the body is the means of refutation here, it is also the means of encounter. "Weighted," the eye drops into the very well of death that the ornaments of the book try to screen off. Encased in concreteness, Bishop's speaker plunges into the safety of holy burial, the places where the world is purified. But in each case she finds that this promise is actually the watery promise of freedom, that the cocoon opens instantly onto unsheltered flight. There are two parallel agonies here: first, the pain of the ignited book, the purge of meanings all around the naked eye that was defended by them; and second, the pain of experience itself in a fragile body, the desert wind full of sand that stings the exposed eyes of the tourist (who lacks her local guide's "burnoose"). Thus the poem is unified, despite its awkward transition between the cultural problem of representation and an individual's experience of travel: both sections are about thought embodied.

What is missing in each section, however, is the substance of thought itself. It is to be sought only in what they share, the element that unifies the poem: the blankness between the stanzas, the crystalline purity of the page and the sky. Ocean's openness, the freedom that the mind craves when it dwells silently in itself, belongs properly both to cultural and to physical experience. It is an ideal as well as a natural fact. Both in the world and the mind, this freedom's poverty ("watery") and its richness ("prismatic") merge in its double character as a "white-and-blue" thing. A single experience is born from the two opposite problems of Bishop's laboratory-poems. The grotesque self-regard of the monumental book and the cold, indifferent chaos of the world meet at the surface of the page, the surface that the speaker's eye traverses.

Neither problem can be solved: the speaker of this poem must "see through" religion's containers for death, and she must still always *see* through them. Her eye is weighted; embodied in culture, she must wear its trappings. Caught and freed at once, the Emersonian mind undergoes simultaneously both of the opposite experiences of Bishop's "Sonnet": dragged into the book, it is turned loose upon the world. It is aware of the openness into which the eye drops and of the heaviness that makes it drop, committing it to sensation. The reciprocal quality of these formulas suggests a transcendentalist solution: perhaps the artist can be both the human and the God of the work. But to drop the eye into the world is at once a claim and a renunciation: the ripples spread to be extinguished as well as to mark a path. This doubleness of grasping and releasing is the import of the final lines.

What the poet longs to forswear in these final lines is not only the poem's claim to divinity (even to call the fingerprint God's suggested some stable faith, however obsolete) but also its human desire, the poet's desiring sight. In giving up both, both are gained; but this is not a narrative of quick sensory success like Hopkins's spring-poem. In fact, it calls into question the premise of that success, the Christ-child who could act before humanity spoiled nature. Once the knowing eye has been dropped into the world, nothing in the world can satisfy the poet: it is tainted by that very instrument. The fingerprints we dust for always turn out to be our own.

Here, in the extraordinary final verse-paragraph of "Over 2,000 Illustrations and a Complete Concordance," the speaker's only recourse is the book that caused her dilemma in the first place. The eye in the first stanza was weighted both by skepticism and by acquiescence to the gravity of the illustrations. In this last stanza, these two elements are ratcheted up to extremes as both problems of representation — its flimsiness and its inaccessible strength — are felt at once:

> Open the book. (The gilt rubs off the edges
> of the pages and pollinates the fingertips.)
> Open the heavy book. Why couldn't we have seen
> this old Nativity while we were at it?

In the first two lines, an incidental feature of the book, the gilt that "pollinates the fingertips" to offer some hope of magical rebirth, is properly sequestered into parentheses. The initial readerly act, the opening of the book, is firmly reasserted. This mention of gilding is a last gasp of the allegorical way of seeing: a mode in which every fragment absorbs the attention, and "the unremitting expectation of a miracle" or a blossoming is the only hope to cling to. The ornamented book, vessel of encounter with an idea, is here subordinated to some essence inside. The parentheses that cordon off this detail are wildly uncharacteristic of Bishop; she seems to be trying to set aside the difficult materiality her poetry is founded on.

Looking at the open book and at its referent — both invoked by the word "Nativity," which refers to the engraving and to the birth it depicts — the speaker brackets her allegorical way of seeing. She is preparing to confront something more like the Romantic symbol — in fact, the original symbol, Christ, the double essence that authorized successful representation for poets like Hopkins. Meaning and sensation will merge. She is about to set aside the incidental details of the book, suddenly known to be a mere husk or container, and bear down on its content. She has gotten serious.

But of course the speaker does not see the quintessential symbolic scene, the scene in which idea and bodily fact are unified in the Incarnation of God. It is missed as soon as she turns the page to it. It is "this" in these lines, right at hand, yet it cannot be touched and does not touch her.

> Why couldn't we have seen
> this old Nativity while we were at it?
> — the dark ajar, the rocks breaking with light,
> an undisturbed, unbreathing flame,
> colorless, sparkless, freely fed on straw,
> and, lulled within, a family with pets,
> — and looked and looked our infant sight away.

The eyes' numbness in this poem's conclusion verges toward the death of vision that Bishop's poems have always craved, the death that would accompany imagination's birth into a world of things. This encounter offers the worst as well as the best of both worlds: the scene cannot be "disturbed" by the eye that plunged powerfully into the book to know its finitude; but it does not "breathe" like the infinite, windy world behind that book. The dilemma of the poem has centered on the nature of the space that vision needs: the book's enclosure was not enough, and the open world was too much. But with the extraordinary pun of the last line, this tableau presents both problems at once: it is impossible either to get rid of it or to get enough of it.

The richness of ideal vision, then, is missing in this second encounter with the book — the heart of this scene is not "prismatic" but "colorless." But ideal vision's burning pain and aridity are missing too — the heart of this scene is not "painfully ignited" and "watery" but "sparkless" and "freely fed on straw." All the dilemmas of this poem are dissolved, as sight descends and does not descend into the picture. The eye persists without consuming its objects, yet its weight is forgotten as it merges lightly with the light, unmarked areas of the picture. Flame replaces the suffocating and homogeneous water images of book and world. And most important, the speech that mars experience by making souvenirs of it, the speech inherent to poetic sight itself, is quieted: "infant," the key word of the last line, etymologically means "unspeaking." The subject and object of sight are one in these words, when no word is spoken.

> Open the heavy book. Why couldn't we have seen
> this old Nativity while we were at it?
> — the dark ajar, the rocks breaking with light,
> an undisturbed, unbreathing flame,
> colorless, sparkless, freely fed on straw,
> and, lulled within, a family with pets,
> — and looked and looked our infant sight away.

The paradox of the last line, where desire gets rid of its object and itself, is tragically perfect: it finds new possibilities for art in impossibility. Not speaking in this scene enables speech. In regarding the Word wordlessly, the poet cleanses herself of the desire for innocence, exactly as she takes on that innocence herself. The double grip of language and experience is released all at once: each tightens so much, into the aching words of regret, that it turns inside out. Loss and satisfaction — a miracle seen through, and seeing through a miracle — happen at the same instant. They could never coincide in real space, which is bound to be either open or closed. This scene could never happen in the world or the book "while we were at it." Its happening takes place in a sort of bubble merging reading and experience, an incarnation of the Incarnation; to its recursive power the reader has no access.

Still open, the book goes on the shelf. But reading cannot conclude: this Nativity is born into the poem in the regret of the lyric speaker at never having confronted it. Neither read nor experienced, the unspoken Word would mean freedom both from the book's apparatus and from the horizon's encompassment. The Nativity of these last lines is a sealed bubble-artifact — an astonishingly light globule in which paradox resolves. Its birth is nothing other than the eye's own souvenir of the world it plunged into, laden with the desire for knowledge. Stung by wind and sand and straining to know its place in the blankness of nature, the poet's eye is both too delicate and too ambitious. It gets an eyeful of ocean; the lids close at once. But as the eye closes darkness opens, and as vision succumbs to grit and vastness something liquid and self-contained is absurdly born. One tear — this poem's last sentence — contains all the tragedy of Bishop's work: as it drops, the world's salt and the eye's roundness greet each other in one horizon. This souvenir of not seeing is one that the poet has forever.

7 Merrill's Expansiveness

Poetry of knowledge is often a solitary endeavor. For the Emersonian poet, the detachment of the poem's object, which "sits for its portrait"[1] as the mind finds the forms to represent it, has tended to coincide with detachment of the poetic speaker from society. Reproachful of conversational forms, the epistemological poet often stands apart; her work is on a promontory between two realms, and she can neither be contained by society nor absorbed by sublimity. Though a member of this tradition, and an especial admirer of Bishop, James Merrill sought a poetics that respected his own contained gregariousness. In all his writings, he kept in mind the materiality of his forms, and the difficulty of finding words in a void. In his poem "Marsyas," the elements of formal rigidity and creative choice are reflected in the "stiff rhythms" and "gorgeous rhymes" of the poem of the Apollo figure, a strong rival poet whose power pulls the poem's protagonist out of himself. The first element of that dyad imposes formal control; the second offers beauty and plenitude. The tension between these two poetic challenges — order and submissive awe — would culminate in Merrill's extended poem of education, *The Changing Light at Sandover*. Even in that prosiest of American poems, it would find resolution in the same lyric instantaneity that, in the stories of Marsyas, Semele, and other annihilated singers of ancient Greece, merges pride with abjection.

The vulnerability of human flesh is one message of the Marsyas myth: at the end of that story, the god of poetry flays the (intrinsically) inadequate human singer. The obvious response for a formalist writer is to center anxieties about pride and weakness on objects rather than on innate capacities. In Merrill's most autobiographical poem, "The Broken Home," the title object — the house, rather than the people involved — absorbs the poet's attention in the poem's final lines. Redemptive power emerges not just from a reckoning with events but also from the opening of an actual window in the house that leads to "the unstiflement of the entire story." It is the house, not the storyteller, that lacks breath. The poet needs only to expose inner space to outer in order to clear away the stultifying mythic overlay of this poem about his parents, whom he calls "Father Time and Mother Earth, / A marriage on the rocks." In his gloss on this passage, Merrill pointed away from the autobiographical: "That bit in 'The Broken Home' . . . isn't meant as a joke. History in our time *has* cut loose, *has* broken faith with Nature" (*Recitative* 177). This claim has ecological resonance, to be sure, but it is at the same time a commentary on a failure of contemporary philosophy. Considering experience as a set of events in which relationships evolve, history-obsessed Hegelian philosophy neglects experience's instantaneous power, its meanings in a moment of encounter with space and objects.

This passage anticipates an important feature of Merrill's magnum opus, *Sandover*: the engine of the text is the Emersonian double question of language in nature and nature in language. Though he is often treated as a poet of life stories, Merrill is, more importantly, a poet of houses and sensation, and his art of conversation and relationship should be understood in that context. This chapter will turn to *Sandover* to find out how that oxymoron, a sociable Emersonian voice, is possible, but first it will examine how Merrill defines himself in the lyric tradition, as a nature poet. Before he turned to developing systems of collective reincarnation and striving, Merrill was a pastoral poet: a solitary shepherd developing a Congregationalism of one.

MERRILL'S METAPHOR for himself in the poem "Syrinx" is the reed — isolated in a natural setting, shaped for the piper's woodsy music with little need of an audience, and above all else grounded in sensory experiences:

> . . . foxglove
> Each year, cloud, hornet, fatal growths,
> Proliferating by metastasis
> Rooted their total in the gliding stream.

The strength of the reed — poetry's strength — is in its delving roots, which give it the anchorage to sum up a world of uncomfortable facts in a single structure. It totals up an array of transient objects to ground them firmly in the flow of a Jamesian stream. Its stiffness makes it a reed to be read, something unlike the other plants because it is self-contained and static, instead of metastatic. Like a well-made poem, it is an object that resonates when the reader adds breath. The "metastasis" of the large natural world, an exponential multiplication that quickly grows out of conceptual scale, can nonetheless be summed up, in the calculus of poetry, to a unity — one centering self in a centered world, the reed that stabilizes itself even in the stream of experience.

Merrill is well known as a puzzle builder, but in all the analyses of "Syrinx" no critic has bothered to solve the equation that makes the poem distinctive, the bizarre experiment in orthography that sets the stage for the experimental deployment of the four winds on the page at the poem's close. In the summation of this being in nature — the reed that somehow crafts a variety of swirling objects into a single tone formed by the shape of its body — the totality of the world is expressed in a mathematical equation whose complexity is worth analyzing. That totality is named in an algebraic expression:

Some formula not relevant any more
To flower children might express it yet

Like $\sqrt{\left(\frac{x}{y}\right)^n} = 1$

— Or equals zero, one forgets —

The y standing for you, dear friend, at least
Until that hour he reaches for me, then

Leaves me cold, the great god Pain . . .[2]

Unlike the work of many of the other poets who advance this Emersonian project, Merrill's calculus is multivariable: he will strain to accompany the x factor of his poetry — himself ("X my mark") — with the y factor, "you," a reader who is also a fellow poet and supplies the breath for the poem's music. Sociability and eros ("Who puts his mouth to me") are indeed crucial factors in this image of the poet; but underlying them are familiar problems of knowledge in nature.

Every rift in this passage is packed with ore — for example, in asserting the irrelevance of "flower children," Merrill makes a comment on sixties youthculture's simplistic, uncalculated claims of unity with nature; on high modernist poetry's finding of beauty in harsher realities rather than in flowers; on the impossibility of homosexual procreation; and on the maturity of a stiffened self that can no longer be fed on "formula." But it is the equation itself that holds the most interest. As Stephen Yenser has pointed out, it is partly a recasting of the poem's title word, with the "S" and "r" of "Syrinx" becoming "square root," the "i" orthographically resembling an "I" (as Merrill seems to have directed in the publications of this poem), and the other letters of the word all appearing as themselves. But the formula here is not just an amalgamation but also an equation, a set of relations in which the unity of the world, the total of objects, is defined as both one and "I," the poetic self. That unity of (controversial) unities stems from the mutual cooperation, or productive disharmony, of three elements.

Since 1 squared and 0 squared are both just themselves, we can set aside the radical sign as mathematically insignificant (it provides the "S" and "r" as well as playing on the poem's program of "roots" and "radicalism"). One solution for this equation then finds that x and y are equal. The poet ("X my mark") and his inspiring addressee represent equal entities, and because they do their ratio — which is also the sum of the world, and the lyric's speaking self — is one. It is a simple, satisfying conclusion — but in the following lines, as "Pain," rather than a beloved "you," begins to blow the poet's tune, more complexity is suggested. The failure of love suggests a very different relation between x and y than that of identity. Even as it propels us forward to the bleak flux of the four winds in the final lines, "Nought Sought Eased Waste," this realization should return us to the equation, in which one term has been neglected.

There is another possible solution: if n is an even number, x and y could be opposite rather than identical. If the poet and his addressee, or the poet and his subject, are fundamentally opposed, mirror images (if, that is to say, $x = -y$), we must rely on the third term — "n," nature, the unspoken word of every lyric poem in this tradition — to balance the equation and avoid the nihilism either of −1 or of 0. The square root of a negative number cannot be anything but imaginary: all imaginary numbers, in fact, include $\sqrt{-1}$ as a factor, a nonsense term represented by a lowercase "i" that here threatens to supplant the well-rooted, erect "I" that is resembled by the number one. Only when nature is the exponent can a lyric poet expound confidently the communion of humanity.

All of this is to say that despite his ingenuity, Merrill is a nature poet, and that this fundamental fact animates his concept of the poet's work. Experience in nature is his first theme from the time he composed "The Black Swan" for his first book, and it remains the crucial element through which his poems mediate among people. His poems function, then, because of their abiding faith in the evenness of the natural world, cold and painful as it is — an even-ness that can cancel out human negativity and difference by replicating it against itself. Thus before considering the personalities, the *x*'s and *y*'s, of Merrill's poetry, we must consider the materiality of his imagination, the natural realm in which his poems self-consciously place themselves.

THE OPENING and close of *Sandover*'s first volume, *The Book of Ephraim*, describe two very different versions of the writer's regret: it has been the task of the volume to get from one state of chagrin to the other. *Ephraim* teaches itself not to regret what it might have been, and instead to regret what it is.

Few important works of literature are marked so prominently by doubt about their own compositional choices. But for Merrill, such doubt is intrin-sic to the philosophical lyric — not a consequence of his far-fetched method but part of the work of any poem that is absorbed with knowing. Merrill's cosmology is thus a descendant not of the relatively unselfconscious myth-systems of Yeats and Blake, but of the lyric craft he himself claimed as an influence, especially that of Bishop. The reading of *Sandover* proposed here culminates in Merrill's poem of homage to Bishop, "Overdue Pilgrimage to Nova Scotia." This method suggests that only after Merrill's composition of *Sandover* and the perfection of its linguistic negotiation of space did such a pilgrimage become possible. In coming to terms with its identity as a lyric text, *Sandover* enables a shift in Merrill's attitude toward his own sociabil-ity, the salient feature that distinguished him from his poetic predecessor. By decoupling sociable writing and multivocal writing from their usual settings in the novel, *Sandover* allows Merrill to integrate his gregariousness fully into the lyric in his final volume of short poems.

In its first few lines, *Ephraim* occupies itself with apologizing for the mis-match between its chosen genre and its subject matter:

Admittedly, I err by undertaking
This in its present form. The baldest
Reportage was called for. . . .

In a word, the poet worries that *Sandover*, his relaying of Ouija-board experi-ences to a world of readers, should be, and should have been, written in prose. Merrill's abandoned Sandover novel (with its suitable narrative themes of time, loss, and the American West) is a recurring preoccupation of the first half of *Ephraim*: but those novelistic issues appear in *Sandover* primarily as a foil to the lyric concerns of sensory knowledge, naming, and self-presence.

By the end of *Ephraim*, however, more fundamental regrets have replaced the second-guessing of the first few lines. It turns out that the tragedy of the lyric is not its difference from the novel, its failure to tell an engaging story well. Rather, the lyric problem is the problem of the poem's own composition: a deed that draws the writer of sensation and thought out of the material that inspires him, away from the world he used to visit reliably, and into the world of text, its equipment both more rigid and more ephemeral than what it describes. Merrill's response to this paradox is not synthesis but exaggeration: at the same time he opens up his poem to the void and hunches all the more closely over his alphabet. He creates a tight linkage between the far-fetched and the domestic, between the airy premises of the cosmologist and the merely drafty premises of the homeowner.

In Dante, the stars are a recurring image of stability and arrival, and the word "*stelle*" closes each canticle of his *Commedia*. The pilgrimage of *Sandover*, though, is an interior one; the protagonist JM stands in the last lines of each canticle in the same building where the poem began. At the most, he has traded one kind of chagrin for another: this is a poem of education but not of conversion. In answer to the outer world's reproach, the poet offers only his attentive presence, and offers it only from indoors. The stars are seen differently at different moments in the crypto-epic of *Sandover*. At the end of the first book of the trilogy, the poet is silent in response to Mother Nature's nighttime reproach; at the end of the second, an overabundance of light mirrors the overflow of discursive, humane explanation. And at the close of *Scripts for the Pageant*, the final volume of the trilogy, the stars outdoors are brought indoors, scrupulously, to the poet's table, as he returns to read his own words out loud:

A star trembles in the full carafe
As the desk light comes on, illuminating
The page I open to.

This reflection on the decanter answers Merrill's anxieties about the mismatch between stiff human forms and the beauty of the world's illuminations. It invokes at the same time the image of an actual star and that of the just-activated interior light, the desk lamp associated with the craftsman's work.[3] The "star" on the vessel belongs both to sky and to desk; the two possibilities are mutually exclusive, but the poem makes them coexist. Such inside-out representation is *Sandover*'s crucial trope, beginning with the sunny moment in the first section of *Ephraim* when the poet gives up on time's power to tell the story and writes it himself, in form, because "January draws this bright line down the page." It is a story that "time," by contrast, "would not tell." In synchronic images like that of a star activated by a human switch, nature's power and the poet's power are made coextensive on the surface of a domestic object.

Merrill employs a poetics both of stars and of desk, of the unaccommodated self in space and of its accommodations. The lyric simultaneity of these images makes it necessary to dissociate *Sandover* from novelistic form; but their substance in turn gives poetry an important element of hospitable generosity. The star at the end of *Sandover* does not shine on a glass, and certainly not on an empty teacup; it shines on a "full carafe." The drinks can soon be poured, since the poet and his collaborator have a guest in the flesh. Thus *Sandover* has brought to the fore Merrill's poetic sociability, and reconciled it with his lyric formality. The poem decouples that gregariousness at last from the novelistic arts of temporality and incident.[4] In his final volume of poems, *A Scattering of Salts*, he integrates that sociable artistic paradigm back into the short lyric form on which his career was founded.

The first poem in *A Scattering of Salts* is an experiment in which unadorned cosmology and the unadorned body are considered at the same time, starkly. The protective house is nowhere in evidence, and only the thin armature of wordplay and metaphor defends the vulnerable artist from abject exposure. Titled "A Downward Look," the poem ultimately manages to identify the intimidating, surveying gaze of a sun god with the self-regard of its protagonist. Featuring "limbs," "faults," and "a delta thicket," this world seen from far above is also the bathing poet's own body. Linking the warmth of shelter and firmament, the poem inhabits both the extremes of lyric privacy and universality. The smallest and the largest comprehensible scales of vision are one. But like its companion-poem, "An Upward Look," this extreme version of knowledge and self-knowledge is chastened by sorrow: as the poem closes, its protagonist

... hardly registers the tug

When, far beneath, a wrinkled, baby hand
Happens upon the plug.

The depth and wholeness the downward look embraces are recast at the close in the isolated encounter between a grasping hand and the object it grips. The final lines center the poem not on the warmth and radiance of the sun, but on the drain, the coming chill, and the highly localized warmth of the auto-erotic. The sky that such extreme poetry embraces shrinks to a single point of contact. Without other people to moderate these negotiations of scale, the trope of the inside-out veers toward extremes: the largest possible vision of the world, the smallest possible "plug" to drain its luxury.

Later in the volume, the nude poet of "A Downward Look" and "Swimming by Night" clothes himself, donning a jacket that is also a world map. This act in the spirit of the microcosm implicates him instantly in the protective technologies of the narrow culture of his day. Like the furnace of *Ephraim*, the title object of the poem "Self-Portrait in Tyvek$^{(TM)}$ Windbreaker" both enables and diminishes the poet's presence in his larger world. Tyvek, the synthetic substance that Merrill notes was "First developed for Priority Mail," is both representation and insulation. As eco-merchandise, the world-map jacket celebrates the atmosphere globally and blocks the wind locally. In relocating Bishop's trademark object, the world map, onto his sojourning body, Merrill adjusts her lyric problem of materiality to the idiosyncratic social realm he lives in. Other people claim a place in the poet's brooding, even going so far as to touch Merrill's chest above his heart and say "Voila mon pays" (This is my country).

The poet puts the jacket on "Over my blood-red T-shirt from the Gap" to unify his split physical and social self, to invoke his kinship with the unity of the globe. The "Guilty knowledge" of the poem is the difference between this stylish windbreaker, which represents all the world's water and land, and the real "breaker upon breaker on the beach," the clean outer world that smug environmentalists claim solidarity with. (That world is itself broken due to the clever pun linking wave and jacket, the beach polluted with the fragmentation of language — notably, Tyvek was "First used for Priority Mail," and this fabric-strewn beach is thus, like the one in "The Bight," "Littered with old correspondences.") To protect oneself from the weather with a synthetic jacket as a way of expressing one's awareness of the environment emblematizes, for Merrill, deeper estrangements intrinsic to artificiality itself: "Erotic torrents flash on screens instead / Of drenching us." This volume's final broken-hearted poem, "An Upward Look," with its failure of eros in nature and its split lines, is anticipated here, and anticipated more subtly than in the typographical aporia at the close of "Self-Portrait."

All these issues are under negotiation in the homage to Bishop, "Overdue Pilgrimage to Nova Scotia." In this final volume, *A Scattering of Salts*, Merrill is more self-consciously a nature poet than anywhere else in his body of work, and more conscious of his debt to Bishop. As they leave her hometown at the end of this oddly oblique elegy, the travelers in the poem admire a light rainfall: the drops, called "self-belittling brilliants," are both emblems of nature's power, like the stars, and images of Bishop's modest sensibility governing the pilgrimage in her honor. But the poem locates itself, in its final stanza, in an enclosed space in which human mechanisms of ornament and communication somehow coincide with that presiding spirit. Awkward near misses are the result: the hometown of the poem's opening is, after all, not Merrill's own but Bishop's; and the things he sees there are often not her relics but merely relatives of the things she lived with, objects in a museum "Miles later and hours away." The objects of the poem are just things nearby that happen to remind him of her writing, metonymies rather than actual mementos of her own historical youth. Moreover, there is no chronological method for encompassing and resolving the elegiac project.

In accord with Bishop's attitude about the absurd allure of the souvenir, Merrill spends a surprising amount of time on the inessential features of his pilgrimage — for example, features of the car and the drive *from* the village (rather than the drive to it, which a narrative version of pilgrimage would highlight). The poet and his companion "fill up" on thoughts of Bishop's "Filling Station" as they refuel their car, and this energy becomes meaningful on the drive out of town. They may know the poet "by heart," and therefore "foreknow" all the relics of her village, but the town itself "touches" them only "By not knowing how": as they drive away in sunlight, in the poem's first lines, "A shower of self-belittling brilliants" fall.

The storm makes itself seem less stormy as its elements are illuminated. Such is the experience of the observant tourist in nature, aware of many differently sized objects: her encounters with the world are marked and disrupted by incidental particles that distract her from the whole. This line also, one suspects, describes Merrill's experience of Bishop herself, a writer and conversationalist of "self-belittling brilliance." The third line of "Overdue Pilgrimage" thus offers a perfect and suggestive metaphor; it is easy to imagine it as the poem's final line. But it appears *first*, a perfect overview and synthesis of large and small — a synthesis itself doomed to be overwhelmed by particularity (the belittling details of the trip) as the poem continues. Dislocated from the conventional storyline of narrative pilgrimage, this poem lacks a satisfactory point of arrival. It has instead moments of lyric intensity, which may appropriately be analyzed out of order.

The challenge of this particular elegy is to resolve itself with an image that honors Bishop and also honors her modesty. As self-belittling as the raindrops may be, the lines that describe them are not belittling. Without becoming trivial, the poem must earn its smallness carefully. Revising the image of the raindrops, which are both crystalline and liquid, the final image of this poem is a very different meeting of the particulate and the watery.

The open terrain, it turns out, offered a false metaphor for the poet's work: her job is not to refract and sharpen the sky's light, or even to bring dynamism to the mucky particles of the world, as the waterfall does in a later stanza. The best emblem of the journey is instead a scene of darkness and of not being touched, a scene in which the storm of art's power, and the "emotions" with which it is artificially associated, are held away from the speaker by a necessary shell, the equipment of pilgrimage that has been obstructing its objects.

> So here we sit in the car-wash, snug and dry
> As the pent-up fury of the storm hits: streaming,
> Foaming "emotions" — impersonal, cathartic,
> Closer to both art and what we are
> Than the gush of nothings one outpours to people
> On the correspondence side of bay and steeple
> Whose dazzling whites we'll never see again,
> Or failed to see in the first place. Still, as the last
> Suds glide, slow protozoa, down the pane,
> We're off — Excuse our dust! With warm regards, —
> Gathering phrases for tomorrow's cards.

The car wash offers a better metaphor for art, as Merrill understands it via Bishop, than any piece of nature did. As always in this self-conscious poetics, the artificial space offers access to an experience that immediacy itself cannot.

Sitting in the dark, however, is a strange position for a pilgrim. Here the inside-out images of *Sandover* are recapitulated in a complex nesting, both of storm within storm and of warmth within warmth. The private storm that the protagonists occupy at the end of this poem, the car wash, offers both refuge from the power of the weather and access to it. Merrill finds his place in nature inside a shell that both sustains his experiences and seals him off from them. Indeed, in a paradox any reader of Bishop will recognize, those two effects are one: just as Bishop's village "Touched us by not knowing how," the "pent-up" emotional force of the Nova Scotia sky is released only in the dark, generic structure of the car wash.

Meanwhile, though, refusing to grieve, Merrill writes postcards, recording for the benefit of his friends an experience quite unlike the one he is having. The bright beauty of the picture postcard is the flip side of the darkness of its inked message, words that say from within a terrain charged with significance, "Wish we were here." This lyric pilgrimage, lacking the resources of narrative form, is saved from disappointment by the compensation that *Sandover* makes possible: the countryside's chilly sights somehow meet their match in the artificial snugness of the poet's warm regards.

This homage to Bishop, though, is not all about writing; the physical experience matters. In the crucial second stanza of "Overdue Pilgrimage," Merrill works to look through Bishop's eyes at her village (or perhaps at a different village) as it charmingly fails to be touching or evocative. This stanza about nature is the emotional core of the poem; moreover, it maps with suitable awkwardness the conceptual core of the Emersonianism featured in the present analysis. The manipulations of size that the poem stages feature the two critical images of this book, the house and the ocean; in each case, outsized nature and human shelters interact more closely than one would expect.

> The child whose mother had been put away
> Might wake, climb to a window, feel the bay
> Steel itself, bosom bared to the full moon,
> Against the woebegone, cerebral Man;
> Or by judicious squinting make noon's red
> Monarch grappling foreground goldenrod
> Seem to extract further essence from
> Houses it dwarfed.

In this passage from the second stanza, both scenes are crucially concerned with size — one features open water that is also closed to humanity, the other closed buildings somehow opened in nature. Bishop's mother, "put away" in an asylum, sets the theme of enclosure. The following visual experiences answer this fear by allowing the protagonist, a young Bishop within Merrill's imagination, to contemplate the freedom of open water and the consoling possibilities of making a home in nature.

Neither view, of sea or house, is possible without the frame provided by its counterpart: only the window on an upper floor makes nature's strength visible, and only the butterfly outside the houses makes it seem possible that there is sweetness within them. Indeed, to some degree these paradoxes undermine the things themselves: the bay stiffens within the frame of the conceptualizing window, while the insect seems to bring a titanic appetite that sucks the house dry, moving its legs violently to infuse the "gr" of "grappling" into the identity of the picturesque flower. The visionary requires herself to find both strength and nourishment in the world, but each dwindles as the other swells.

The mediating substance of these principles, as we have seen, is the grittier reality of dirt, its grains briefly translated into the silver of the fish scales and the twinkling planet but acknowledged as the final stanza opens to be a darker fact, both of nature and of relationships. The poem must culminate with the "dirty look" that the world turns on the rigorous Emersonian poet, whose imposition of personality is matched by an overwhelming sensitivity to the world's response. This is a look that nature poetry must both include and assuage. The description of a synthesizing, symbolic waterfall addresses this double mandate by being both the object and subject of a gaze. (In "McKane's Falls," a waterfall expresses this double status with a clever pun that also invokes Emerson's attention to the materiality of our lenses on the world: "So you've seen through me, sang the cataract.")

Bringing his vision of nature into human-made darkness, where weather can be best experienced, Merrill declines the child personae of Bishop's "To a Tree" and his own "The Broken Home." A simple look out a window cannot resolve the paradoxes of inside-out sight that he feels so sharply. (This is why *A Scattering of Salts* ends with the bleak and passionate poem of soil, "A Downward Look.") Not enabled by the artifacts of the village or even by the crafted phrase "self-belittling brilliants," the transition to a less self-regarding awareness of earth is made possible by other objects: the trees of the penultimate stanza. Like the reed of "Syrinx," these trees ground an eager, bright vision in seeing-equipment that (unlike the window and the flimsy, out-of-focus goldenrod) cannot be made transparent. Once the stubborn materiality of wood against the sky is acknowledged (albeit in passing), the poem is ready to acknowledge the materiality of dirt on the road of pilgrimage — and in the pilgrim's own "dust," his fragile body.

The trees bridge the first few stanzas' Wordsworthian quest for authenticity — involving shared memory, childlike whimsy, and human sympathy through imagination — and the collapse of that search, in the final stanza's celebration of the fake, with its tight juxtapositions of dark and light, cleanliness and dirt, and commerce and nature. This stanza of transition, with its apparently arbitrary image of the trees, activates a complex mode of confessional poetry for the purposes of the final stanza. In this mode, the point of reference is not the soul-searching letter but the breezy postcard, an object that marries an experience one might not have had with a "correspondence side" where the natural world's meanings are reduced to a collection of phrases.

The claim to be merely "Gathering phrases" is a surprising finish for a poem that began with the symbolic simplicity of the rain and the authentic, bio-graphically rich shyness of the late poet's hometown. The transitional stanza, then, is of crucial importance: even though the last stanza successfully embod-ies both the tourist's grit and his desire for catharsis, the penultimate stanza brings awkwardly together grounded self-consciousness and the symbolic mode of the outdoor pilgrimage. To a reader unaware of Bishop's interest in the solid, strange objects that enable visions of size, this transitional stanza might seem merely eccentric; but as an homage to Bishop the conversational geographer it is highly appropriate.

Look, those were elms! Long vanished from *our* world.
Elms, by whose goblet stems distance itself
Taken between two fingers could be twirled,
Its bouquet breathed. The trees looked cumbersome,
Sickly through mist, like old things on a shelf —
Astrolabes, pterodactyls. They must know.
The forest knows. Out from such melting backdrops
It's the rare conifer stands whole, one sharp
Uniquely tufted spoke of a dark snow crystal
Not breathed upon, as yet, by our exhaust.

The trees in this stanza have the features of the window and the flower from stanza two: they can be looked through, like wineglasses, and made to contain for savoring the natural space beyond them. Distance is the key theme the poet uses to locate his voice in this poem of homage and reportage. Without a theory of space he cannot know where he stands. He cannot begin to imagine "standing whole" without having encountered the late-winter forest — its trees made partial and inaccessible, not only bare but blurred by the car's velocity.

The cognitive crux of "Overdue Pilgrimage" resides in the wistful sentences that describe the apparition of the bare elms in the thawing threshold-coldness of very early spring. "They must know," the poet says: "The forest knows." The mysteries of the poem, not directly spoken, are mysteries of integration with the landscape, the "stems" of stability that provide a handle on distance itself: mysteries of Emersonian knowledge. The forest, forlorn and cumbersome, somehow has this knowledge. Though wooden, it is one with open natural space. Strikingly, though, the metaphors for this unity are eminently human ones: the trees are the vessel for the spirit of nature, "goblets" that make it possible for the connoisseur to handle it; and they are leftovers of some other experience, "old things on a shelf." Somehow in all their alien and cumbersome character the trees remind Merrill of the family crystal — they are glasses through and in which, on special and self-conscious occasions, the world can be seen and consumed.[5]

SUCH POETRY, celebrating both the gaps opened by art and the gaps it fills, is more true to Emerson's philosophy than he himself consistently was. This lineage in the poetics of incommensurability outdoes its founding writer: a prime example is Merrill's revision of Emerson's own key tropes of "Each and All." Like that poem of experience and souvenir, "The Blue Eye" centers on a beach that prominently features a seashell. Inconveniently, though, this favored poem of Merrill's in its last line alters Emersonian cognitive questions, to ask how one can know a person, rather than an object: "How shall we know him, then? By the light in his blue eye." Before turning to the epistemological shoreline-poem, then, one final consideration of lyric sociability in Merrill's work is called for.

As that line suggests, Merrill's poetry often handles distinctively socialized versions of the Emersonian problems of knowledge and the absolute.

Hence the negotiations of distance, size, and outdoor space deeply inform the construction of *The Changing Light at Sandover*. In the final scene of that poem, a newly widowed friend, Vasili, interrupts the climactic reading of *Sandover* itself. He arrives just as the reading is about to commence in Merrill's cottage — and also before an assembled otherworldly court, comprising dead souls that have been communicating by Ouija board with Merrill and his partner. As we have seen, the illumination of both scenes, the domestic and the cosmological, is achieved when Merrill turns on the desk light on this evening; the "stars" on hand are both real and imaginary. To describe the evening's staging of the difference between deeply felt life and poetically constructed afterlife, Merrill uses Emersonian terms of size, rather than morality or time: Vasili's bereavement, his close experience of death, makes him "Gulliver" to the Lilliputian poet.

That difference in scope between the mourning lover and the poet-philosopher, though, is minor when compared to the size of the gap at which the lover grieves, the abyss of death itself. Thus Gulliver (Vasili), dwarfing the poet, is himself dwarfed, more dramatically, by the magnitude of his sorrow, "the sucking waves." A stupefying vastness begins to loom over the scene. As Merrill starts to read his poem (and finishes writing it), he feels with new sharpness the difference between world and otherworld, our earthly home and the horizons of ultimate knowledge — and yet the text entangles them all tightly. The poem ends with the following passage:

> . . . Both rooms are waiting.
> DJ brighteyed (but look how wrinkled) lends
> His copy of the score to our poor friend's
> Somber regard — captive like Gulliver
> Or like the mortal in an elfin court
> Pining for wife and cottage on this shore
> Beyond whose depthless dazzle he can't see.
> For *their* ears I begin: "Admittedly . . ." (559 – 560)

The ambiguity here is intense: is the all-important audience, the "ears" of the last line, the "elfin court" or the mortals at hand? Which shore is "this shore" — that is, which world do we imagine, and which do we know? Are we transcribers (and readers) of a cosmology, or writers of it? At first, Merrill attempts to finesse the split between this world and the one elsewhere with the pliable word "both" ("Both rooms are waiting"); however, the final shoreline meta-phor deliberately eliminates that sense of the two chambers' proximity. That which is outside experience and that which is inside — ideal desires and present pain — confound each other entirely. The dazzle is both here and entirely elsewhere; so is the home; and Vasili is at once Odysseus and Penelope. As in the case of the shell-gatherer, knowledge's confinement to a domestic space coincides with an apprehension of "depthless dazzle."

In this intensely difficult passage at the culmination of Merrill's epic of learning, the poet and the reader must attend to the many and multivalent claims of cosmology, emotional work, and aesthetics. Fortunately, Merrill's lyric oeuvre offers us a simpler handling of these Emersonian problems of knowledge. The problem of incommensurability, the seashell problem of "Each and All," is treated directly in "The Cosmological Eye" — the very early poem that Merrill revised during the writing of *Sandover*, thirty-five years later, and renamed "The Blue Eye."[6] Both versions of the poem center on a persona who uses artificial means to confront nature, hoping to compensate for the unreliability of his senses. The nearsighted protagonist brings a mirror to the beach, hoping that he might see more precisely by bringing nature close as a framed representation. Of course, he is disappointed by the representation just as he was by the world itself; attributing his own myopia to the mirror's "parallel vagueness," he decides to regard only the stable and formless blue of the sky, believing that it is "realest." Not blurry like everything else, the blanks of sky and tilted mirror are identical — yet the protagonist insists on studying blue in the artificial frame of the mirror.

In "The Cosmological Eye" (1946), the protagonist's lapse from worthwhile earthy knowledge is blamed on the "horizon":

Blue of horizons made of yes and no
Clasps him from his fulfillment, from seeking blue
Shells and a blue wet feather.

Because the horizons of possibility and oblivion fascinate the protagonist, he neglects the particulars of the scene, the proper objects of knowledge. Those objects, "Blue shells," are "of less / Being to him than ideal blues," so he turns his mirror of art, which was supposed to bring things into focus, to frame the open sky that defies focal depth. The writer of "The Cosmological Eye" flatly condemns this turn to sky, asserting that poetry should be "keener-eyed," should be about objects rather than abstraction. It is an assertion any reader of modern American poetry will recognize and affirm: indeed, it is the key to the standard modern critique of Emerson's poetry (see chapter 1).

In a way, though, Merrill's tragic vision of cognitive weakness in the 1946 poem is too easy. It locates the poem's failure only in its protagonist, and implies with satisfaction that the poet himself knows fulfillment, in the suggestive sky blue of the shell and the feather. Only the wetness of the feather, an object dropped by the "elegant" birds of an earlier stanza, hints at the bedragglement of beach objects that Emerson bemoaned in "Each and All," when he described the seashells' failure to contain the beauty of experience's wholeness. The strength of Emerson's poem, indeed, was shown in chapter 1 to reside in the fundamental challenge posed by that episode to any simple idea of the relation between things and their context. In "The Blue Eye" (1981), decades later, a subtle revision transforms Merrill's *ars poetica* of shoreline from a self-satisfied recommendation of minuteness in poetry to a rigorous probing of Emerson's philosophy of part and whole.[7]

Minor adjustments to the staging alter the poem's emphasis: in 1981, the eye, like the mirror framing sky, becomes "blue"; and the mirror, like the eye seeking wholeness, becomes "oval." No longer are we to blame art for the failings of human perception, the problems of knowledge Emerson knew to be primal. However, the bizarre tableau of the mirror on the beach is not outgrown. On the contrary, it becomes a metaphor for experience itself. As Emerson puts the metaphor: "It is very unfortunate, but too late to be helped, the discovery we have made that we exist. . . . We have learned that we do not see directly, but mediately, and that we have no means of correcting these colored and distorting lenses which we are" ("Experience" III.43). For Merrill, both an affinity with sky (the eye's blue color) and nearsightedness (the blurring of nature's objects) are human characteristics, features of writerly knowledge — that is, Emersonian knowledge. Merrill now confesses to sharing Emerson's infinite philosophical ambition (and its accompanying numbness and uncertainty), of which in the earlier poem only the protagonist was guilty. Thus the poet, too, feels Emerson's essayistic urge to know "something more" than objects' imprint.

Of course, in 1981 as in 1946, Merrill also knows that the reading of such objects offers all the fulfillment we can expect. The poem must therefore locate incommensurate types of vision, myopia and presbyopia, in the same eye. The challenge is then set for the last stanza's lyric handling of the each and the all. A powerful pun and a new list of objects invite pragmatic readings of the poem, readings in which somehow the whole might be seen within the frame of the particular — but finally the most important strength of the passage is precisely its useless stasis, the blindness of its all-seeing Emersonian eye. As the poem nears this resolution, the protagonist rejects both abstraction and mute appreciation of nature, and vows that he will report the world, somehow. At the moment of representation, though, something more happens:

> Henceforth it is his pride no sooner to
> Frame in a sense the blood-and-thunder Sea
> (Its egg acrawl with noon deflecting summary)
> Than flash! horizons made of yes and no
> Tilt him beyond all telling — empty shell,
> Dropped feather, footprint drained of sky. How shall
> We know him, then? By the light in his blue eye.

Success is the opening note of the final stanza. The ambiguous, dynamic relationship between eye and mirror, experience and art, is perfectly encapsulated in the pun of the stanza's first line. To hold a mirror up to nature, as art does, is indeed in a sense to frame it; and to open an eye on nature is indeed to frame it in a sense. (A less clever pun closed "The Cosmological Eye" with similar ambiguity.)

However, this perfect doubleness, resolving the troubles of "Each and All" pragmatically by exploiting the flexibility of language, is "no sooner" achieved than Merrill undermines it. The "blood and thunder" of the sea are acknowledged, recording the scene's impact on senses besides framing sight. The poem registers oceanic depth and instability (inadequately depicted in critical art's flat, oval mirror) by calling the sea a three-dimensional "Egg deflecting summary." No phrase can summarize the scene: in a context as absolutely whole as the ocean, with its binary horizon (where only "yes" and "no" can be said and each obviates the other), experience moves out of language, "beyond telling," into a "tilted" realm of Dickinsonian obliqueness. There is no studying the moment, just as for Emerson there was no studying the shell. Here at the sea, in the space of transition, we feel the despair of "The Poet," "The inaccessibleness of every thought but that we are in"; here "On the brink of the waters of life and truth, we are miserably dying" (III.19).

This is the moment of transcendent experience that Emersonian poetry cannot forgo. There is nothing easy about it: the writing self's inadequacy and the eye's triumph in the landscape are both presented at once. "Fulfillment" here means an experience of wholeness — an experience coupled with the attention to small objects that "The Cosmological Eye" recommended. In the final lines, though, this doubleness is not accommodated in flexible language; Merrill turns here (and "henceforth") not to the pun but to the stiff and tiny emblem. The disappointing focal object takes the same form here as it does in "Each and All," the form of the "empty shell" — unconnected with its context except by an abrupt dash, and evoking both death and knowledge. Discontinuity, not spiraling ascent, is the dominant mode.

> Flash! Horizons made of yes and no
> Tilt him beyond all telling — empty shell,
> Dropped feather, footprint drained of sky.

This list of mere objects, with no progress written into it, encapsulates the poetics of "The Blue Eye": no longer claiming to mediate part and whole, the poem reports their incommensurability.

The stakes are higher here than in "Each and All," since retreat from the scene is never an option; in fact, the protagonist is drawn into it more deeply in the last stanza. Emerson's seashell, still empty of meaning, is joined here by a "Dropped feather" and a "footprint drained of sky" — these final two items, though lacking all narrative vigor, evoke the scene of Icarus's flight. Those icons of failure, the beach souvenirs already drained of meaning, are at the same time emblems of poetic surmounting. Perhaps (as the blue shell in "The Cosmological Eye" implied) they are objects "of sky." Such upward progress was the theme of Holmes's reading of the shell, but Emerson knew that higher cognitive ambition only increased the urgency of the fundamental problems of seeing and writing. Here those paralyzing problems are registered in the shoreline scene's total stasis, and in the corresponding lack of a verb to create a relation between these bare objects and their context.

At the close of "The Blue Eye," as if in preparation for *Sandover*, a question about personality intrudes into this poem full of objects: "How shall we know him, then?" The poet himself is now among the objects for reading on the beach. This final question echoes: it asks simultaneously how we can know about Icarus's heroism (by his dropped feather?); how we can discern the "winged" poet that Emerson called for (by her quill, or print?); how we can identify a body nature washes up before us (by Holmesean study of the corpse?); how we can know the dead (by animating an arbitrary "shell," like *Sandover*'s Ouija-board cup, to act in language?). These types of knowing — mythic, textual, scientific, elegiac — are all involved in the final question, which is itself a response to the list of disheveled beach objects that add up to no whole. Synthesis by puns has already been rejected; the question is too serious for that.

And yet the answer to these cognitive questions is, or seems, frivolous: we shall know the poet "By the light in his blue eye." Perhaps truth is being located in playful wit, in winking conversation like those that constitute *Sandover*. Such energies may, after all, offer adequate hints of the Icarean poet-figure's transcendent experience of sky. Indeed, the near rhyme of "eye" with "sky" reminds us of Emerson's linking of eye-circle and horizon-circle, which in turn suggests that the light in the blue eye might be the Platonic Sun (the ultimate Idea) or a sun god. A light in the eye, after all, is a reflection from elsewhere, even though we regard it as emerging from a core of personality. Like the turbulent cochlea echoing in a shell held up to the ear, this sparkling cornea offers to synthesize natural and human power, knowledge's subject and its object. The playful eye might be a symbol of the poet: both fully transparent and fully reflective, it might unify the powers of the mirror and the sky.

That possibility, however, cannot quite dispel the Emersonian seashell problem of small knowledge. The final stanza of "The Blue Eye," featuring so prominently and starkly the beach objects Emerson despaired of knowing in context, is anything but light. In such close proximity to emblems of the deathly body — especially the un-sightly shell from "Each and All" — the eye open for our examination cannot subordinate the boundless and turbulent world to itself and its sparkling personality. The seeing self must also be subordinated to the infinity it encounters. The absolute largeness of the shore-line context overwhelms the protagonist: the horizon "tilts" him toward the horizontal, and he becomes one of the clues of nature strewn on the sand. The poet is his own fossil, a shell of himself — dead in his tracks, his plume dropped as soon as it begins to write. We "know him" by infinity's reflection in his glazed eye.

Only in this last line, as it reflects without blinking the oblivious sky, does the protagonist's eye take on the suggestive blueness that the poem's title assigned to it. Emerson bequeathed to the American lyric this moment of aspiration "beyond all telling," the static moment in which the writer's eye strenuously finds itself among the puny trophies of boundless space. Criticism must learn from poets; at present, it has only old names for this fresh and agonizing failure of knowledge. The Emersonian writer is always Icarus, all washed up in the instant he leaves his feet; always Semele, burned out in a flash.

As I stood there alone and forsaken,
and the power of the sea and the battle
of the elements reminded me of my own
nothingness, . . . then all at once I felt how
great and how small I was; then did those
two mighty forces, pride and humility,
happily unite in friendship.
— Søren Kierkegaard,
    July 29, 1835

It is one of the *feelings* of modern philosophy
that it is wrong to regard ourselves in a *historical*
light as we do, putting time between God
and us; and that it were fitter to account every
moment of the existence of the Universe
as a new Creation.
— Ralph Waldo Emerson,
    September 23, 1826

Epilogue

All the value of an approach to literature can be found in its interpretive outcomes: the foregoing chapters must therefore justify themselves. Even so, I should acknowledge the philosophical framework undergirding the present analysis — not to enhance the argument's persuasiveness, or to paper over its idiosyncrasies, but just to situate such idiosyncrasies on their proper foundation. Tendentious, heedless of history, reductionist, eschewing methodical labor, impelled constantly to retrace tragic dichotomies: such a temperament, whether it befits the reader of Emerson or not, finds its justification in the philosophy of Søren Kierkegaard. The literary analysis undertaken in these pages is inspired by his manner of accounting for human sensation and insight: that is, in the stark and cold light of stringent theology.

Despite their shared iconoclasm, Kierkegaard and Emerson are contemporaries rarely mentioned in the same breath. Cognoscenti, asked to assign the attributions to the two facing epigraphs, would show little hesitation in assigning each writer's quotation to the other.[1] Of necessity, the two thinkers are opposed whenever power and accomplishment are at issue. From that perspective, they can hardly come near each other: Emerson preaches self-reliance, and few modern characters were less robust, on the page or in person, than Kierkegaard. But power and confidence are not the only categories of description. When a different interpretive perspective is chosen, the two philosophies snap into place, revealed as parallel epistemological endeavors. There is good sense in the writers' channeling of each other in the Epilogue's two epigraphs. Their disparity on the matter of puissance comes to seem not only inconsequential but also appropriate — they are, after all, thinkers for whom "Pride and humility happily unite in friendship." A certain set of philosophical choices, indeed, intertwines robustness with its opposite, in order to expose instead, on the cross section, issues of knowledge and human scope.

Unlike Emerson's, Kierkegaard's writings resist excerpting — it takes significant space to represent his thinking in his own words, rather than merely explaining his thoughts. In part, the extended quotations below serve to acknowledge the vast stylistic differences separating the existentialist Dane from Emerson, the incisively quotable American scholar. In another way, though, these Kierkegaardian rhapsodies must be displayed to show his oddity and unmannerliness, especially in *Philosophical Fragments*, a series of whimsical, self-mockingly pedantic thought-experiments. He can rarely be associated with an image or an aphorism, and speaks without gravitas; nonetheless, he is the primary patron of the shoreline ethos this book has described as an Emersonian property. His philosophy returns inexorably, abashed, fruitlessly, to the brink of infinity. As abstractly as he writes, he writes of the same sea.

> The paradoxical passion of the Reason thus comes repeatedly into collision with the Unknown, which does indeed exist, but is unknown, and in so far does not exist. The Reason cannot advance beyond this point, and yet it cannot refrain in its paradoxicalness from arriving at this limit and occupying itself therewith. . . . But what then is the Unknown? To say that it is the Unknown . . . does not satisfy the demands of passion, though it correctly interprets the Unknown as a limit; but a limit is precisely a torment for passion, though it also serves as an incitement. . . .
>
> What then is the Unknown? It is the limit to which Reason repeatedly comes, and in so far, substituting a static form of conception for the dynamic, it is the different, the absolutely different. But because it is absolutely different, there is no mark by which it could be distinguished. When qualified as absolutely different it seems on the verge of disclosure, but this is not the case; for the Reason cannot even conceive an absolute unlikeness. (35)

This cognitive boundary, the edge of absolute alienation, in the same moment incites and frustrates the passion for more knowledge.[2] Since there is nothing beyond it, there is nothing to be gained by confronting it. It blocks the curious mind just by removing all barriers. As Emerson, always more succinct than the philosopher of irony, put it in his most existentialist essay, "Experience": "Suffice it for the joy of the universe that we have not arrived at a wall, but at interminable oceans" (III. 42).

In this excerpt, Kierkegaard's insistence on constant return to a limit, without any advance beyond it, indicates how stubbornly his philosophy opposed itself to the diachronic system of knowledge Hegel had built. Practically conceding that he would persuade no one, Kierkegaard set out to needle Hegelians rather than to win them over. Achieving nearly nothing, epistemologically or rhetorically, was part of his project. He thought philosophical achievement was overvalued, and scorned Hegelian truth for having been "conceived in advance." For similar reasons, the Emersonian poetics designed in opposition to Hegel promulgate a sensibility that should rightly be called "Dickinsonian" (without the overtone of flightiness that that term has acquired). Like much of Emerson's philosophy, Dickinson's poetry of knowledge is not about accomplishment — or indeed, any kind of change. Publication was usually an afterthought, and within her texts even "Adventure" is an internal phenomenon (see poem 817). The poems that resulted from her extraordinarily strained stillness, and followed on it for several generations, embody prospectiveness without prospects; they are sensory poems of stasis. They cannot refrain from counterpoising humanity and that which is absolutely different. This tendency makes them remarkably impervious to today's most relied-upon interpretive instruments: for one of the most stalwart, and well-equipped, bastions of Hegel's mode of thought can be found in modern literary criticism.

Much recent interpretation of literature, absorbed with narrative change in history and making use of a dynamic epistemology superbly adapted to the novel, describes human knowledge as advancing inexorably (though not without difficulty). In such criticism's well-conceived cognitive schemes, time is the governing principle.[3] Epistemology is put into motion, and becomes hermeneutics. Tacitly adopting the premise of noncontradiction, such analysis assumes that a literary object, if it is to express opposite extremes of experience, requires sensible transitions. Some process must mediate between vigor and infirmity, winter and summer, gigantism and puniness. Under this interpretive lens every text is, in a way, a slice of an autobiography, and partakes of the same chronological sensibility that, to Western minds, unifies the parts of a lifetime. The text arranges opposite experiences into different moments, and mediates between them through the dialectical or progressive operations of narrative.

Thanks to its heritage, then, criticism in such a Hegelian grain usually constructs — whether under the guise of paraphrase, exposition, or contextualization — a "story of the text." For good reason, the critic seeks to shape unified stories out of opposed principles, and seeks to mitigate or overcome "[t]he inaccessibleness of every thought but that [which] we are in." Insofar as she is an instructor, then, ushering readers into well-formed structures of thought, the critic is (thankfully) no Emersonian of this tradition. A critic who arrays opposites reasonably across a timeline, buffering them with transitional processes, grounds that endeavor on the premise of noncontradiction — a premise that Dickinsonian writers tend not to share. In the case of the lyric, which may lack an intrinsic narrative element, the interpretive storyteller tends to default to textual biography, an accounting of how the text came to be written; thus the poem as an accomplishment draws more theoretical interest than the poem as an object. (Though it applies to the ungainly biographical criticism of twentieth-century philosophical poets, this tendency is especially pronounced in Dickinson studies. In older criticism, of course, there is a hint of condescension in the emphasis on Dickinson's "accomplishment"; in recent politically motivated criticism, there is a more worthy hidden agenda.) This critical maneuver, in its many sophisticated iterations, results from a bias toward narrative logic that has tended to plague even the least distractible interpreters of texts ever since Hegel transposed problems of Knowledge into processes of History.

With a stable footing in reasonable hermeneutics, scholarship about U.S. writing is enabled to consider relations of power, social imagination and negotiation, and human self-actualization. The essays of Emerson, on the other hand, if taken together as an aesthetically complex experience in a Dickinsonian vein, set fissures branching through the ground of knowledge. Acknowledgment of this American epistemology's basic strangeness might encourage new critical stances in the study of the U.S. lyric. Simply by emphasizing nature, in fact, Emerson's philosophy already parts company from the Hegelian worldview that governs much of our most useful modern self-understanding.[4] Hegel's project has to do with things that actually happen, through human device or the associated development of human spirit. He believed critical and philosophical thinking must cease to be static and hermetic: instead, his philosophy "aims at realizing the conviction that what was *intended* by eternal wisdom, is actually *accomplished* in the domain of existent, active Spirit, as well as in that of mere Nature" (*Philosophy of History* III.17). This axiom is congenial to both of the current trends in U.S. literary studies: not only historicist criticism but also renewed interest in pragmatism as a way writing is unified with activeness.

But Emerson generally directs his readers toward "mere Nature," the same realm that Hegel takes for granted and dismisses. Dickinson, never complacent, emphasizes that nature's meagerness; Frost its stubbornness; Bishop its artificiality; and Merrill its awkward domesticity. None of these emphases extends perception into new capacity or new insight; progress and achievement are not the goals. Each poetic seems in some way, instead, to turn perception inside out. In their philosophical texts, Emersonian poets in Dickinson's line do not attempt to work through problems of knowledge, but to embody those problems in outdoor space. In the resulting tableaux, equally composed of language and of spatial experience, they register the crisis of writerly experience that Emerson expressed in "Circles": "Our moods do not believe in each other. . . . I am God in nature; I am a weed by the wall" (II.182). As Emerson poses it here, the problem of reconciling such different sensations is a problem of belief — not one of accomplishment or even anticipation. Striving to address both the large and the small, temporally unmediated Emersonian writing engages the world not hopefully, in history, but strenuously, in space. To write is to inhabit opposite extremes, in disbelief: "On the brink of the waters of life and truth, we are miserably dying" ("The Poet" III.19).

The writings of Kierkegaard, no less than those of Hegel, address themselves to the problems of epistemology that have perennially been regarded as central to an understanding of nineteenth- and twentieth-century U.S. literature. Chapter 4 suggested that for Dickinson, Christology lies at the root of all rigorously conceived sensory knowledge in space. It goes without saying that the influence of theology is less overt in the later poets examined here, but the Dickinsonian recourse to sensation and to intensely felt paradox has Christological overtones in their work as well. In the subtleties of their respective epistemologies, moreover, these Emersonian writers partake of a long tradition of Augustinian thought, one that highlights irreconcilable opposites, rather than processualism or synthesis.

Opposites that go unmediated are anathema to Hegelian thought, as they are to narrative generally. If such oppositions turn out to be a basis of the lyric mode discerned in these writers, literary study will need complements to its predominantly story-oriented analytical technique. Kierkegaard is well suited to accompany the present proposal for one such kind of synchronic analysis, because of the way he compresses cognitive complexities into a single moment. In order truly to oppose a dynamic idea of knowledge, one must develop ways to characterize stasis, and give it texture: the alternative is speechless or unanchored awe. The shoreline, even as it creates just that feeling, can be seen as a response to this problem: a way of embodying, in nature, Kierkegaard's central paradox about knowledge. For his own part, Kierkegaard describes knowledge's pivotal moment not in a natural setting, but in a textual one, using theological discourse that is informed by (and also refreshes) the idea of the Incarnation. Without moving beyond its initial scenario, ignoring aftermaths of all kinds, his philosophy presents us again with the tragically clenched knot that unites the physical and the ideal — the puzzle at the root of all epistemology.

THE ANTECEDENT dilemma of knowledge is classically expressed by Kant, who asks how any relation can be established between phenomena outside the self and the creations of thought. What do the exterior and the interior have to do with each other, and why should we expect knowledge to link them reliably? Kant argues that we should let go of that expectation — but at the same time he concedes what Emerson feels, that the mind is drawn to experiences of the sublime, as the glimmer of an "unavoidable illusion" (*Prolegomena* 98). Kierkegaard imagines how that glimmer could come to be a human reality, and pierce the consciousness: he concludes that such an interaction can come only with radical, instantaneous change, at infinite price. Emerson, meanwhile, indicates without irony how such a price might be worthwhile. He addresses himself most forcefully of all Kant's successors to the seductive promise of infinite reach: the horizon's apparent suggestion that absolute knowledge is possible, not only commensurate with the human spirit but touchable by the eye.

The deep chasm that opens for Emersonian writers, despite this promise — between the small and the boundless, the particular and the general — is a challenge of natural history rather than history. In other words, it has to do with the ways people organize knowledge internally, into discrete categories, rather than the way they spread it contiguously across a timeline. In connection with Emerson's development of a philosophical posture in the Paris natural history museum, Lee Rust Brown points out that "[h]istory in the sense of its Greek root — as a systematic description of a fully present subject . . . — survived into the nineteenth century only in the term 'natural history'" (269n41).[5] Even that relic of the classical, static idea of history seems not to have survived into the twenty-first century: but it is this "full presence" of the world to humanity that Emerson urges constantly on his readers. For him, the point of thinking is to apprehend the structure of nature as the structure of the mind.

History itself was interesting to Emerson only as he perceived it: stepwise, in moments. This is the import of his claim "There is no history, only biography": in stating this, at the beginning of the essay titled "History," he does not mean that individual lives taken together add up to history—but precisely the contrary. Each life contains all history within it. (This why the next sentence reads "Every mind must know the whole lesson for itself—must go over the whole ground.") For Emerson, the individual mind was the fundamental molecule of cosmic integrity, the place where the world's unification exists first or not at all. For this reason, he often has more in common with American poets of nature, who find their perceptions significant without the benefit of company, than with Wordsworthian conversation-poets or American novelists of communal progress.

Among systematic answers more positive than Kant's about the basis of the human claim on true knowledge, almost all the classic solutions before Emerson are based on chronological arrangements.[6] Time is the governing principle of the key knowledge systems of Europe: Platonic knowledge is generated by regained access to prebirth omniscience;[7] Hegel's *Weltgeist* drives us forward through history to afford occasional glimpses of the absolute; and the elect Christian's knowledge is authorized by its relation to after-death omniscience. Absolute knowledge in all these cases inheres in the human, but is held away *at present*, for one historiographic reason or another (forgetfulness in the case of Plato, culture in the case of Hegel, and sin in the case of the elect Christian). Along the axis of time, ignorance and knowledge are arranged and disentangled without simply divorcing them.[8]

Secretly, though, such temporal solutions to the physical/ideal dilemma actually make experiences that happen — events of apparent consequence — less important rather than more. In the sweep of narrative, meaning tends to emerge precisely as detail and texture recede. Kierkegaard, in his inimitable way, explains why this is so. If profound truth can be accessed directly, through dialectics or concerted prayer, there is no need for excitement when it happens — because fundamentally, nothing has changed. "The underlying principle of all [progressive] questioning is that the one who is asked must have the Truth in himself, or be able to acquire it by himself. The temporal point of departure is nothing; for as soon as I discover that I have known the Truth from eternity without being aware, the same instant this moment of occasion is hidden in the eternal" (8). The emphasis on time, Kierkegaard claims, actually downgrades the significance of temporal experience, of real transition between qualitatively different states. The respective midwiferies of Socratic dialogue, Christian good works, and Hegelian world progress only draw out intrinsic human sapience and power; the whole story, ultimately, is germinated into humanity. Experience, in such a philosophy, adds nothing to the quintessence of the self. There is no such thing as learning, only manifestation.

Philosophical Fragments, however, opts to disagree with that foundational Hellenic premise, the postulate that knowledge's source is distant only in time (lapsed or in embryo). The first fact about humanity in Kierkegaard's philosophy is its capacity for true learning, which is to say, its remoteness from the truth. Thus begins an uncanny line of thought that leads the philosopher to eternity rather than history. Without the axis of time to arrange ignorance and knowledge, the philosopher acknowledges (observing our smallness) that truth is after all not inherent and entire within humanity. Knowledge comes at least in part from outside the human mind: from the world of bodies, objects right at hand, rather than the Platonic house of Forms that Kant condemned. The birth of knowledge is therefore not solely the human spirit surmounting and realizing itself; however — and here arises the particular difficulty of Western philosophy of the absolute — it must also not be solely an external fact, must not negate the self who craved it. The individual is not to be absorbed into the miasma of her own salvation.

In a philosophy of the moment, without buffering transitional stages, the discontinuity between ignorance and knowledge must be real and total, and yet human subjectivity must survive the break. To embrace these contradictory cognitive requirements, and to avoid a strict Kantian amputation of mind from truth, Kierkegaard holds that some sort of initial "teacher" is required, one who both participates in human fallenness and is distinct from ignorant humanity. Epistemological trouble focuses, then, on the moment of this teacher's incarnation (a birth in flesh that creates a distinctive emphasis on the physicality of knowledge, yet does not lead to anything recognizable as empiricism).[9] Ultimately, Kierkegaard focuses his speculation on the character of the "teacher" in this moment of paradox, the only moment in which absolute knowledge occurs: Christ, who is both entirely unlike humanity and entirely human.

In light of the consistently disappointing quality of human events, it is a strong point in favor of temporal philosophies that they do not hinge on how things turn out at any given point. But in order to believe in learning, Kierkegaard insists on an individualized story of true change, in which history is both consequential and surmountable by the human. Without an incarnational mystery, humanity might, per Hegel, spiral indefinitely toward absolute knowledge without ever needing to arrive at it. With such a sensational moment made thinkable, though, it becomes possible to focus on singularity rather than historical sweep: "Now if things are to be otherwise, the moment in time must have a decisive significance" (8). Why should things be otherwise, so that the "moment" of encounter with difference matters philosophically? Why should an instantaneous experience offer the only fullness time can possess? Kierkegaard will not engage this question; he knows there is no beating Hegel at his own game. He replies only that he is describing a different kind of epistemology: "The projected hypothesis indisputably makes an advance on [says something different than] Socrates. . . . Whether it is therefore more true than the Socratic doctrine is an entirely different question, which cannot be decided in the same breath" ("Moral" 93). Nonetheless, the purpose of his project is to defend the moment of intense encounter with the unknown from the status of mere jumping-off point, the relative obscurity to which Hegelian History would relegate it.

TO BELIEVE IN the importance of the human moment is to believe that human endeavors matter. Hence the human characters in Elizabeth Bishop's "At the Fishhouses," a fisherman and a writer, take on the charge of crafting lives and livelihoods almost directly out of cold vastness. The fisherman does this work dynamically, through oscillation: he must constantly negotiate "The water's edge," where

> Up the long ramp
> descending into the water, thin silver
> tree trunks are laid horizontally.

For this pragmatic task he has tools and substrates — the trees themselves, and the fish he fetches home from the ocean and renders ugly: "He has scraped the scales, the principal beauty, / from unnumbered fish with that black old knife." The protagonist, on the other hand, has only eyes and hands; and it is not her job to "clean" the sea's products for consumption, but to keep beauty intact.

"At the Fishhouses" is a better poem than the more anthologized Bishop text "The Fish," because in the latter poem Bishop attempts to blend the characters of poet and laborer. Like the Frost of "Two Tramps in Mud-Time," she works as a hobbyist to sample the nourishment from nature that others would extract on an economically meaningful scale. In the absence of economic meaning, her day of work must develop some other kind of narrative closure — and thus "The Fish," a superbly descriptive poem of encounter with an uncanny natural object, ends with the least rigorous image, and the least captivating two lines of verse, in all of Bishop's work. The image transforms seafaring equipment — the oil from an old outboard motor — into a promise of future redemption, and of forbearance from the flood that required the boat in the first place: "Everything was rainbow! rainbow! rainbow!" This shortcut to a vague redemptive future stems from the poem's true underlying weakness: its proclivity for narrative shape and closure of its own. It longs to be a fish story, rather than a poem about a perch.

The force of Bishop's poem is all in her eye (or should be). The fish's eye resembles isinglass, and the drama of its presence comes only from the way Bishop's words operate upon it. The object between worlds, a piece of nature in a poem, is itself simply a fish out of water, and in a lyric framework its destiny is of no inherent interest. But once the poem is thought of as a narrative, and the poet as a kind of laborer, the writer who lives in details has to will intrinsic value retroactively into the essence of her object. Bishop does this here by granting her object total freedom from the eye that made it worthy of attention: "And I let the fish go." Environmentally responsible though this choice may be, poetically it is a claim to eat one's fishes and then have them too. It implies that nature can be both small in the hand and at large in the sea. Narrative is the culprit here — only on a timeline can both a capture and a release be unproblematically real. The reader's feeling of anticlimax is not the result of poor narration, but of narration out of place, directing an experience whose interest should be in sensation rather than incident.

As she ambles along the shoreline, away from the fisherman's shed, in the body of "At the Fishhouses," Bishop's speaker finds her attention repeatedly drawn outward to the ocean. There are describable objects on the shore, and inland, but description keeps turning toward the unknown and unnamable. In that impulsive, outward look are all the mysteries Kierkegaard found it necessary, for no particular reason, to address.

Cold dark deep and absolutely clear,
the clear gray icy water . . . Back, behind us,
the dignified tall firs begin.
Bluish, associating with their shadows,
a million Christmas trees stand
waiting for Christmas. The water seems suspended
above the rounded gray and blue-gray stones.
I have seen it over and over, the same sea, the same
slightly, indifferently swinging above the stones,
above the stones and then the world.
If you should dip your hand in,
your wrist would ache immediately,
your bones would begin to ache and your hand would burn
as if the water were a transmutation of fire
that feeds on stones and burns with a dark gray flame.

When she lacks recourse to redemptive equipment like the Christmas trees, the body is the poet's only locus of meaning. Since the season can never change during the span of a poem, here in the lyric, such equipment as the trees can only "wait" indefinitely for deployment. In the moment itself, though, impossible sensations can be imagined. The mind projects itself not forward in time, to Revelation, but forward in space, into the water before it. The imagination, touching nothing, touches the all that is the water — absolute, inhuman cold.

The Emersonian perceiving mind has an instinct to reckon with just what is least amenable. In this worldview, in which transcendence is a human endowment, uncanniness is part of thinking: Socrates, for example, according to Kierkegaard, "could not make up his mind whether he was a stranger monster than Typhon, or a creature of a gentler and simpler sort [merely] partaking of something divine. This seems to be a paradox. However, one should not speak slightingly of the paradoxical; for the paradox is the source of the thinker's passion. . . . But the highest pitch of every passion is always to will its own downfall" (29). Thus far this passage echoes strongly with Emerson's ruminations on the questions of a human's infinite nature — what sort of hybrid is this stalky biped, who feels himself also to be titanically powerful? Their similar urgings against habit and tedium indicate that Kierkegaard shares Emerson's sense of the world's oddity, and of human power. But the metaphor he chooses next is quite inconsonant with the conventional Emerson with whom the student of American literature is familiar. The following sentences focus not on the mystery of human surmounting, but on the mystery of falling. Kierkegaard's message here sounds more like that of Jonathan Edwards. "So for example the scientists tell us that our walking is a constant falling. But a sedate and proper gentleman . . . thinks this to be an exaggeration, for his progress is clearly a case of mediation; how should it occur to him that he is constantly falling when he religiously follows his nose!" (29). The word "religiously" here is used sarcastically, in Edwardsean disdain for the genteel Hegelian religiosity of moderation and synthesis. (Edwards disrupted his church community, and was forced out of the pulpit, by his insistence that bourgeois family solidarity had nothing to do with salvation.) Kierkegaard is an advocate of extremity, and his vertigo develops from the same basis — the same fallingness — as the Puritan sensibility undergirding Emerson's most rigorous aesthetic.

The truth about the ocean, as Bishop asserts powerfully in "At the Fishhouses," is that it cannot be left alone, and it cannot be consumed: "If you tasted it, it would taste bitter, / then briny, then surely burn your tongue." The sequence of these adjectives is important: the flavor-word "bitter" is replaced not by its commensurate term "salty," but by the empirical, nonculinary word "briny." As the analysis of Holmes in the Introduction showed, the sea is too foreign and too vast to be alimentary. Its impossible size says along with Kierkegaard's paradox, lyrically, irrationally, "Comedies and romances and lies must needs be probable, but why should I be probable?" (42). Its characteristics cannot be acculturated — indeed, they cannot even be spoken. The burning tongue of the poet at the end of Bishop's sentence represents the fact that not even flatly descriptive language like "briny" can make any linguistic claim on the seawater: it overwhelms any sense one brings to bear, acting violently upon the fleshy implements that are assigned to act upon it. And yet, she says in the closing lines of "At the Fishhouses," it can be named in the homeliest of terms: "It is like what we imagine knowledge to be."

The final lines of "At the Fishhouses" are justly admired for their beauty, and in contemporary poetry criticism they are famous for all the wrong reasons. Like Dickinson's line "I dwell in Possibility," the poem's last phrase, "flowing, and flown," has become a buzzword for critical predilections that are in many ways alien to the full meaning of the passage. The phrase often becomes a tool for critics, a handy crowbar by which other poetic phenomena, sometimes even in other oeuvres, can be opened and unfolded.[10] Luis Alberto Brandão Santos writes one of the most moving declarations along these lines, telling a story of the lyric remaking itself as progressive narrative. In arguing that "At the Fishhouses" sheds light on the close of Bishop's "In the Waiting Room," he asserts that the waters of this poem can be sampled, to enable a sacrament that returns the little girl of the other poem to her proper self after her vertiginous lyric experience: "Historicized, identified, the subject who describes becomes the narrator subject. In the waters of history, the subject is finally baptized" (in Almeida et al., 88). For Santos, the lyric moment needs to end at long last, and the historicized textuality emerges to rescue the historical subject from being dissolved by poetry.

Such handling of an ocean-poem is highly germane and mannerly in our present critical moment. Scholarship is relatively uninterested in lyric modes, except as they help us understand the differences among subjects carefully situated on a demarcated timeline of shifting identity concepts. But to make *water* the vessel of granulated history is to colonize it for understanding in the terms of human knowing. Historicist analysis tries to call to the sea in the language of History that Hegel developed for the space of "accomplishment," inland sites of contestation. Such interpretation, despite its better instincts, elides difference rather than acknowledging it — finding in ocean flux the same directed dynamism that characterizes inland work, and finding in what Bishop calls quite explicitly and emphatically "The same sea, the same" all the historiographic differentiation one can desire. Moreover, and most important, it neglects the possibility of something happening than which "Nothing stranger had ever happened," and "Nothing / stranger could ever happen." To the poet of "In the Waiting Room," that *something* is simply incarnation.

Most readings of these last lines of "At the Fishhouses" take for granted that Bishop's words mean what historical criticism is always saying, the outcome it has conceived for good reasons in advance — that knowledge must be contextualized, that conceptual and social structures contain the objects of poetry, and that suffering can be reduced with a properly educated sense of human limitation. All of these things are probably true; but there is scant evidence for them in "At the Fishhouses" — with its placid, unaltered setting; its featureless water on the brink of swallowing all human-made objects; and its motionless encounter with fiery waters through which no one can pass. The embrace of "history" in its final lines, instead of celebrating temporal contextualization, names this Emersonian aesthetic's antipathy toward narrative itself.

In these last lines the water, which has continued to tug at the speaker's attention, occupies her thoughts entirely.

> It is like what we imagine knowledge to be:
> dark, salt, clear, moving, utterly free,
> drawn from the cold hard mouth
> of the world, derived from the rocky breasts
> forever, flowing and drawn, and since
> our knowledge is historical, flowing, and flown.

This sentence is almost universally taken to express the subjection of the human to the flow of History, and her enlightenment about her own puniness in context before its unending chronological power. The key principle in such readings of this poem is dynamism, the *rivus* (brook) of the word "derived." But in such a case, Bishop the perfectionist would have known how to make it clear that mightier forces than her own imagination are at work. For one thing, to leave herself out of the picture, she would have opted for the present rather than the past participle, and made "derive" an intransitive verb. The independent power of History's knowledge, if that is what this passage is about, would have been expressed more properly. Surely in its own tidal strength it would not be "derived" but "deriving from the rocky breasts forever." Instead of crediting the waves with their own force, though, the speaker locates agency elsewhere — in herself, standing with senses awake in the scene and creating anthropomorphisms of the seafloor; and in "us," the ones who with her imagine knowledge into existence at every moment. This is why the first line of this passage is so strange and willful, in its Bishopian determination to convert oblivion into factuality, beleaguered insularity into conceptual mastery (an effort that is the precise obverse to Thoreau's claim about the useful well: that in it you should see the ocean and your own smallness). This is why knowledge is said to be "drawn" from the world rather than issuing spontaneously for the sailing or surfing human to engage. It moves itself and yet is under the gravity of the mind. "The eye is the first circle; the horizon which it forms is the second" — likewise, the seawater that is like knowledge does not exist until the knower sees it.

A diachronic reading here reflexively pounces on the word "historical" — and indeed, no word seems better calibrated to vindicate historicism's insistence on presence within a particular cultural moment, on contingency and spontaneity, on instability. But Bishop could not have foreseen that "histori-cal" would come to mean "culturally imbricated" rather than (as philosophers used it) "non-eternal." If knowledge is a "drawing" — that is, an artist's depic-tion as well as an emergence or a deed — this word takes on different shadings. One way to shade it, with chapter 3 in mind, is to notice the oceanic power of the speaker in these lines — unable to dip her hand into the water, she is none-theless able to move as freely as it does under its surface, surging gently with the powerful small kicks of her own commas in the second line quoted above. Another way to shade it, with chapter 2 in mind, is to notice the hard objects of the enjambments, the "hard mouth" and "rocky breasts" of the body, the Frostean objects that make that motion seem merely decorative, a futile kick-ing against the stoniness of impenetrable existence.

Yet a third way to encompass the term "historical," so that it fits properly into the beauty of this perfectly balanced poem, stems from Kierkegaard's championing of synchronic Christology. As we have seen, the philosopher claimed that it is only in a Christological system of knowledge that a moment can be decisive. In the Hegelian worldview, any particular moment is insig-nificant, because the flood of History cannot be essentially affected by it: "As long as the eternal and the historical are external to one another, the histori-cal is merely an occasion" (49). Bishop in these lines dreams of making them internal to one another, for the ocean's movement is "forever" and yet also "historical" — and it is somehow also "like what we imagine knowledge to be." In the ocean metaphor for knowledge's most extreme possibility, eternity and historicality are mutually containing categories.

In the course of insisting that no temporal gap can forestall access to re-demptive meaning, Kierkegaard names the necessary mutual interdependence of the eternal and the historical. For him, as for Dickinson, "Gethsemane" is not an event but "A Province — in the Being's Centre" (670). The ocean there-fore would matter to Kierkegaard, not just because it interacts with — and is historicized by — the human imagination, but because at the same time it never changes.

Whatever can be essentially differentiated by time is *eo ipso* not the Abso-lute.... [T]hough the Absolute is declinable in all the *casibus* of life, it re-mains itself ever the same; and though it enters continually into relations with other things, it constantly remains *status absolutus*. But the absolute fact is also an historical fact. Unless we are careful to insist on this point our entire hypothesis is nullified; for then we speak only of an eternal fact. The absolute fact is an historical fact. (84)

For these two writers, the "historical" is the sharply felt counterpart to eternity — not victorious over eternity but entangled with it. "The absolute fact is an historical fact" — historicity is an element of all knowledge, not an implement of terminology with which the scholar can needle the belletrist.

Because Bishop's ocean refuses human scale, it threatens to make the poem that would contain it an insignificant thing — in Kierkegaard's words, "a mere matter of memory," rather than of knowing (8). And indeed the final line seems at first to suggest the importance of memory — like Keats's nightingale song, the sea and the knowledge it resembles are "flown" in the final phrase. It seems the poet is impotent before the ravage of time — a wide perspective cancels out the poet's deriving power, the Emersonian energy with which she confronts nature. But the word "flown," even while it contains and puts out of reach the flowing world, is also still contained by "flowing." The movement of the poem continues all the way through its last word. The power of the moment of vertigo "above the stones" persists in these last lines (as perhaps it does not in the very last lines of "In the Waiting Room," and as it certainly does not in the last line of "The Fish"). In a way, paradoxically, the poet succeeds at capturing the flux. To understand this doubleness — this mutual containment — criticism needs a Kierkegaardian perspective.

The historical nature of boundless knowledge is precisely what Kierkegaard sets out to preserve — as he says, "This is what makes it so difficult to effect an [absolute] understanding: that the learner becomes as nothing *and yet is not destroyed*; . . . that he understands the Truth and yet that the Truth makes him free" (24, emphasis added). Living in time, on land, must not become inconsequential, no matter how transcendental the pure, cold knowledge that supervenes. Without drowning the writer whose solid materiality constitutes her, then, the unknown ocean must be encountered in its absolute otherness. This philosophical dilemma can be regarded as a practical problem of representation. The dynamic, "flowing" presence of the tide must coexist with the secure, indoor absence of the writer, who tries as part of her land-bound livelihood to write down that "flown" vista. As soon as the writer becomes aware of the way her senses draw nature's characteristics forth, she is already drawing her object — and therefore already absent from it, already writing, her object already escaped into the remoteness of the seascape.

Thus in the moment itself writerly absence is the troublesome reality of experience. For Kierkegaard and for Bishop, this is an insoluble problem of belief, even for those who (like the dreaming speaker in the final lines of "Over 2,000 Illustrations") witness Christian miracles with their own eyes. "Though a contemporary learner really becomes an historical eye-witness, the difficulty is that the knowledge of some historical circumstance . . . does not make such an eye-witness a disciple" (Kierkegaard, *Philosophical Fragments* 49). For Kierkegaard, this is true of nature as it is of Christ. Presence and "immediacy" cannot substitute for the deeper, ontological knowledge that no sensory input can do more than suggest. "Everything that has come into being is *eo ipso* historical . . . nature has a history . . . This is nature's imperfection[:] that it has no history in any other sense; but it is a perfection in nature that it nevertheless has this suggestion of a history[:] *namely that it has come into being*. This constitutes its past, the fact that it exists is its present" (62). Absurd as this definition of history may seem, it has an impressive pedigree: indeed, when taken in this sense the word "history" denotes a task assigned to writing in antiquity, a task that Emerson and these successor poets manifestly undertake. And as pointless as this definition of history may seem, it is an alternative that might be important for other reasons in the early twenty-first century: Witold Gombrowicz wrote, "It is only by opposing History as such that we can oppose today's history."[11]

In dividing nature, the lyric writer believes that there is only one division that matters: between what is known and what is not known. Not content with the resulting subset of the world that is within her range, she undertakes with Emersonian ambition to account systematically for that primal act of division itself. The edge she constantly retraces and the fall from wholeness of which it is the scar are elemental to her definition of the human. Her elemental belief is: she has things to learn.

In presence itself, then, and not necessarily in the march of time, is the vanishing point of Emersonian sensory reality, which like the horizon is always flown as it recedes before the opening eye. The American writer, a beachcomber who encounters the brink of continental space, must engage with the idea of history rather than the promise of History. She is first and always a natural historian. For her, knowledge is no ongoing experience, but a sciential flash, a violent instant of contact between the mental and the phenomenal. The historicity of knowledge predominates in the heart of the least historic of land-scapes, the shoreline — and exists there more purely and with more difficulty than anywhere else. Hence no historicism can touch as directly as aestheticism does the historical knowledge that most thrills the Emersonian eye.

And, to be sure, the eye cannot touch it either, any more than it can encapsulate the horizon. These philosophers of natural history, unlike students of culture, can offer no answers. Yet the stark airiness of this landscape gives it the greatest bearing — not the least — on problems of human marking, problems of representation in time and of embodied thought. More perfectly than anything else, the beach horizon occupies the spread hands of the American poet as she draws them together with the world; yet ironically, this historical power relies on the perfect abstraction of the way it represents eternal, unmediated size. At the brink of infinity, within this soul-built horizon, the "cold hard mouth" of the flowing world can never be more chilling, never more indifferent, and never more miraculously eloquent.

Notes

One. The Beachcomber's Horizon

1. It is notable, in this light, that matters of epistemology play little role in current studies of Emerson (he is more often admired as a theorist of Thoreau's antitheoretical hermeneutics). But it is even more remarkable that Emersonian cognitive efforts are so often called triumphalist, even though they so often fail.

2. Richard Poirier, in *A World Elsewhere*, expresses a narrative problem that might at first seem similar: "The creation of America out of a continental vastness is to some degree synonymous in the imagination with the creation of freedom, of an open space made free. . . . Describing the situation in images which most often embody it in American literature, we can say that American writers are *at some point* always forced to return their characters to prison" (7, 29, emphasis added). This claim is different from mine because Poirier's emphasis is on a hope dashed by events rather than on a vision paralyzed by philosophical necessity.

3. Other members, of course, might be T. S. Eliot, Hart Crane, H.D., A. R. Ammons, and even Walt Whitman; on the other hand, the dynamic seascape poetry of Wallace Stevens is the most powerful antagonist to this line. His poetic project is rigorously conceived and perfectly opposed to the ones examined here.

4. The field offers many precedents for this reciprocal methodology. To choose a pertinent example: critical vision of Emerson's narrative power came to fruition in Poirier's *A World Elsewhere*, a reading of Emerson through the lens of later American novels. My project reads Emerson through the lens of lyric poetry instead, with the aim of beginning to trace a lyric Emersonianism parallel to the narrative one Poirier described.

5. This gap is one that Cavell feels more tragically in other places, and one that Richard Rorty strives cleverly to span. In response to the challenge, Cavell, Poirier, Elisa New, and other pragmatist readers have shown that the Emersonian imagination is found as well as founded, that it is receptive as well as concupiscent. This finding in turn has greatly enriched the doctrine of Joel Porte and others that, from the very beginning, "The fictional quest for knowledge of the wilderness was synonymous — as in the Emersonian equation — with the desire and need to explore the self" (*Romance* 228).

6. It is now fourteen years since Elisa New wrote, "It is beginning to be noticed how much of our theory is narrative theory" (*Regenerate Lyric* 8); with few exceptions, theory of the lyric since then has become more narrative rather than less.

Memory and hope, and the obstacles to them, now govern and enable many excellent readings of poems, just as they govern our readings of history and novels. This book is an experiment in neglecting those temporal categories in favor of spatial ones. The experiment will be justified if it can show how these poets invite and reward such atemporal reading.

The narrative approach extends well back into Emerson scholarship as well: Stephen Whicher's intellectual biography of Emerson sees him progressing from liberation to acquiescence, and H. H. Waggoner makes the narrative approach a central element of Emerson's own thought: "It seemed to Emerson that man's situation was at once precarious and immensely hopeful" (181) — that is, oriented toward future events. Sacvan Bercovitch, less universalizing, treats classic American literature as a supple and ongoing negotiation of collectivist and individualist concerns — again, an unfolding story rather than an examination of moments. Jonathan Levin aligns Emerson with the pragmatists, and asserts that for Emerson, "If no fact is sacred in itself, it is because its sacredness is instead a function of its transitional unfolding" (2).

7. Myra Jehlen has argued convincingly (in *American Incarnation*) that this paradox can be a useful screen for other agendas: it creates the American leverage on the landscape that enables many economic claims on the world as "property."

8. Leo Marx's *The Machine in the Garden* closes by lamenting exactly this lack of a middle ground.

9. Emerson to Mary Moody Emerson, quoted in S. Whicher, 18.

10. "Sinners in the Hands of an Angry God," in Baym et al., *Norton*, 480.

11. See Bercovitch, *American Jeremiad*.

12. Foremost among these critics is Richard Poirier, who in *Robert Frost, The Renewal of Literature*, and *Poetry and Pragmatism* has argued for a highly effective Emersonian epistemology of linguistic flex and skeptical self-attenuation. An extension of this pragmatic Emersonianism of nature is found in New (*Line's Eye*), and Levin deploys temporal terms to the same end in analyzing the Stevensian poetics of "transition."

13. *Representative Men*, "Goethe: or, the Writer," *Collected Works* IV.151.

14. Cognitive success of this type, identifying part and whole, undergirds our ideas about critical knowledge as well as knowledge of nature. The central premise of the New Criticism (Cleanth Brooks: "What is true of the poet's language in detail is true of the larger wholes of poetry" [192]) is still a necessary premise for most literary-critical writing, since analysis must focus on evidence much smaller than the textual whole it seeks to describe.

15. See also Cameron, *Writing Nature*, on Thoreau's journals' disciplines of encounter with nature, and Buell, *Environmental Imagination*, 118, on the "romantic poet . . . beginning also to become the natural historian."

16. The primacy of Emersonian authority in constantly refreshed American analytic thought is anticipated in Emerson's own cheery formulation of Harold Bloom's influence theory: "All minds quote. Old and new make the warp and woof of every moment. There is no thread that is not the twist of these two strands" (quoted in Holmes, *Emerson* 296).

17. Lee Rust Brown describes this dynamic brilliantly without extending it to the

troublesome category of infinity: "Emerson upsets empiricist epistemology with a more extreme empiricism, asserting that the leading edge of experience cuts its way through the world at a point beyond the direct grasp of knowledge" (173). This phenomenon becomes problematic at the horizon, which is not only the leading edge of knowledge — it is a kind of edgelessness.

18. See crucially New, *Regenerate Lyric*. While relying heavily on New's championing of theology in U.S. poetry, the present study seeks to show that Emerson should be included in, rather than poised against, this poetic of incommensurability.

19. In Holmes, *Autocrat*, 97.

20. Holmes, *Emerson*, 309.

21. "Each and All," in Emerson, *Essays and Poems*, 448. The central episode of this poem hints at issues of literary representation and criticism as well as of experience in nature. It was Wordsworth, in the "Dream of the Arab" episode, who first equated the fragile readability of book and shell; for us, the seizing of the shell from its vast context may serve to characterize our contemporary writerly reader, the critic who extracts a quotation from context and transports it into her own textual space. The resulting problem of incommensurability between the quotation and the full text of which it is a sample seems, appropriately, to cause special trouble for critics of Emerson.

22. David Porter, expressing the critical consensus, associates readerly disappointment in the final lines of "Each and All" with Emerson's abstraction, his neglect of nature's particulars. Porter's critique is that "retreating from the complicated and apparent to the abstract was the inevitable result of Emerson's enormous impatience for the clarity of large truths: '. . . The only way . . . [is] to kick the pail over, and accept the horizon instead of the pail'" (*Emerson* 8 – 9). In this poem, however, which Porter condemns most strongly for such a retreat, Emerson's speaker flees from just such a clear, uncomplicated horizon, clutching a beachcomber's pail full of shells, and goes out again only as far as the river. Remarkably, he avoids his self-imposed poetic task not by turning to a bare horizon, but by failing to return to it.

Two. An Everywhere of Silver

1. *Representative Men*, "Goethe: or, the Writer," *Collected Works* IV.151.

2. The pioneer of such criticism is Richard Poirier, who argues for Frost's "satisfaction not in the results of his labor but in the labor itself" (*Robert Frost* 288). In the crucible of work, in Poirier's reading of Frost, resistance and consent to nature's objects come to be one. Systematic criticisms have been built on this foundation. Jonathan Levin, for example, praises the "[r]adically qualified will" in "transition" that characterizes the Emersonian self. Elisa New finds the American experiential difference in the ability to mediate and blend cognitive dynamism and receptivity: "The peculiar discovery of American philosophy is that what really matters is not what comes first, mind or world, our power or its power, but rather the instant in which the potentiality or force of both are caught up together in a specific operation" (*Line's Eye* 13). Bonnie Costello follows on New's work with a consideration of seven

more recent U.S. poets, in the 2003 volume *Shifting Ground*: "Landscape, that pro-spective gaze in which man dominates over the scene, must submit to the reciprocal gaze of nature" (87).

3. Interpreting this sentence, Bercovitch transposes it into a narrative of his own device: in his reading, this infinitely receding America may be "unapproachable today, but tomorrow (Nature had whispered to him) [it would be] the city of 'the lords of life'" (*Puritan Origins* 179). Allowing the future (here in a snippet from the essay's timeless epigraph) to dominate the present, Bercovitch shows the difficulty of ideology's "[p]recarious leap from the first term to the last" (*Puritan Origins* 180). Poirier's understanding of such moments in Emerson is stricter, and more pertinent for the purposes of this book: "Emerson himself recognized the limits of his own enterprise, [and] had a tragic view of the disparity between desire and possibility, all the more so because the physical continent of America sometimes seemed like a bridge between the two" (*Renewal of Literature* 70).

4. Hence, for example, this clause from the opening sentence of Budick's book-length study, *Emily Dickinson and the Life of Language*: "Dickinson chose, in effect, perhaps even with full philosophical self-awareness, to concern herself, not with ob-jects or people or events, but with words themselves" (preface).

5. The proposals for sufficiency trotted out in those sentences of "Experience" — ocean as "hint" of vigor, ocean as a setting for the "vector" of human longing, human longing as "impulse to believe," impulse to believe as proof of unmediated power, unmediated power as transcendence of space — recover the essay's jauntiness. But at the end of this sophistry, space itself is reduced to meaninglessness: "I exert the same quality of power in all places" (a boast undermined immediately by what should be a needless exhortation, "Onward and onward!"). The claim is given the lie throughout an American literature obsessed with self-location within even its most fancifully contrived spaces.

6. Barbara Packer's is far and away the strongest version of a narrative Emersonian philosophy. She describes him as seeking "[a] theory of origins that can explain both how nature came to resemble us and why it presently holds itself aloof from us" (43). Hence, for Packer, Emerson's project is much less about sensation than about myth.

7. See New, *Regenerate Lyric*, 168, on the theological importance of Dickinson's unwillingness to go directly against the grain.

8. A more fragmentary poem mulls this same image as both a figure of mutability and intercourse and a residue or shard of selfhood in the aftermath of loss:

Each that we lose takes part of us;
A crescent still abides,
Which like the moon, some turbid night,
Is summoned by the tides. (1634)

9. Not incidentally, the poem is founded on its inability to place the copula be-tween Love and Thought that it needs. Instead, they are connected by the "and" of the title, like the distinct but linked "Each" and "All" of "Each and All." One notable difference is that "Bond" and "Free" are adjectives, and therefore potentially appli-cable both to the same noun.

10. Indeed, this is the thrust of Brett Millier's short discussion of "Sandpiper" (334–335), which cites a letter in which Bishop praises binoculars' power to bring fascinating "details" of a harbor scene closer. Interestingly, though, even in that letter Bishop also expresses disappointment with the binoculars—after she trains them, as she does first, on the ocean: "I adjusted them immediately and it is just too bad there aren't any interesting ships on the sea at the moment." The blank horizon magnified looks the same as it does unmagnified.

11. In a much later speech, Bishop reads "Sandpiper" to be about precisely her own fascination with the ocean: "Yes, all my life I have lived and behaved very much like that sandpiper—just running along the edges of different countries and continents, 'looking for something.' I have always felt I couldn't *possibly* live very far inland, away from the ocean; and I *have* always lived near it, frequently in sight of it" (Millier 517). The speech, with which Bishop accepted a poetry award, was given in Norman, Oklahoma, and Bishop dwells for fully two-thirds of the short talk on her life on shores and the unfamiliarity of being so far inland.

Three. Privacies of Storm

1. See, for other examples, David Porter, *Emerson and Literary Change*: "He insists on dissolution. . . . The emphasis is on rhetoric and not rhyme. . . . Unrestricted form both releases and gives voice to the flowing figures of nature" (178–179); Jonathan Levin, *The Poetics of Transition*: "Art is [for Emerson] the perpetual exercise of transitional imaginative energies" (40); Harold Bloom, "Emerson: The American Religion": "If no two disciples can agree upon Emerson's doctrine, and they cannot, we can grant the success of his evasion. Yet there is the center: evasion" (*Emerson* 118); Sacvan Bercovitch, *The Puritan Origins of the American Self*: "Emerson's Scholar-Teacher-Natural Philosopher . . . compensates for political failure by collapsing nature and society, history, biography, and autobiography, into the eschatological Now which is Emerson as the representative American" (174); and, most important, Richard Poirier. Evan Carton and Julie Ellison, on the other hand, maintain interest in both language's fluidity and its solidity.

2. Porter writes, "There was an essential contradiction in his imaginative makeup: the inclusiveness of his organic conception of existence was everywhere thwarted by the closed space of poetic expression" (*Emerson* 168). Emerson's style, to Porter, was cramped by his own poetic form, and liberated only by prosiness.

3. U.S. culture's deployment of Emerson supports such a reading: aphoristic detachability, not breadth and fluidity, is the feature of Emerson's writing that invites readers to scavenge various chunks from the essays and cart them off into other texts.

4. Lawrence Buell, "The Transcendentalist Poets," in Parini and Millier, 119.

5. Awkwardly, the success of such an argument depends on the success of the critic's synecdoche, claiming a bit of evidence as representative of the whole—even though the larger claim is that in small Emersonian objects, synecdoche captures our interest because of the way it fails.

6. Stanley Cavell asserts that "the puzzle of the Emersonian sentence must find a piece of its solution in a theory of the fragment" (*Unapproachable America* 21).

7. He would write allegorically in "Crossing Brooklyn Ferry," "the wolf, the snake, the hog [are] not wanting in me." These animals are emblems of particular human urges, and as emblems are unlike the list of animals in Emerson's passage. The whimsy of the journal, not Whitmanian expansiveness, dominates Emerson's published version of this "occult relation" idea. In the volume *Nature*, "the very scorpions" are replaced by "the vegetable": instead of elaborating on this odd phrase, Emerson simply claims that the vegetative "fields and woods . . . nod to me, and I to them" (I.10).

8. For important work on this topic, see Julie Ellison's chapter "Transition and Detachment" in *Emerson's Romantic Style* and Lee Rust Brown's chapter on the Coleridgean "fragment," "Ruins in the Eye," in *Emerson Museum*.

9. The representational solutions at the close of "The Snow-Storm," temporal crosscutting and verbal accommodationism, would later be adopted in the flickering poetics of Stevens, with more success. His late poetry's deployment of apposition, of quick transition and myriad handedness, relies on sentences' temporal movement, "The intricate evasions of as," to resolve contradiction ("An Ordinary Evening in New Haven"). It might even manage to overlap the time of thaw with the occasion of the storm, in defiance of the seasonal shifts that dictate the poem's drama. But oxymorons, like the one to which Emerson resorts in the final line, are not dynamic; they are restatements of static difficulty. Such a trope leads to synthesis by verbal accommodation, falsely stabilized epigrams like "frolic architecture," "volitant stabilities," or "Ghostlier demarcations." The conjunctive power of the Stevensian "as" contains the spirit of compromise much more effectively than any conjunction of adjective and noun.

10. Located "At the garden's end," this human dwelling is juxtaposed with an Edenic space but has an ambiguous position relative to its comfort (and to the amoral force of Satan): it is both in the garden and beyond it, just as its occupants are both contained by it and out in the storm.

11. In one reading, the prepositional phrase "of storm" subordinates privacy to the whirling wind: the storm owns the privacy. In the other reading, "storm" is merely an attribute of that privacy: this is a privacy of the sort correlated with storm. This verbal technique of superimposition, with container and contained, essence and ornament, constantly switching places, is one that Dickinson would master with similar deployments of the word "of" — "Processes of size"; "Of Immortality/His Strategy." The difficult pun in Bishop's phrase "The art of losing" functions the same way.

12. In describing Emerson's prose, critics have tended to emphasize its slipperiness and vagueness — what he himself, writing of nontextual knowledge, famously called "lubricity" ("Experience" III.29). See especially Poirier, *Renewal of Literature*: "[V]agaries are the very substance of his writing. . . . He wants to evade formulas even while indulging in them" (74); and *Poetry and Pragmatism*: "As pragmatism recommends, [vague language] points toward future realization, toward the existence of things which it cannot verbally re-present" (148).

13. *Journals*, quoted in Ellison, 181. Ellison calls the two principles highlighted in this analysis "transition" and "detachment."

14. This is the emphasis Eduardo Cadava places on the weather's power in his study of Emerson, although he also assigns that power a human teleology. This blending of atmospheric and human phenomena strongly suggests Cadava's reliance on Hegelian foundations for his project. Indeed, in a personal communication (September 2002), Cadava described intensive study of Hegel as a primary formative experience of his scholarship.

15. See *Oxford English Dictionary* (OED) example 8c (online).

16. According to the OED, the verb "wreck" was used almost solely in nautical contexts until 1878. In an 1865 instance, the verb was applied to the destruction of houses, but it was placed in quotation marks, as a self-conscious metaphor. One apparent exception to the word's exclusive nautical usage is a lexicographic error. An instance from Spenser's 1592 *Amoretti* — "That tree . . . am I, whom you do wreck, do ruine, and destroy" — is misconstrued. Spenser's poem has a tripartite structure culminating in the parallel triad "wreck," "ruin," and "destroy." The first quatrain is about a ship, and the final couplet reads in its entirety "*That ship*, that tree, and that same beast am I, / Whom you do wreck, do ruine, and destroy." The last line's verbs correspond to their respective nouns in the previous line.

17. For this emphasis on the "framework stout" as an emblem of Bishop's poetics, I am indebted to Peter Sacks (seminar discussion, fall 1996).

18. This is a pun also noted by Stephen Yenser in his discussion of time in *Ephraim*.

Four. Dickinson Outdoors

1. In another place, using the theological language of the "type," Emerson says that "The body of man is the type after which a dwelling-house is built" (quoted in S. Whicher 115). Such odd claims are a long way from the culturally entrenched Puritan ideology of typology, the "Figurative Terms" that Gurdon Saltonstall called "obvious" (Bercovitch, *Typology* 5).

2. For Dickie, who is more attentive to this poem, the Dickinson lyric is about openness, as opposed to the confinement of prose (see 69). At the other end of the scale, with an interest in confinement, the superb historicist critic Karen Sánchez-Eppler notes the simultaneity and paradox of the poem in a very suggestive sentence: "Dickinson represents poetic possibility as both domestic and unbounded; she celebrated domestic liberty, but the manner in which she does so demonstrates that it is a contradiction in terms" (113). Primarily, though, she is interested in the house but not in its identity with sky.

Lesley Wheeler uses the poem to buttress her assertion that "Dickinson, finally, insists on the lyric as an enclosure," by claiming after a rote paraphrase of the poem's extraordinary images ("sky for a roof," and so forth) that "[e]ven the idea of possibility becomes an enclosure" (40). Though less attentive than Sánchez-Eppler, Wheeler provides a useful and up-to-date summary of the polarity in Dickinson studies. The critical disarray she mentions has particularly stymied collective understanding of this poem: "No consensus exists . . . on the extent to which Dickinson practices a formally closed or radically open version of the lyric" (20).

3. One exception is found in the exceptional critical book *Emily Dickinson and the Problem of Others*, in which Christopher Benfey asserts that "possibility, in this poem, requires small, enclosed, protective spaces" (34) on the way to arguing in the other direction that "for all her emphasis on privacy and solitude, Dickinson . . . is more a poet of other people than [even] Whitman is" (83).

4. For more on the unacceptability of the poem's deferral to poetics, see New, *Regenerate Lyric*, 1–14; for more on the unacceptability of the finite serving the eternal, see Kierkegaard, *Philosophical Fragments*, 19–22.

5. Stanley Cavell writes: "The explicit temptation of Eden is to knowledge, which above all means: to a denial that as we stand, we know" (*Quest* 49). This last phrase, with its metaphor of "standing," that is, simply being in space, is a reminder that gathering even with the eye is a kind of claiming, and that all knowledge is instantaneously rapacious; it always takes hold of the world, even, or especially, when relaxing.

6. In fifteen instances of the word and its cognates, only one clearly refers to an activity rather than a presence (Rosenbaum 536). None refers to a profession in our modern sense.

7. New discusses the relevance of Kierkegaardian philosophy to Dickinsonian emotion over against the sublime (*Regenerate Lyric* 159), but the two have not been methodically linked on epistemological grounds. For more on the theoretical implications of Kierkegaardian (rather than Hegelian) criticism, see the Epilogue.

8. Notably, as Cynthia Hallen points out, Dickinson "[t]reasured a well-marked copy of Thomas a Kempis's *Of the Imitation of Christ*" (77). I am indebted to Katie Peterson for highlighting this fact.

9. Recent scholarly interest in the variants haunting each Dickinson manuscript page exemplifies this urge, since under such attention the dynamism of the reader's eye seems to be demanded by the document itself. Instability and flux allow us to treat Dickinson's objects as we do novels: her process of choice (or, in the case of Cameron's *Choosing Not Choosing*, the heuristic of choice) can sometimes be more interesting than her choices.

10. To be sure, a strain of recent work emphasizes the material status of Dickinson's poem in the fascicles: see especially Cameron, *Choosing Not Choosing*. The goal of this work, though, is to discern dynamism and constant renegotiation within the text, and to free the poet from the prison of her own objects. Without reading the poems as a sequence, such analyses usually make a narrative from Dickinson's task of self-publication, and from later liberatory reading. In the end they make it impossible for the poet not to choose not choosing.

11. One claim often advanced in feminist readings of Dickinson is that inaction is elevated to the status held in patriarchal writing by the excursive imagination: as Vivian Pollak puts it, Dickinson "tended to substitute observation, feeling, and reading for more active forms of experience" ("Literary Allusions" 54). Debra Fried, in her adroit study of quotation *Valves of Attention*, counters that reading itself is an active and interlocutory activity (120).

12. Temporal frameworks for reading have now been set deep into the bedrock of literary study. The intellectual foundations of these techniques, laid in the mid-twentieth century, are examined in the Epilogue. Today they often go without saying.

In a representative instance from 2001, Betsy Erkkila makes them seem almost un-questionable: "Insofar as Dickinson lives *in time* rather than *outside* of it, and insofar as language is in Bakhtin's terms a dialogic medium, all her poems . . . have a social and historical dimension" (71). No one could disagree with either of the first two clauses as they stand. But they operate along with unspoken additional premises: first, that the poet's life (in time) is also the life of her poems; and second, that Bakhtin's dynamic terms describing the "novelistic" also apply to lyric utterance.

13. Lee Rust Brown's remarkable study links Emerson's thought with static, spec-imen-oriented pre-Darwinian natural history. He argues that in emphasizing expe-rience, Emerson defies the Platonic premises that persist into Hegel's philosophy: "Emerson does affirm a reality transcending history, but he indicates that it hides somewhere in empirical activity" (171). For Hegel, it might be said that History is the reality transcending history.

14. Roland Hagenbüchle offers as background to his discernment of an (avowedly Hegelian) "aesthetics of process" in Dickinson just such an intellectual history: "To understand Dickinson's epistemological revolution, it is necessary to sketch, however briefly, some of the mid-nineteenth-century developments. The period was vitally influenced by the element of process, of change" (135).

After this contextualizing paragraph, Hagenbüchle sets aside historicism and un-dertakes a project much like David Porter's. They are the language-oriented critics par excellence: "If meaning, as is the case in Dickinson's work, is increasingly generated in language alone, concrete life — as the occasion for the poems — tends to recede into the background" (142). It is not clear which of these phenomena is meant to cause the other, but the present book disputes both.

15. See Brown's suggestive sentence: "History in the sense of its Greek root — as a systematic description of a fully present subject . . . — survived into the nineteenth century only in the term 'natural history'" (269n41).

16. See most recently Wolosky and Dickie, who take Emerson as a foil; for readings positing a tighter relation, see G. Whicher and Waggoner. Diehl argues that Dickin-son leverages terror to subvert the optimistic scheme of her precursor Emerson; her essay postulates that "[i]t is power that lies at the center of Dickinson's relation to Emerson" ("Emerson, Dickinson, and the Abyss," Bloom, *Emerson*, 683).

17. See Gilbert and Gubar (narrating the story of the poet "achieving the author-ity of self-creation" [585]), Juhasz, Eberwein, Pollak, Wheeler, and others. Pollak's formulation is representative: "Her poems are . . . in quest of an object. . . . [Yet] her imagination is activated by those relational losses against which she protests most vehemently. For this reason, social powerlessness is Dickinson's most thoroughly ex-plored, consistently interesting, and intransigently feminist theme" (*Dickinson* 132). Cristanne Miller completes the story expeditiously: "Dickinson . . . transform[s] the world's inadequate language into an adequate language of her own" (147). This ver-sion of Dickinson might be described roughly as constituting a "historicist" strain in Dickinson studies, with feminism as its animating principle. Suzanne Juhasz points out that the essays collected in *Feminist Critics Read Emily Dickinson* all accept "the premise that Dickinson's *actions* make sense" and "are dedicated to the continued exploration and definition of Dickinson's power" (17, emphasis added).

18. See Porter (*Dickinson*), Cameron (*Lyric Time*), Gelpi, Budick, Carton (arguing that Dickinson pursues power through paradox), and Stonum (deploying Thomas Weiskel's "three-phase sequence" [69] of sublime encounter to show how power pursues Dickinson). Porter's formulations are representative: "The elementary experience . . . is living after things happen" (9); "The elemental act [is] bonding language to discrete experiences that are both inescapable and unutterable" (29). These scholars, mapping the transition from a muscular imagination into the aphasia of the poems, might be described roughly as constituting a "linguistic" strain in Dickinson studies.

19. One critic, Cristanne Miller, is aware of bestriding this fissure, and expresses interlocking "fascination" and "frustration" in doing so (19). A passage in her introduction incisively describes the fundamental dilemma of the Dickinson scholar: "Dickinson uses both the strategy of the weak, in her attempt to win over the world as lover, and the strategy of the strong, in her attempt to win against it as rival. The narratives of most poems adopt some version of the former strategy; the language of all her poetry reveals the latter" (18). Both weak and strong, Dickinson is for Miller in either case seeking a sort of victory: the story of history or the descent into language drives the poems' quest. Under the rubric of the epistolary, though, Miller resists the urge to complete either story, settling instead for several outcomes, magisterially named "various explanations" (184). Miller's method, so aware of the dangers of choosing any one storyline, is unimpeachable, although the dialectical nature of letter writing seems hardly to exhaust the possibilities of the poems' split character. The present study chooses outdoor epistemology rather than epistolary phenomenology to govern the dilemma.

19. In historicist criticism about accomplishment, poetry "[h]as the potential to order emotions that are inherently disordered" (Pollak, *Dickinson* 27); definition can be imposed on chaos. In the language-oriented discourse, "absences and omissions," not artifacts, are the true sites of meaning — the poet's ineffable selfhood only condescends to "[e]stablish[] her individuality within the inherited system of language" (Porter, *Dickinson* 6). In other words, in the feminist view the inexpressible works to achieve expression, while in the semiotic view pure expressivity infuses itself into language, and often shatters it.

20. The incommensurability of indoor and outdoor absorbs Emerson's attention, not only as a metaphor for philosophical trouble but also as an experiential vexation. He describes the writer's trouble as one of two irreconcilable settings: "What is the hardest task in the world? To think. . . . We all but apprehend, we dimly forebode the truth. We say I will walk abroad, and the truth will take form and clearness to me. We go forth, but cannot find it. It seems as if we needed only the stillness and composed attitude of the library to seize the thought. But we come in, and are as far from it as first" ("Intellect" II.196).

21. See especially Poirier. Levin, *Poetics of Transition*, follows on this work with analysis of highly un-Dickinsonian writers such as Stein and Stevens, none of them likely to occupy what Stonum calls her "[p]eculiarly hesitant sublime" (190). Cadava, in a sophisticated historicist deployment of "transition," describes history's elusiveness as the meaning of Emerson's elusive nature and its weather: "Nature is in fact

always another name for writing" (3), and writing in turn is deployed "to transform the relations in which we live" (6). Julie Ellison is less goal-oriented in her analysis of Emerson's rhetoric, and the Emersonianism exercised here owes much to the Emerson described in her chapter "Transition and Detachment," in *Emerson's Romantic Style.*

22. "We ought to say a feeling of *and,* a feeling of *if,* a feeling of *but,* quite as readily as we say a feeling of *blue* or a feeling of *cold*" (James, *Principles of Psychology* I.245).

23. The critical fascination with Dickinson's agoraphobia neglects not only the poems' focus on nature but that of the letters as well: in her second letter of self-introduction to Higginson, for example, Dickinson writes "Of my Companions[:] Hills — Sir — and the Sundown — and a Dog — large as myself, that my Father bought me — They are better than Beings — because they know — but do not tell — and the noise in the Pool, at Noon — excels my Piano" (*Letters* 261). Why should not Dickinson also have enjoyed regular Wordsworthian walks?

24. See Miller, 2 – 5, for the most patient and insightful analysis of this poem as a story of poetry.

25. The variant final line, "In Spiceless Sepulchre," serves only to demonstrate how jejune the more narrative second stanza might have been without this last image. If death is merely the absence of life, a flavorless void, then artistic work impinges upon human mortality and its meanings not at all.

Five. Frost and the Unmoving World

1. Richard Poirier's influential text *Robert Frost: The Work of Knowing* made this case masterfully, and was itself preceded by Frank Lentricchia's choice to use "the mediation of William James" to place Frost "within an international, modernist philosophical context" (xii). See more recently New, *Line's Eye,* and Costello, *Shifting Ground.*

2. "Take Something Like a Star."

3. *Selected Letters,* 344. This "setting" associates the poem with the central object of "The Witness Tree," a cairn with an "iron spine" watched over by a scarred tree. The objects are witness to "My proof of being not unbounded."

4. In a passage about particularly American, Romantic knowledge of objects and natural systems, Lee Rust Brown holds that "Emerson's imagination . . . located possibilities of remove not just on speculative promontories but also in the closest views of specific details and facts" (70).

5. "Take Something Like a Star."

6. "Two Tramps in Mud-Time," the Frost poem in which the wanderer and the worker from Wordsworth's "Resolution and Independence" appear (with their social classes switched, and the poet in the role of the watched rather than the watcher), is notably unsuccessful at making social meaning out of the warm working mood described so powerfully in "Mowing" and hinted at in the offstage lumberyard of "Good-By and Keep Cold."

7. The populace, whose members wear their characteristics loosely, also challenges

Frost's own descriptive work (New Hampshire "has one I don't know what to call him"; "I don't know what to say about the people") — but this latter problem of representation is one that he shrugs off, with flexible sentences, when playing the public role of folksy pragmatist.

8. See *American Jeremiad*, 75.

9. I have substituted the 1849 reading of the second sentence (I.288). The editors of the *Collected Works* here opt for the 1836 variant "and vulgar things."

10. Thoreau, by contrast, asserts that "time is but the stream I go a-fishing in" in the course of laying claim to a stability beneath its flux: "While I drink I see the sandy bottom and detect how shallow it is. Its thin current slides away, but eternity remains. . . . I do not wish to be any more busy with my hands than is necessary" (351).

11. This poem is thus locked in conversation with the central idea of Poirier's *Robert Frost: The Work of Knowing*: the idea that excitement and use are made one in Frostean pragmatic poetry. Elisa New pursues a similar theme across even more of U.S. literary culture in *The Line's Eye*.

12. If we feel that in the end the poet of "A Star in a Stoneboat" simply has the better kind of knowledge, we are surely missing half of the diptych. If nothing else, the farmer knows his own strength in a way that the poet, who does not actually lift anything (or mend any wall), does not.

13. "The Figure a Poem Makes," *Collected Poems, Prose, and Plays*, 777.

14. For more on an instance of this debate, see the description of a panel of pragmatist thinkers at which it was addressed directly, in Norwood, "Finding What Will Suffice," 26.

15. For Rorty, the reason to be satisfied is in order to look to the future with hope; he deplores political academics who "prefer knowledge to hope [in a] turn away from secularism and pragmatism" (*Achieving Our Country* 37).

16. In *The Performing Self*, Poirier asserts that "we are all confused, and it is not necessarily bad that we are" (xviii), and he elaborates that literature is "energy in motion, an energy which is its own shape" (xxiii). In "Rose Pogonias," as Elisa New has argued, that shape coalesces painfully into an oval that displays the skewing vector of human desire in a nature of circular wholeness (*Regenerate Lyric* 234).

Jonathan Levin defines pragmatism neither as a mode of provisionality nor one of prospectiveness, but as a vector: "For a pragmatist, art is neither an ornament to life nor a form of leisured indulgence. . . . It is the *process* whereby humans devise and test the values, pleasures, and meanings that make life worth living" (5, emphasis added).

17. See Richard Poirier's argument to this effect, in *Robert Frost*, 291–299.

18. Brower, for example, says that the poem "is absorbed with states-between . . . where real and unreal appear and disappear" (26).

Six. Bishop's Weighted Eye

1. "At the Fishhouses." For extended treatment of this ocean-poem, see the Epilogue.

2. "The Riverman."

3. It is of course fair to ask about the humans who confronted nature in South America before any Europeans did; but Bishop does not think of that. "Our eyes," for her, are North American eyes. Clearly, not all humans believe that art and experience are as tightly entangled as an Emersonian lyric poet does; but this chapter is just about Bishop.

4. Bonnie Costello's crucial study *Elizabeth Bishop: Questions of Mastery* executes dozens of superb readings exactly by focusing on the relation between "observation and metaphor" (3). In separating the two sharply, though, Costello considers the drive for mastery to be distinct from observation itself — supposing that observation could be innocent if not for the development of a mastering impulse, an impulse that for Costello results from the problematic of "seeing *in time*" (2, emphasis added). Costello introduces time and flux as categories wherever possible, as the critic's antidote to the dangers of Emersonian "stability": Bishop's "excursive sight," she says, "replaces transcendence and mastery with pleasure in discovery and surprise" (150), that is, with progressive knowledge.

5. Costello points out (68) that the dogwood is a traditional symbol of Christ's body.

6. This observation about the label's similarity to Hamlet in excess of the objective correlative emerged in a class discussion led by Peter Sacks at Harvard in fall 1996.

7. To put this into the literary-critical terms established above: the first poem mulls the problems of allegory, the second the problems of symbol. In allegory, the world is left out of the text's artifice; in a (natural) symbol, the poet is left out of the intense exchange between the thing and its meaning.

8. Unfortunately, the modern defenders of allegory are rhetorically crippled by their other commitments: Walter Benjamin's *The Origin of German Tragic Drama* and Paul de Man's essay "The Rhetoric of Temporality" in the second edition of *Blindness and Insight* are unlikely to make clear, convincing cases for its usefulness. It is worth attempting here to summarize their claim: allegory is severed from the thing it should mean, and stands alone in the world with a pathetic majesty all its own. Because it is so sharply aware of its failure to include its meaning, it is a more suggestive form than the Romantic symbol, which seeks to obscure the vast difference between thing and idea by mere rhetorical hand waving. (Bishop's iceberg, which is a symbol, evades this indictment by representing no comprehensible human idea: it "adorns only itself.")

One result of allegory's failure is a focus on materiality and decay. The constitutive feature of allegory is the sadness with which pathetic tokens are proffered in the stead of transcendence. Bishop's monument, isolated in the laboratory of this strange poem, is likely the clearest example in English of the allegory that Benjamin and de Man praise for its rigor, its failure, and its melancholic beauty. The landscape of this poem, in its facticity, exaggerates the eye's tendency to make nature into a piece of art — an emphasis that Benjamin would approve: "The theory that every image is only a form of writing . . . gets to the very heart of the allegorical attitude" (*Origin* 214).

9. The stack of boxes expresses perfectly the melancholic attitude of Benjamin's "brooder," who is doomed "[t]o pile up fragments ceaselessly, without any strict idea

of a goal . . . in the unremitting expectation of a miracle" (*Origin* 178). Likewise, the encounter with the monument can only point away from itself toward some other resolution: in the final line of "The Monument," we are enjoined absurdly to "Watch it closely."

10. Luis Alberto Brandão Santos has argued powerfully (in "Map of Waters," in Almeida et al., *Art of Elizabeth Bishop* 84 – 89) that the interest in fluidity in Bishop reveals her gradual acquiescence to history and change. He charts a progress in her oeuvre "[f]rom earth to water, from space to time, from description to narrative, [and] from Geography to History. . . . From conquest to loss" (89). Within each poem, then, "[t]he descriptive look sees itself confronted by the inevitable narrative reflections" (87), as associative meanings progress from one to the next in a way that develops contingent and historicized human meanings. Santos seeks narrative correctives to what he considers dangerous, "Emersonian" sight.

11. This metaphor about the channel's fossilizing sediment is Bonnie Costello's (*Elizabeth Bishop* 182).

12. Notably, the poem was inspired by a visit to Duxbury not in March but in late May (*One Art* 586, 587). The poem is dedicated to the owners of the house, who had loaned it to Bishop and her partner, Alice Methfessel; Methfessel's being left out of the retirement house is more noteworthy as an emblem of solitude than the exclusion of a less important walking companion might have been.

13. Susan Stewart writes of the souvenir's metonymic character that "the souvenir is by definition incomplete," but she goes on to argue that this incompleteness merely invites the superaddition of a sentimental aura of narrative: the souvenir "[w]ill not function without the supplementary narrative discourse" (136).

14. Gary Fountain has described Bishop as a collector: in testimony from her friends, "[w]e sense that her residences were exhibition spaces" (Almeida et al., *Art of Elizabeth Bishop* 260), full of objects from her travels.

15. In "The Poet and His Public," cited in Costello, *Questions of Mastery*, 3.

16. Walter Benjamin foresaw this development in the nature of allegory. He wrote in an unpublished work begun after the completion of *The Origin of German Tragic Drama* that "the key figure of the early allegory is the corpse. The key figure of the later allegory is the 'souvenir'" ("Central Park," quoted in Pensky 175).

Indeed, the book is a perfect example of the allegorical structure as Lloyd Spencer has analyzed it: "Its internal coherence, or 'compellingness,'" is primary; it "depends on the reader's grasp of an interpretive *context* not given"; and it is characterized by "a high degree of optical awareness, the implication of a hierarchy of values, and a stable hierarchised organisation of existence" (62).

17. In a later letter, Bishop acknowledged that this move made the poem confusing, and regretted including the Seven Wonders of the World. Obviously, though, it was not a mere oversight or confusion; Bishop knew what belonged in a Bible. In fact, she remarked to Robert Lowell that she did an experiment with a Bible when mulling the book title "Concordance," "one of those test samplings, you know": "My finger came right down on the concordance section, so I felt immensely cheered" (*One Art* 223). Bishop's adoption of a fundamentalist's exercise, picking a Bible passage at random, in

order to help her decide on a title, is a perfect emblem of the tongue-in-cheek religiosity that "Over 2,000 Illustrations" tries to arrive at.

18. See Vendler, "Domestication, Domesticity, and the Otherworldly."

19. It should go without saying that any number of reactionary impulses can be discerned in the desire to reconcile book and world; each such impulse is marked with the sexism of the "fat old guide" who "made eyes"; the heterocentrism of the Englishwoman who randomly announces the pregnancy of a stranger; or the fascinated Orientalism of the engravings in which Arabs indicate a Christian holy site while "Plotting, probably, / against our Christian Empire" (Vendler, "Domestication").

20. William James described the conundrum of the second verse-paragraph aptly: "Things are 'with' one another in many ways, but nothing includes everything, or dominates over everything. The word 'and' trails along after every sentence" (*A Pluralistic Universe*, in *Works of William James* 145).

Seven. Merrill's Expansiveness

1. Emerson, "Intellect," II.199.

2. The publishers of *From the First Nine*, uninterested in the mathematics of this poem, nonsensically extend the radical line to cover the "=1" part of the equation; in the volume *Braving the Elements* the equation is reproduced correctly.

3. One critic, in a review Merrill took to heart, accused his more highly wrought work of "smelling of the lamp" (see Yenser 20); this line may be his final response to that indictment.

It is hard to imagine how Merrill, the inveterate dealer in ambiguity, could have avoided seeing the delicious pun available here in the word "decanter." As someone about to sing his poem forth, he could have located the star in himself even as he placed it on the surface of the glass. I would speculate that in fact "decanter" once appeared in this line, but was replaced as Merrill reminded himself of the highly material program of *Sandover*, a program in which the transmutation of the body into light has no appropriate place.

4. The introduction of poetic fire and uncanny beauty into a sociable situation depicts the oddity of this initial coupling in Merrill's work, in the strange and brief poem "Charles on Fire." A capricious party guest touches

> a lit match to our host's full glass.
> A blue flame, gentle, beautiful, came, went
> Above the surface. In a hush that fell
> We heard the vessel crack. . . .
> Steward of spirits, Charles's glistening hand
> All at once gloved itself in eeriness.
> The moment passed. He made two quick sweeps
> And then was flesh again. "It couldn't matter less,"
> He said, but with a shocked, unconscious glance

Into the mirror. Finding nothing changed,
He filled a fresh glass and sank down among us.

5. The trees dwell in the mind on the same shelf with the words "astrolabe" and "pterodactyl" — quaint, uncommon words describing obsolete facts. The concepts behind these words are relevant, of course: the astrolabe, an instrument for surveying the sky, orienting sailors in open oceanic space, is similar to the trees that offer goblet "stems," or handles, for distance itself. And the etymology of "pterodactyl," "wing-finger," suggests that unfettered movement through open space and manipulation of objects might possibly be linked. But in the hands of the reader, these words are first and foremost uncanny chunks of language, linguistic souvenirs of other worlds. These simplest of poetic objects, the trees in the landscape, share some essential strangeness with them.

6. *From the First Nine*, 361 and 5, respectively.

7. Merrill himself felt the changes to be noteworthy: he had "The Cosmological Eye" reprinted as an appendix to his collection *From the First Nine*, intending it to exemplify his early, "inept" attention to "[c]ertain lifelong motifs" (361).

Epilogue

1. Kierkegaard, *Journals*, in *A Kierkegaard Anthology*, 3; Emerson to Mary Moody Emerson, quoted in S. Whicher, 18.

2. Elisa New cites this same passage in the course of linking the theologies of Kierkegaard and Dickinson, in contradistinction to a transcendentalist Emersonianism. In her reading of this paragraph, though, the Kierkegaardian limit is placed in single quotation marks; it is not a geographic fact but a metaphor that helps to chart his place in the history of ideas. The present book, linking Dickinson's experience of this geography not only with the status New claims for her ("the most confirmed kind of Protestant" [*Regenerate Lyric* 162]) but also with her own brand of Emersonian idealism, claims that Emerson's style of positive experience in nature governs the sensuous exercise of this negative theology.

3. The tradition of discerning Hegelian energies in American writers begins as early as Feidelson, who writes that Emerson's "[p]rimary question is not the locus of form with relation to subject and object but rather the locus of subject and object with relation to a formative *process* evident in both" (129, emphasis added). The philosophical mind was freed from dualism by Kant; in Hegel, it finds knowledge to be dynamic. Thus Richard Poirier writes in the first paragraph of *A World Elsewhere*: "Let us for the moment assume with Hegel that 'freedom' is a creation . . . of consciousness, that freedom is that reality which the consciousness creates for itself" (4). Under this vital assumption, the heroism of action is also for Poirier the heroism of writing: "The greatest American writers really do try, against the perpetually greater power of reality, to create an environment that might allow some longer existence to the hero's momentary expansions of consciousness" (15).

4. Lee Rust Brown argues that in emphasizing experience, Emerson defies the Pla-

tonic premises that persist into Hegel's philosophy: "Emerson does affirm a reality transcending history, but he indicates that it hides somewhere in empirical activity" (171). For Hegel, it might be said that "History" is the reality transcending history.

5. See also one of the OED definitions of "history": "A systematic account (without reference to time) of a set of natural phenomena, as those connected with a country, some division of nature or group of natural objects, a species of animals or plants, etc. Now *rare*, exc. in Natural History." (In this sense following the similar use of ιστορια by Aristotle and other Greek writers, and of *historia* by Pliny.)

6. Stanley Cavell expresses the motivation here straightforwardly enough: "The dissatisfaction with such a settlement as Kant's is relatively easy to state. To settle with skepticism . . . to assure that we do know the existence of the world . . . the price Kant asks us to pay is to cede any claim to know the thing in itself, to grant that human knowledge is not of things as they are in themselves. You don't — do you? — have to be a romantic to feel sometimes about that settlement: Thanks for nothing" (*Quest* 31).

7. In the *Meno*, Plato claims that "the soul, since it is immortal and has been born many times, and has seen all things . . . , has learned everything that is" (364).

8. It is appropriate, then, that the maturation of literary criticism as a discipline has corresponded with the blossoming of "historicism" into predominance. Reliable knowledge, traditionally, must be situated in time, and mythmaking and historiography can satisfy this requirement with almost equal felicity.

9. *Philosophical Fragments* proceeds to describe some features of the decisive moment of knowing: one notable feature of that moment is that reason is seized by epistemological paradox, and found inadequate, at precisely the moment in which it seems that the opposite is the case. To describe this moment of paradox, Kierkegaard chooses imagery of the inside out: "The reaction of the offended consciousness is to assert that the Moment is folly, and that the Paradox is folly, which is the contention of the Paradox that the Reason is absurd, now reflected back as an echo from the offended consciousness" (41).

10. Emphasis is added in the following quotations: "[There is an] enigmatic 'knowledge' Bishop *anticipates* in 'At the Fishhouses,' where *continuity rests in the narrative rupture of history*: 'and since'" (Doreski 34); "Belief [in a passage of Merrill's], as in the postmodern perspective generally, is necessarily *provisional and processive*, as Bishop says, 'flowing, and flown'" (Jonathan Keller, in Rotella 141); "'Historical' assumes a double meaning: Our knowledge is necessarily historical inasmuch as it occurs in time . . . ; but it is also knowledge *of* history, of the lives and events that precede our own and give it meaning" (Gilbert 145, emphasis in original); "These waters offer no reflection, figurative or literal, for they represent the essence of *motion and change*" (Costello, "Vision and Mastery" 362); "Though it remains both dangerous and *elusive*, [the water's] powerful finality is [here] diminished. Both burning and cold, its paradoxical nature *invites us to approach it*, for it is not all unequivocally one reality" (Fast 366). Can all these readers really be looking at "The same sea, the same," that we see before us?

11. Quoted by Milan Kundera, "Weltliteratur," in the *New Yorker*, January 8, 2007, 28.

Works Consulted

Almeida, Sandra Regina Goulart, Glaucia Gonçalves, and Eiana Reis, eds. *The Art of Elizabeth Bishop*. Belo Horizonte, Brazil: Editora UFMG/CNP, 2001.

Bachelard, Gaston. *The Poetics of Space*. Boston: Beacon Press, 1994.

Baym, Nina, Wayne Franklin, Francis Murphy, and Hershel Parker, eds. *The Norton Anthology of American Literature*. Vol. 1. 5th ed. New York: Norton, 1998.

Benfey, Christopher E. G. *Emily Dickinson and the Problem of Others*. Amherst: University of Massachusetts Press, 1984.

Benjamin, Walter. *The Origin of German Tragic Drama*. Trans. John Osborne. New York: Verso, 1977.

———. "The Task of the Translator." In *Illuminations*, 69–82. Ed. Hannah Arendt. Trans. Harry Zohn. New York: Shocken Books, 1985.

Bercovitch, Sacvan. *The American Jeremiad*. Madison: University of Wisconsin Press, 1978.

———. *The Office of the Scarlet Letter*. Baltimore: Johns Hopkins University Press, 1991.

———. *The Puritan Origins of the American Self*. New Haven, Conn.: Yale University Press, 1975.

———, ed. *Typology and Early American Literature*. Amherst: University of Massachusetts Press, 1972.

Bishop, Elizabeth. *The Collected Prose*. New York: Farrar Straus Giroux, 1984.

———. *The Complete Poems, 1927–1979*. New York: Farrar Straus Giroux, 1995.

———. *One Art: Letters*. Ed. Robert Giroux. New York: Farrar Straus Giroux, 1994.

Bloom, Harold. *Elizabeth Bishop*. New York: Chelsea House, 1985.

———. *A Map of Misreading*. New York: Oxford University Press, 1975.

———, ed. *Ralph Waldo Emerson*. New York: Chelsea House, 1985.

Brooks, Cleanth. *The Well-Wrought Urn: Studies in the Structure of Poetry*. New York: Harcourt, Brace, 1947.

Brower, Reuben. *The Poetry of Robert Frost: Constellations of Intention*. New York: Oxford University Press, 1963.

Brown, Lee Rust. *The Emerson Museum: Practical Romanticism and the Pursuit of the Whole*. Cambridge, Mass.: Harvard University Press, 1997.

Budick, Emily Miller. *Emily Dickinson and the Life of Language*. Baton Rouge: Louisiana State University Press, 1985.

Buell, Lawrence. *Emerson*. Cambridge, Mass.: Belknap Press of Harvard University Press, 2003.

———. *The Environmental Imagination: Thoreau, Nature Writing, and the Formation of American Culture.* Cambridge, Mass.: Belknap Press of Harvard University Press, 1995.

———. *Literary Transcendentalism: Style and Vision in the American Renaissance.* Ithaca, N.Y.: Cornell University Press, 1973.

Cadava, Eduardo. *Emerson and the Climates of History.* Stanford, Calif.: Stanford University Press, 1997.

Cameron, Sharon. *Choosing Not Choosing: Dickinson's Fascicles.* Chicago: University of Chicago Press, 1992.

———. *Lyric Time: Dickinson and the Limits of Genre.* Baltimore: Johns Hopkins University Press, 1979.

———. *Writing Nature: Henry Thoreau's Journal.* Chicago: University of Chicago Press, 1985.

Carton, Evan. *The Rhetoric of American Romance: Dialectic and Identity in Emerson, Dickinson, Poe, and Hawthorne.* Baltimore: Johns Hopkins University Press, 1985.

Cavell, Stanley. *In Quest of the Ordinary: Lines of Skepticism and Romanticism.* Chicago: University of Chicago Press, 1988.

———. *This New Yet Unapproachable America: Lectures after Emerson after Wittgenstein.* Albuquerque, N.M.: Living Batch Press, 1989.

Coleridge, Samuel Taylor. *Biographia Literaria.* Ed. James Engell and Walter Jackson Bate. Princeton, N.J.: Princeton University Press, 1983.

Cook, Reginald Lansing. *Dimensions of Robert Frost.* New York: Rinehart, 1958.

Costello, Bonnie. *Elizabeth Bishop: Questions of Mastery.* Cambridge, Mass.: Harvard University Press, 1991.

———. *Shifting Ground: Reinventing Landscape in Modern American Poetry.* Cambridge: Cambridge University Press, 2003.

———. "Vision and Mastery in Elizabeth Bishop." *Twentieth Century Literature* 28, no. 4 (Winter 1982): 351–370.

Cox, James, ed. *Robert Frost: A Collection of Critical Essays.* Englewood Cliffs, N.J.: Prentice-Hall, 1962.

Dante Alighieri. *Inferno.* Trans. Robert Hollander and Jean Hollander. New York: Doubleday, 2000.

de Man, Paul. *Blindness and Insight: Essays in the Rhetoric of Contemporary Criticism.* Rev. 2nd ed. London: Methuen, 1983.

Dickie, Margaret. *Lyric Contingencies: Emily Dickinson and Wallace Stevens.* Philadelphia: University of Pennsylvania Press, 1991.

Dickinson, Emily. *The Manuscript Books of Emily Dickinson.* Ed. R. W. Franklin. Cambridge, Mass.: Belknap Press of Harvard University Press, 1981.

———. *The Poems of Emily Dickinson.* Variorum Edition. Ed. R. W. Franklin. 3 vols. Cambridge, Mass.: Belknap Press of Harvard University Press, 1998.

———. *Selected Letters.* Ed. Thomas H. Johnson. Cambridge, Mass.: Harvard University Press, 1985.

Diehl, Joanne Feit. *Dickinson and the Romantic Imagination.* Princeton, N.J.: Princeton University Press, 1981.

——. "Emerson, Dickinson, and the Abyss." *ELH* 44, no. 4 (Winter 1977): 683–700.

Dobson, Joanne. *Dickinson and the Strategies of Reticence: The Woman Writer in Nineteenth-Century America*. Bloomington: Indiana University Press, 1989.

Doreski, C. K. "Proustian Closure in Wallace Stevens's 'The Rock' and Elizabeth Bishop's *Geography III*." *Twentieth Century Literature* 44, no. 1 (Spring 1998): 34–52.

Eberwein, Jane Donahue. *Dickinson, Strategies of Limitation*. Amherst: University of Massachusetts Press, 1985.

Ellison, Julie. *Emerson's Romantic Style*. Princeton, N.J.: Princeton University Press, 1984.

Emerson, Ralph Waldo. *The Collected Works of Ralph Waldo Emerson*. 4 vols. Ed. Alfred Ferguson and Jean Ferguson Carr. Cambridge, Mass.: Harvard University Press, 1971, 1979, 1983.

——. *Essays and Poems*. Ed. Stuart Sherman. New York: Harcourt, Brace, 1921.

Erkkila, Betsy. "Book Review: *Emily Dickinson: Monarch of Perception*." *Emily Dickinson Journal* 10, no. 2 (2001): 68–74.

Fast, Robin. "Moore, Bishop, and Oliver: Thinking Back, Re-Seeing the Sea." *Twentieth Century Literature* 39, no. 3 (Fall 1993): 364–379.

Feidelson, Charles. *Symbolism and American Literature*. Chicago: University of Chicago Press, 1953.

Feuerbach, Ludwig. *The Essence of Christianity*. Trans. George Eliot. Buffalo, N.Y.: Prometheus Books, 1989.

Fried, Debra. *Valves of Attention: Quotation and Context in the Age of Emerson*. Ann Arbor, Mich.: UMI, 1990.

Frost, Robert. *Collected Poems, Prose, and Plays*. Ed. Richard Poirier and Mark Richardson. New York: Library of America, 1995.

——. *The Poetry of Robert Frost*. Ed. Edward Connery Lathem. New York: Henry Holt, 1979.

——. *Robert Frost and Sidney Cox: Forty Years of Friendship*. Ed. William R. Evans. Hanover, N.H.: University Press of New England, 1981.

——. *Selected Letters*. Ed. Lawrance Thompson. New York: Holt, Rinehart, and Winston, 1964.

Gelpi, Albert. *Emily Dickinson: The Mind of the Poet*. Cambridge, Mass.: Harvard University Press, 1965.

Gilbert, Roger. "Framing Water: Historical Knowledge in Elizabeth Bishop and Adrienne Rich." *Twentieth Century Literature* 43, no. 2 (Summer 1997): 144–161.

Gilbert, Sandra M., and Susan Gubar. *The Madwoman in the Attic: The Woman Writer and the Nineteenth-Century Literary Imagination*. New Haven, Conn.: Yale University Press, 1979.

Goldensohn, Lorrie. *Elizabeth Bishop: The Biography of a Poetry*. New York: Columbia University Press, 1992.

Grabher, Gudrun, Roland Hagenbüchle, and Cristanne Miller, eds. *The Emily Dickinson Handbook*. Amherst: University of Massachusetts Press, 1998.

Haack, Susan. *Evidence and Inquiry: Toward Reconstruction in Epistemology.* Oxford: Blackwell, 1993.

Hagenbüchle, Roland. "Emily Dickinson's Aesthetics of Process." In *Poetry and Epistemology: Turning Points in the History of Poetic Knowledge,* ed. Roland Hagenbüchle and Laura Skandera, 135–147. Regensburg: Verlag Friedrich Pustet, 1986.

Hallen, Cynthia. Review of *Nimble Believing: Dickinson and the Unknown. Emily Dickinson Journal* 10, no. 2 (2001): 75–78.

Hegel, Georg Wilhelm Friedrich. *The Philosophy of History.* Trans. J. Sibree. New York: Dover, 1956.

Herbert, George. *The Poems of George Herbert.* Ed. F. E. Hutchinson. London: Oxford University Press, 1972.

Holmes, Oliver Wendell. *The Writings of Oliver Wendell Holmes.* Vol. 1, *The Autocrat at the Breakfast Table.* Boston: Houghton Mifflin, 1900.

———. *The Writings of Oliver Wendell Holmes.* Vol. 11, *Ralph Waldo Emerson.* Boston: Houghton Mifflin, 1922.

Hopkins, Gerard Manley. *Poems of Gerard Manley Hopkins.* Ed. W. H. Gardner. New York: Oxford University Press, 1948.

Jacobson, David. *Emerson's Pragmatic Vision: The Dance of the Eye.* University Park: Pennsylvania State University Press, 1993.

James, William. *Essays in Philosophy.* In *The Works of William James,* ed. Frederick Burkhardt, Fredson Bowers, and Ignas K. Skrupskelis. Cambridge, Mass.: Harvard University Press, 1978.

———. *Principles of Psychology.* 3 vols. Cambridge, Mass.: Harvard University Press, 1981.

Jehlen, Myra. *American Incarnation: The Individual, the Nation, and the Continent.* Cambridge, Mass.: Harvard University Press, 1986.

Johnson, Greg. *Emily Dickinson: Perception and the Poet's Quest.* Montgomery: University of Alabama Press, 1985.

Juhasz, Suzanne, ed. *Feminist Critics Read Emily Dickinson.* Bloomington: Indiana University Press, 1983.

Kant, Immanuel. *Prolegomena to Any Future Metaphysics.* Ed. James W. Ellington. Trans. Paul Carus. Indianapolis, Ind.: Hackett, 1977.

Keats, John. *The Complete Poems.* Ed. John Barnard. New York: Penguin, 1988.

Keller, Jonathan. *The Only Kangaroo among the Beauty: Emily Dickinson and America.* Baltimore: Johns Hopkins University Press, 1979.

Kellner, Hans. "However Imperceptibly: From the Historical to the Sublime." *PMLA* 118, no. 3 (May 2003): 591–596.

Kierkegaard, Søren. *A Kierkegaard Anthology.* Ed. Robert Bretall. Princeton, N.J.: Princeton University Press, 1962.

———. *Philosophical Fragments.* Trans. Howard Hong and Edna Hong. Princeton, N.J.: Princeton University Press, 1985.

Lentricchia, Frank. *Robert Frost: Modern Poetics and the Landscapes of the Self.* Durham, N.C.: Duke University Press, 1975.

Levin, Jonathan. *The Poetics of Transition: Emerson, Pragmatism, and American Literary Modernism*. Durham, N.C.: Duke University Press, 1999.

Lopez, Michael. *Emerson and Power: Creative Antagonism in the Nineteenth Century*. De Kalb: Northern Illinois University Press, 1996.

Lynen, John. *The Design of the Present: Essays on Time and Form in American Literature*. New Haven, Conn.: Yale University Press, 1969.

Merrill, James. *The Changing Light at Sandover*. New York: Knopf, 1996.

———. *Collected Poems, James Merrill*. Ed. J. D. McClatchy and Stephen Yenser. New York: Knopf, 2001.

———. *The (Diblos) Notebook*. New York: Atheneum, 1965.

———. *A Different Person: A Memoir*. New York: Knopf, 1993.

———. *From the First Nine: Poems, 1946–1976*. New York: Atheneum, 1982.

———. *Recitative*. Ed. J. D. McClatchy. San Francisco: North Point Press, 1986.

———. *A Scattering of Salts*. New York: Knopf, 1995.

Miller, Cristanne. *Emily Dickinson: A Poet's Grammar*. Cambridge, Mass.: Harvard University Press, 1987.

Millier, Brett. *Elizabeth Bishop: Life and the Memory of It*. Berkeley: University of California Press, 1993.

Mitchell, Domhnall. *Emily Dickinson: Monarch of Perception*. Amherst: University of Massachusetts Press, 2000.

Nabokov, Vladimir. *Speak, Memory*. New York: G. P. Putnam's Sons, 1966.

New, Elisa. *The Line's Eye: Poetic Experience, American Sight*. Cambridge, Mass.: Harvard University Press, 1998.

———. *The Regenerate Lyric: Theology and Innovation in American Poetry*. Cambridge: Cambridge University Press, 1993.

Norwood, Kyle. "Finding What Will Suffice: Pragmatism and the Incommensurable in Twentieth-Century American Poetics." Ph.D. diss., University of California at Los Angeles, 1994.

Packer, Barbara L. *Emerson's Fall: A New Interpretation of the Major Essays*. New York: Continuum, 1982.

Page, Carl. *Philosophical Historicism and the Betrayal of First Philosophy*. University Park: Pennsylvania State University Press, 1995.

Parini, Jay, and Brett Millier, eds. *The Columbia History of American Poetry*. New York: Columbia University Press, 1993.

Paul, Sherman. *Emerson's Angle of Vision: Man and Nature in American Experience*. Cambridge, Mass.: Harvard University Press, 1952.

Pensky, Max. *Melancholy Dialectics: Walter Benjamin and the Play of Mourning*. Amherst: University of Massachusetts Press, 1993.

Plato. *Meno*. Trans. W. K. C. Guthrie. In *The Collected Dialogues of Plato*, ed. Edith Hamilton and Huntington Cairns, 353–384. Princeton, N.J.: Princeton University Press, 1985.

Poirier, Richard. *The Performing Self: Compositions and Decompositions in the Languages of Contemporary Life*. New York: Oxford University Press, 1971.

———. *Poetry and Pragmatism*. Cambridge, Mass.: Harvard University Press, 1992.

———. *The Renewal of Literature: Emersonian Reflections.* New Haven, Conn.: Yale University Press, 1988.

———. *Robert Frost: The Work of Knowing.* Stanford, Calif.: Stanford University Press, 1990.

———. *A World Elsewhere: The Place of Style in American Literature.* New York: Oxford University Press, 1966.

Pollak, Vivian R. *Dickinson, the Anxiety of Gender.* Ithaca, N.Y.: Cornell University Press, 1984.

———. "Emily Dickinson's Literary Allusions." *Essays in Literature* (Spring 1974): 54–68.

Porte, Joel. *The Romance in America: Studies in Cooper, Poe, Hawthorne, Melville, and James.* Middletown, Conn.: Wesleyan University Press, 1972.

———, ed. *Emerson in His Journals.* Cambridge, Mass.: Belknap Press of Harvard University Press, 1982.

Porter, David. *Dickinson, the Modern Idiom.* Cambridge, Mass.: Harvard University Press, 1981.

———. *Emerson and Literary Change.* Cambridge, Mass.: Harvard University Press, 1978.

Rorty, Richard. *Achieving Our Country: Leftist Thought in Twentieth-Century America.* Cambridge, Mass.: Harvard University Press, 1998.

———. *Contingency, Irony, and Solidarity.* New York: Cambridge University Press, 1989.

Rosenbaum, S. P., ed. *A Concordance to the Poems of Emily Dickinson.* Ithaca, N.Y.: Cornell University Press, 1964.

Rotella, Guy, ed. *Critical Essays on James Merrill.* New York: G. K. Hall, 1996.

Sacks, Peter. *The English Elegy: Studies in the Genre from Spenser to Yeats.* Baltimore: Johns Hopkins University Press, 1985.

Sánchez-Eppler, Karen. *Touching Liberty: Abolition, Feminism, and the Politics of the Body.* Berkeley: University of California Press, 1993.

Spencer, Lloyd. "Allegory in the World of the Commodity: The Importance of *Central Park*." *New German Critique* 34 (1985): 59–77.

Spengemann, William C., ed. *Nineteenth-Century American Poetry.* New York: Penguin, 1996.

Steiner, Wendy. *Pictures of Romance: Form against Context in Painting and Literature.* Chicago: University of Chicago Press, 1988.

Stevens, Wallace. *The Collected Poems of Wallace Stevens.* New York: Vintage Books, 1990.

Stewart, Susan. *On Longing: Narratives of the Miniature, the Gigantic, the Souvenir, and the Collection.* Baltimore: Johns Hopkins University Press, 1984.

Stonum, Gary Lee. *The Dickinson Sublime.* Madison: University of Wisconsin Press, 1990.

Thoreau, Henry David. *The Portable Thoreau.* Ed. Carl Bode. New York: Viking, 1964.

Torricelli, Robert, and Andrew Carroll, eds. *In Their Own Words: Extraordinary Speeches of the American Century.* New York: Kodansha International, 1999.

Vendler, Helen. "Domestication, Domesticity, and the Otherworldly." *World Literature Today* 51 (1977): 23–28.

Waggoner, H. H. *American Poets, from the Puritans to the Present*. Rev. ed. Baton Rouge: Louisiana State University Press, 1984.

———. *American Visionary Poetry*. Baton Rouge: Louisiana State University Press, 1982.

Weisbuch, Robert. *Emily Dickinson's Poetry*. Chicago: University of Chicago Press, 1975.

Wheeler, Lesley. *The Poetics of Enclosure: American Women Poets from Dickinson to Dove*. Knoxville: University of Tennessee Press, 2002.

Whicher, George F. *This Was a Poet: A Critical Biography of Emily Dickinson*. New York: Scribner's, 1938.

Whicher, Stephen E. *Freedom and Fate: An Inner Life of Ralph Waldo Emerson*. Philadelphia: University of Pennsylvania Press, 1971.

Whitman, Walt. *Leaves of Grass and Selected Prose*. Ed. Lawrence Buell. New York: Modern Library, 1981.

Wills, Garry. *Lincoln at Gettysburg: The Words That Remade America*. New York: Simon and Schuster, 1992.

Wolin, Richard. *Walter Benjamin: An Aesthetic of Redemption*. Los Angeles: University of California Press, 1994.

Wolosky, Shira. "Dickinson's Emerson: A Critique of American Identity." *Emily Dickinson Journal* 9, no. 2 (2000): 134–141.

Wordsworth, William. *The Prelude, 1799, 1805, 1850: Authoritative Texts, Context and Reception, Recent Critical Essays*. Ed. Jonathan Wordsworth, M. H. Abrams, and Stephen Gill. New York: Norton, 1979.

Yenser, Stephen. *The Consuming Myth: The Work of James Merrill*. Cambridge, Mass.: Harvard University Press, 1997.

Index

unsuccessful experiments in, 87–89, 114, 152–153

consumer culture, 159, 178

containment: confining, 10, 18, 33, 62, 78, 85, 91, 100, 149–150; and expressive intensity, 51–52, 62–63, 85, 102, 172–173; mutual, 69–70, 74, 96, 169–170, 199, 207–208; necessary for representation, 6, 17, 26, 57–58, 67–68, 73, 98, 102–103, 146, 151–153, 160–161, 168; protective, 18, 37, 59, 61, 86, 103, 165; as vantage on openness, 42–44, 53, 55, 59–60, 76–78, 98–99, 104–105, 162, 164, 166, 181–182, 208. *See also* houses

corporeality. *See* body

Crane, Hart, 211n3

cyclicality, 37, 81, 99. *See also* dynamism; oscillation

Dante Alighieri, 176

deferral: ambiguous, 38, 42, 57, 79; and Hegelianism, 197–199, 201; as recourse of optimism, 18, 31, 38, 79, 147, 203, 223n9. *See also* futurity

Dewey, Jane, 143–144

Dickinson, Emily, 2, 76–105, 197; and containment, 60–63, 65, 66; and eversion, 63, 74, 76–80, 97, 100; exemplifying poetic rigor, 21, 125–126; and openness, 28–31, 32–36, 40, 43, 44; works: "Because I could not stop for Death" [479], 98, 100; "Behind Me — dips Eternity —" [743], 32–35; "A Bird came down the Walk" [359], 92; "Each that we lose takes part of us" [1634], 214n8; "Escaping backward to perceive" [969], 88–89, 102–104; "Essential Oils — are wrung —" [772], 103–105; "An Everywhere of Silver" [931], 35; "Finding is the first Act" [910], 90, 101; "I cannot live with You —" [760], 30; "I died for beauty but was scarce" [443], 98; "I dwell in Possibility —" [466], 76–81, 82, 90, 105, 204; "I felt a Funeral, in my Brain" [340], 28, 126; "I know a place where Summer strives" [363], 94; "I never lost as much but twice —" [49], 66; "I saw no Way — The Heavens were stitched —" [673], 97; "It was not Death" [355], 28–30; "Low at my problem bending" [99], 92; "My Life had stood — a Loaded Gun —" [764], 100; "No Notice gave She, but a Change" [860], 99–100; "One Crucifixion is recorded — only —" [670], 82, 207; "Power is a familiar growth —" [1287], 91; "Safe in their Alabaster Chambers" [124], 92, 98; "A Single Screw of Flesh" [293], 93; "There's a certain Slant of light" [320], 93; "This Consciousness that is aware" [817], 100–101, 195; "This was a Poet —" [446], 86, 102–103; "Time feels so fast that were it not" [858], 8–10; "A Weight with Needles on the Pounds" [294], 93; "When Bells stop ringing — Church — begins —" [601], 95; "The Wind begun to Rock the Grass" [796], 61–63, 68

dynamism: and Hegelian knowledge, 84–85, 195, 201, 205–206; and sensory mediation, 34–35, 78–79, 86, 88–89, 118, 122–123, 180; and pragmatic interpretation, 12–14, 59, 201; twinned with stasis, 43, 58–63, 133, 135, 208–209; unsustainable, 55–56, 124. *See also* compromise

Edwards, Jonathan, 11, 204

Emerson, Ralph Waldo, 1–32, 49–63, 192–199; as aphorist, 49–51, 145, 158, 204; and cyclicality, 37–38; as Dickinsonian, 75–79, 86–92; as empiricist, 39, 96, 109, 115, 141–142, 159, 162–163, 190–191; and incoherence, 8, 20, 31–32, 57–58, 60; and incongruity, 49–55, 101–102; as poet, 19–21, 36, 55–59, 184, 187; quoted in Frost's "New Hampshire," 110–111; works: "Art," 49, 59; "Circles," 18, 23, 27, 46, 51, 52, 60, 90, 102, 197; "Each and All," 16, 19–21, 57, 184, 187–190; "Experience," 4, 7, 8, 22, 23, 24, 27–28, 31–32, 39, 86, 89, 91, 141, 187, 188, 194, 196; "History," 199; "Intellect," 18, 53, 171; "Montaigne," 13, 23, 39, 58; *Nature*, 6, 24–27, 32, 36, 59, 75–76, 109, 115–116, 162; "Nature," 15; "The Over-Soul," 7; "The Poet," 21, 37, 56, 86, 145, 188, 197; "Plato," 50, 58, 86; "The Rhodora," 66; "The Snow-Storm," 55–59, 66, 68, 111

empiricism, 12, 15, 57, 200; defined, 53

emptiness. *See* blankness

enjambment, 2, 63–64, 69, 73, 109, 115, 132, 207

epistemology, 3–7, 193–201; and active/passive binary, 35, 53, 80–81, 88, 103–104; defined, 198; distinguished from hermeneutics, 12, 14–16, 87, 122, 195–196; and history/eternity binary, 199–200, 207–210; and inaction, 1, 12, 15, 59–60, 80, 171; and paradox, 3–7, 16, 26–27, 53–55, 75–81, 100, 137, 197–198, 203. *See also* Christianity

erasure. *See* oblivion

eschatology, 9, 11–12, 18, 39–40, 42–43, 95–96, 135

eversion, 16, 36, 65, 69–71, 161–162, 169, 177–178, 181–182, 207, 227n9; defined artistically, 63; defined epistemologically, 76–78, 207. *See also* Emily Dickinson

excess, 14–15, 18, 25, 27, 30, 56, 63, 75, 115, 130, 135, 146, 187

feminist criticism, 85, 104, 196. *See also* historicist criticism

Feuerbach, Ludwig, 165

Frost, Robert, 2, 107–136, 197; and containment, 63–68; and openness, 36–39, 42; stars in, 109–110, 115–118, 152; works: "After Apple-Picking," 133–136, 138; "All Revelation," 116, 121; "Birches," 118, 128, 130, 133; "Bond and Free," 37–39, 128; *A Boy's Will*, 74, 118–120, 132; "Brown's Descent," 128; "Desert Places," 110; "Directive," 135; "For Once, Then, Something," 108, 124–125; "The Gift Outright," 113; "Good-By and Keep Cold," 63–66, 67, 68; "A Hillside Thaw," 127–128, 134; "Into My Own," 42; "The Last Mowing," 129–132; "Mending Wall," 116, 124, 125; "Mowing," 114, 118–125, 128–132, 134; "Neither Out Far Nor In Deep," 2; "New Hampshire," 110–115, 116, 118, 128; *North of Boston*, 114, 116; "Once by the Pacific," 39–40; "One More Brevity," 125; "Rose Pogonias," 120, 121–123, 129–132, 134; "Spring Pools," 130; "A Star in a Stoneboat," 115–118, 121, 126, 127, 132, 135; "The Star-Splitter," 109–110, 116; "Stars," 121; "Take Something Like a Star," 107, 110, 125; "To Earthward," 108, 118–120, 128–129, 130, 134; "Tree at My Window," 66–68, 118; "Two Tramps in Mud-Time," 202, 221n7

futurity, 17, 27, 31, 34, 42, 84, 91, 98, 121, 144, 156, 202

gender, 33, 37–39, 91, 101, 104

Gombrowicz, Witold, 209

H. D., 211n3

Heaney, Seamus, 126

Hegel, G. W. F., 84–85, 195–199, 201, 219n13

hermeneutics. *See* epistemology

historicist criticism, 84–85, 164–165, 195–196, 204–207, 210, 218n12

history, 7, 33–34, 100, 113, 142, 159,

172, 198–199, 205–210; distinguished from Hegel's history, 199–201, 209, 227n4. *See also* natural history

Holmes, Oliver Wendell, Sr., 17–19, 21, 204

Holmes, Sherlock, 19

Hopkins, Gerard Manley, 138–143, 148, 157, 162, 168

houses, 49–74, 155–157, 171–172, 176, 181

humility: and acquiescence, 11, 79–80, 83, 99, 103, 124, 131, 136, 148–149, 153–155, 164; concomitant with pride, 21, 33–35, 42, 59–60, 62–63, 75, 81, 90, 97–99, 101–105, 112–114, 167–170, 184, 189–191, 192–193, 203; ethical, 121, 132, 204; and mundanity, 72–74, 91, 96–99, 105, 150–151, 159–160, 176–177; and smallness, 25, 41, 45, 50–51, 53, 101–102, 111, 152, 179–180, 185

idealism, 6, 11, 13, 24, 26, 57, 76, 142, 198–199, 206; defined, 53; and egotism, 67–70

ideological criticism, 3, 25–26, 37–38, 86, 104, 109, 113, 196, 205, 223n3

idiosyncrasy, 18, 36, 47, 50, 54, 69, 71, 113, 127, 143, 155–158, 173–174, 178, 183, 193–195, 204

incommensurability: and beauty, 41–42, 55, 75, 131, 146, 184, 209–210; of the concrete and the abstract, 23, 100–102, 131, 198; impossible to mediate, 8, 16–17, 21, 26, 31, 60, 98, 186–189

infinity: as human creation, 24, 46–47, 97, 104–105, 142, 198, 203, 210; and human insignificance, 11–12, 26, 83, 104–105, 190; invoked by anchored objects, 42, 49, 102, 107–108, 190–191; foreclosing action, 5, 53; as representational problem, 1–3, 15, 18, 21, 24–27, 29, 36, 41, 57–58, 89, 116, 152, 154, 194; as rhetorical tool, 31. *See also* incommensurability; openness

James, William, 4, 86, 89, 107

Jarrell, Randall, 158

Jehlen, Myra, 25–26

Kant, Immanuel, 11, 54, 84, 198, 200

Keats, John, 11, 133, 138, 208

Kierkegaard, Søren, 34, 81, 192–210

Levin, Jonathan, 57

linguistic criticism, 23, 29, 85, 104

Longfellow, Henry Wadsworth, 56

Merrill, James, 2, 171–191, 197; and containment, 70–74; and openness, 43–46; works: "The Black Swan," 174; "The Blue Eye," 70, 184, 186–191; *Braving the Elements*, 74; "The Broken Home," 70, 171–172, 182; *The Changing Light at Sandover*, 46, 70, 71–74, 171, 172, 175–177, 180, 185–186, 189–190; "Charles on Fire," 225n4; "The Cosmological Eye," 186–189; "A Downward Look," 177, 182; "Large Mirror Outdoors," 70; "Marsyas," 171; "McKane's Falls," 182; "Overdue Pilgrimage to Nova Scotia," 175, 179–184; *Recitative*, 172; *A Scattering of Salts*, 177, 182; "Self-Portrait in Tyvek™ Windbreaker," 178–179; "Swimming by Night," 43–45, 178; "Syrinx," 172–174, 182; "An Upward Look," 178; *Water Street*, 45

miasma, 1, 21, 31, 34–36, 42, 56–57, 146, 200. *See also* oblivion

mismatch. *See* incommensurability

narrative, 27–28, 35, 72, 110, 124, 156; in literary criticism, 77–78, 84–85, 90, 120, 195–197; in novels, 3, 72, 175–177, 199. *See also* stasis

natural history, 19, 50, 54, 198–201, 209–210

New, Elisa, 30, 213n18

sublime, Romantic, 10–11, 21, 110

Swedenborg, Emanuel, 50, 54

synchrony. *See* simultaneity

synecdoche, 20, 50–52, 199. *See also* part
and whole; souvenirs

Thoreau, Henry David, 21, 25–26, 50,
51

transcendentalism, 8, 14, 40, 78, 87, 111,
165; defined, 78

trees, 60–69, 130–132, 135–136, 182–184,
201, 203

variants in Dickinson, 9, 218n9, 221n25

vertigo, 8, 33–36, 90, 98, 204, 208

waves, 33–34, 40, 44–45, 47, 83, 88, 153,
178, 185, 206

Weisbuch, Robert, 77, 88

Whitman, Walt, 14, 50–51, 54, 86, 109

Whittier, John Greenleaf, 58, 63

Williams, William Carlos, 4, 23, 54

Wordsworth, William, 10–11

Yenser, Stephen, 174